Automobile
Year

PHILIPPSEN

Automobile Year is published by

Christian Philippsen
19, boulevard de Suisse
MC 98000 Monte-Carlo – Monaco
Telephone + 377-9350 9610
Facsimile   + 377-9350 9612
E-mail CP@ChristianPhilippsen.com
www.automobileyear.com

Automobile Year is published
in French as *L'Année Automobile*
(www.anneeautomobile.com)
and in German as *Auto-Jahr*
(www.autojahr.com)

ISBN 2-916206-06-X

Contents

The BMW brand.
A story of success.

BMW Mobile Tradition
Schleißheimer Straße 416
D – 80935 München

BMW repeatedly sets styling milestones with its outstanding designs; innovations have been the hallmark of all BMW products since the first aircraft engines of 1916; and decades of racing victories and world records bear witness to the sporting character of the brand. BMW is a byword for dynamic vehicles, aesthetics, exclusivity and pioneering innovations. In short, Sheer Driving Pleasure.

Fax +49 / 89 / 382 270 22
www.bmw-mobiletradition.com

BMW Mobile Tradition

SIR ALEC ISSIGONIS - MINI 1957

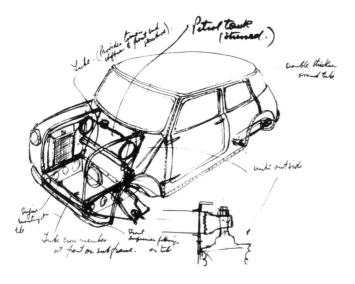

MINI COOPER, winner of the Monte-Carlo Rally, 1965

WAIT.

"MONTE-CARLO 1965" CHRONOGRAPH

Steel case, Girard-Perregaux automatic mechanical movement.
Limited edition to 250 pieces.

GP
GIRARD-PERREGAUX

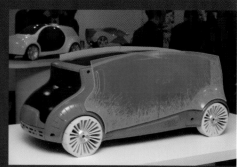

QUELLE AUTRE TECHNOLOGIE OFFRE UNE MEILLEURE MAÎTRISE DE LA ROUTE ?

VIRAGE DANGEREUX DÉTECTÉ

ESP ACTIVÉ

NOUVEAU NISSAN X-TRAIL

EXTREMELY CAPABLE[1]
EQUIPÉ DE LA TECHNOLOGIE INTELLIGENTE ALL MODE 4x4-i.[2]

Avec la transmission All Mode 4x4-i[2], le Nissan X-Trail anticipe le risque de patinage des roues avant, en transférant automatiquement le couple aux roues arrière avant même la perte d'adhérence. Et pour que la route soit encore plus sûre, cette technologie avancée est associée au contrôle de trajectoire (ESP), à l'aide au démarrage en côte (ADC) et au contrôle de vitesse en descente (CVD).

Pour plus d'informations, allez sur **www.nissan-xtrail.fr**

SHIFT_capabilities

ACCROITRE_les capacités

Reliability: proven 10 times over

10 cars on the starting line, 10 cars at the finish line.

Motul lubricants demonstrate their reputation for reliability and performance.

With close to 50% of entrants not crossing the finish line, the 24 H du Mans race deserves its reputation as the world's most difficult motor race. Motul hails the remarkable performance of team Pescarolo Sport who came 3rd overall and 1st among petrol-powered cars, the victories of Aston Martin Racing in the GT1 category and of IMSA-Porsche in the GT2 category, which have made this such an exceptional race.

LMGT1   LMGT2

N° 009 Aston Martin Racing
D. Brabham / R. Rydell / D. Turner

N° 76 Imsa Performance
R. Narac / R. Lietz / P. Long

N° 16 Pescarolo Sport
E. Collard / JC. Boullion / R. Dumas

N° 008 AMR Larbre Compétition
C. Bouchut / F. Gollin / C. Elgaard

N° 007 Aston Martin Racing
T. Enge / J. Herbert / P. Kox

N° 54 Team Oreca Saleen
L. Groppi / N. Prost / JP. Belloc

N° 100 AMR BMS
F. Babini / J. Davies / M. Malucelli

N° 17 Pescarolo Sport
H. Primat / C. Tinseau / B. Treluyer

N° 55 Team Oreca Saleen
S. Ortelli / S. Ayari / N. Lapierre

N° 006 AMR Larbre Compétition
P. Bornhauser / R. Berville / G. Fisken

fluid force

Innovation has good prospects whenever it is cleaner, safer and more efficient.

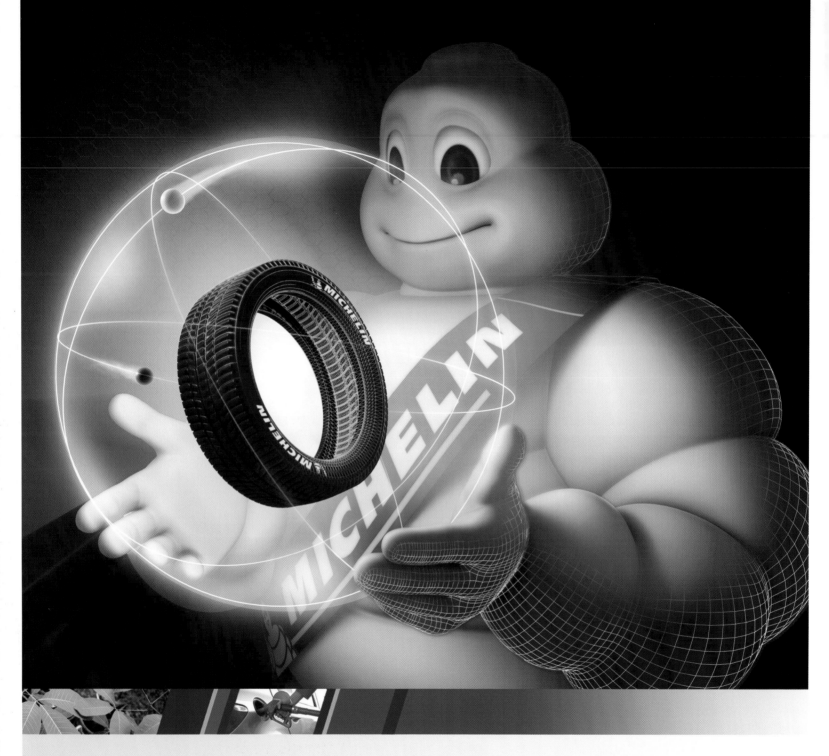

The MICHELIN Energy green tyre lasts 25% longer*.
It also provides fuel savings of 2 to 3% while reducing CO_2 emissions.

* on average compared to competing tyres in the same category.

MICHELIN
A better way forward

1959 Ferrari 250 GT LWB California Spyder
SOLD $4,455,000
Pebble Beach Auctions 2007

Daybreak. By Mikhaïl Gorbachev.

I pour myself a cup of tea and scan the papers for familiar faces.
My bags are barely unpacked and I'm feeling slightly at a loss
as it dawns on me that I'm actually at home, for a change.

Sold exclusively in Louis Vuitton stores. www.louisvuitton.com

LOUIS VUITTON

Editorial

Without further ado, feel free to go straight to pages 134 and 135 and check out the photograph of Kubica's accident at the Canadian GP. It was the most frightening of the year, at least while I write these lines before going to print. Not so long ago, such an incident would have been fatal for the driver, which just goes to prove that the F.I.A.'s insistence on safety over the years has paid off. Even if, as the Belgian journalist Jacques Ickx was wont to underline, "Freedom to risk one's own life is freedom indeed", motor sports certainly doesn't need casualties to be fascinating.

However, having made a flattering comment, I should weigh a little well-aimed criticism against it: F1 regulations have simply become incomprehensible. Spectators are lost in a labyrinth of rules governing the amount of fuel allowed during qualifying and on the starting grid, the tyres and the requirement to use different types of compound during the race, the ban on refuelling while the safety car is out. And that is just the start.

At a time when the F.I.A. is looking into the evolution of the sport, it is perhaps a suitable moment to recall that F1 is above all a drivers' championship. The constructors involved want to demonstrate their technological supremacy, but how many Mercedes or Toyota flags are waved by spectators lining the circuits? Apart from Ferrari, it is the drivers' colours that are seen in the grandstands. Sense dictates that what is needed is a clearly defined, stable set of regulations which levels off performance and budgets, encourages moral values and allows the drivers to make the difference and provide the level of spectacle required of the sport.

Returning for a moment to the subject of safety, let's take a look at road safety. This is an integral aspect of Michelin's Challenge Bibendum which seeks to further long-term mobility. It is not just racing where progress in this field is significant. Our special dossier is dedicated to this subject, while we also investigate the new industry challenges facing manufacturers' design centres.

For the first time ever, Audi and BMW chose the Shanghai Motor Show for world premières. The importance of the Asian economy is becoming stronger every day. At the same time, GM was knocked off its perch as the biggest manufacturer in the world, Ford has been forced to sell off its family jewels to survive, and Chrysler was bought out by an investment fund. But Fiat's recovery demonstrates that all is not lost.

I recall the time I was working for the Belgian Ferrari importer when we saw the arrival of cars like the AC Cobra and other big displacement Detroit metal, and we often poured scorn on them. This last August I had the pleasure of passing a week at the wheel of a Corvette around Michigan. It was a revelation. A 430-hp 6.2-litre V8 for a top speed of over 300 km/h (180 mph), modern running gear, good fit and finish, and a very complete specification both in terms of equipment and safety. And all for the reasonable on-the-road price in the U.S. of the equivalent of €35,000. On a different note, GM's E-Flex technology is a promising novelty. So we should not write off the American manufacturers yet!

New contributors to this year's *Automobile Year* join Pierre Dupasquier and Gordon Murray and our line-up of leading journalists. These include Anne Asensio – finally a lady amoung our ranks! And last, but not least, Bob Lutz. What do they all have in common? They are all engineers, designers, leaders who had, or continue to have important roles in the automotive industry. They are making history and are thus in an ideal position to tell us about it. This is an honour for us, and one we are glad to share with our readers. I am very grateful to them for dedicating their time and energy to us. The French journal *Paris Match* introduced an ingenious phrase: "The power of words, the impact of photos". That is our daily inspiration.

I wish you a happy *Automobile Year*.

Christian Philippsen
Publisher

Industry

California concepts

The Greater Los Angeles Motor Show Design Challenge is a unique annual design contest open
to the many car design studios based in California. For 2006, the challenge was to create "multi-purpose,
environmentally sustainable design entries as diverse as the beach, mountains and deserts that represent
the geographic diversity of LA," according to organizers. As with the previous two Challenges,
entries also had to reflect the distinctive Southern Californian lifestyle, and be innovative and attractive.
The nine participating studios displayed their work in the corridors of the LA Auto Show and the winning
entry was announced at the beginning of the design conference that is also part of "Design LA".
Judges for this year's Challenge were: Bill Van Amburg of Calstart, Tom Matano of San Francisco's
Academy of Art University, Imre Molnar of Detroit's College for Creative Studies and Stewart Reed
of Pasadena's Art Center College of Design. **Sam Livingstone** reports.

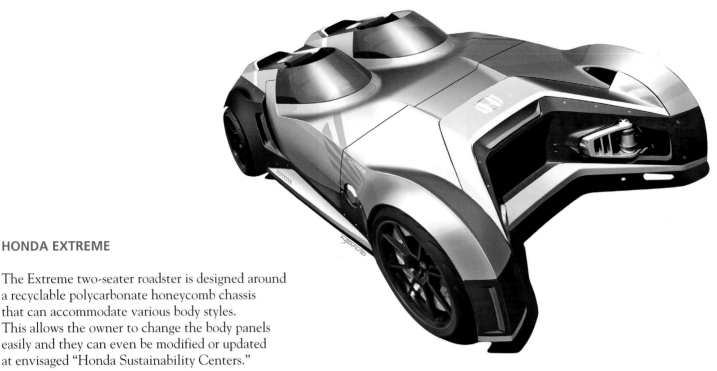

HONDA EXTREME

The Extreme two-seater roadster is designed around
a recyclable polycarbonate honeycomb chassis
that can accommodate various body styles.
This allows the owner to change the body panels
easily and they can even be modified or updated
at envisaged "Honda Sustainability Centers."

VOLKSWAGEN NANOSPYDER

The asymmetrical Nanospyder takes its name from
the nanotechnology that is central to its theme of being
a vehicle capable of being assembled, disassembled
and reassembled on a microscopic level by billions of tiny
nano-machines, to the benefit of its structural efficiency
and recyclability. This most ethereal of entries was also
presented with some of the most powerful illustration work
of the Challenge this year.

TOYOTA RLV

The aluminum, tandem two-seater RLV uses pedal
power, or pedal and electric-assist power. One core
innovation is the way its wheels extend outwards for
high speed (electric-assisted) use, and move inboard
for pedal use on bicycle and pedestrian pathways that
conventional cars and motorbikes cannot access.

HUMMER O$_2$

The winner of this year's Design Challenge was General Motors Advanced Design studio's Hummer O$_2$. Instead of delivering a clever solution that minimized environmental impact, the O$_2$ claims to provide an environmental net gain through a revolutionary phototropic body shell that produces pure oxygen. Algae-filled body panels transform harmful CO$_2$ into pure oxygen that is subsequently released back into the environment. The Hummer also consists of 100 per cent post-consumer materials such as its aluminium structure.

Under the guidance of studio Director Frank Saucedo, designer Jussi Timonen was responsible for the core concept and the almost architectural design direction which has a greenhouse-like form that opens up like a flower to maximize the phototropic panels' exposure to the sun.

MINI BIOMOKE

The BioMoke plays on the name and concept
of the iconic 1960s Mini Moke, and is intended
to be constructed from a single sheet of biodegradable
sandwich panelling impregnated with palm tree seeds.
It is particularly impressive as it was designed by an intern,
Gary Shiu, working at BMW Group Designworks.

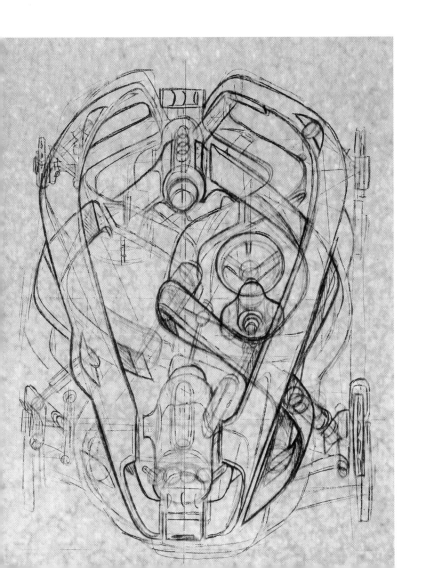

MERCEDES-BENZ RÉCY

Mercedes have chosen to do without the often hard
to recycle plastic content of cars by being made almost
exclusively of wood, metal alloys, glass and rubber.
A sophisticated exterior design taps into the current
fashion for 1970s inspired retro dark woods to give this
concept a particularly unique and very Californian appeal.

AUDI DYNAMIC SPACE FRAME

The Audi is a sleek speedster designed to have a single
space-frame structure through which all fluids and electrical
channels run, including a fluid drive in place of a traditional
driveshaft and suspension components filled with fluid
that responds to electrical current to control the ride.

Jean-Pierre Ploué designs Citroën's future

Jean-Pierre Ploué, head of the *Centre de Création Citroën*, was officially presented with the Louis Vuitton Classic Concept Award for the C-Métisse. The prize rewards excellence in automotive design for the future. **Carl-Gustav Magnusson**, retired head of design at Knoll furniture, an avid car enthusiast and a member of the judging panel chaired by Christian Philippsen, attended the ceremony at the Geneva Motor Show in March 2007.

The C-Métisse is the most convincing expression of Citroën's self-confidence since the groundbreaking DS of 1955. The company's impressive history itself sets the standard for technical innovations that new models must aspire to, but this is no easy task given the benchmarks established in the past. Citroën's best work has always been closer to science than to fashion, based on a thorough approach to the design process. It worshipped mechanics, revolutionized body construction, pioneered the adoption of pneumatics in automobiles, embraced aerodynamics and was an early advocate of ergonomics with excellent results.

Citroën's early history is perhaps best represented by the Flaminio Bertoni period, starting in 1934 and lasting until the early 1960s. The finest exponents of this era were the 1937 Traction Avant or 7CV, the 1948 2CV, and the revolutionary DS. The latter incorporated a series of innovations that virtually reinvented the car: it was the first to use Michelin X radial-ply tyres and pneumatic suspension, and introduced the modern concept of ergonomics through the instrument panel knobs and single-spoke steering wheel. The headlamps turned with the wheels. Stemming from 18 years of development, the DS was a convergence of engineering excellence. Over the next 20 years, Citroën made a million of them and moved on. And yet, the rest of the auto industry is still trying to catch up. 50 years later mainstream manufacturers are introducing headlights that steer with the wheels, while virtually every under-the-bumper radiator opening seen on today's cars was first seen on the DS. In a DS you were in the future.

But Citroën design has not been without its dull moments, in particular between 1980 and 2000, an age which has been described as one of quirky blandness. The designs of that period exemplify a time of following rather than leading. It seems conservative marketing dictated that the road going forward was in the middle lane and well within the speed limit. Metaphors aside, Citroën has passed this stage and is exhibiting leadership qualities that are gathering momentum.

Since 1999 Jean-Pierre Ploué has headed up Citroën's styling studio and has been instrumental in turning the company's fortunes around, introducing a new design language more in keeping with Citroën's proud history. And it was Ploué who attended the Louis Vuitton Classic Concept Award ceremony at the Geneva Motor Show to receive the prize for excellence in automotive design for the future for the C-Métisse.

AUTOMOBILE YEAR: What did you think when C-Métisse won the Louis Vuitton Classic Concept Award?
JEAN-PIERRE PLOUÉ: We were all delighted. The entries were highly competitive with a spirited worldwide selection, and they were judged under rigorous rules by a team of well-respected judges. We felt our work was recognized, which gives us motivation.

AY: How did your passion for car design begin?
J-P P: We lived in Joigny, an old village in Burgundy, and my father sold gardening equipment. My mother worked at the local school and in her spare time was an artist. My interest in design would appear to have started at the age of seven, when my father introduced me to Lego and challenged me to build without instructions. I quickly graduated to Meccano sets.

AY: What and where did you study?
J-P P: I studied interior design in Besançon. I then went on to the Olivier de Serres high school in Paris and studied applied arts. At graduation, Renault offered me a contract after I had finished my military service.

AY: What did you do at Renault?
J-P P: During my nine years at Renault I was able to work on full-scale models and to learn the importance of a three-dimensional approach to design. In the interior design department I got a feeling for colour and trim, and while in the lighting division I got a sense of how the interior could be experienced. I worked on the Twingo and the concept car, Argos.

AY: After Renault, who else did you work for?
J-P P: I worked for VW at the styling centre near Barcelona and then went to Ford in Germany where I worked with J Mays' team on the Mondeo and Focus.

AY: Is it possible to describe the Citroën corporate styling strategy?

J-P P: The strategy is a strong global one to convey the spirit of Citroën: high perceived value, vitality, fluidity and a cultural sense of being French.

AY: And how do you accomplish this?

J-P P: Our *Centre de Création* employs about 180 people including a styling team of 34, led by Gilles Vidal, manager; Vincent Gritt, exterior design; Steven Platt, interiors and Francois Duvis, colour and trim. Overall, it is a mix of young graduates and experienced international designers. As Citroën needs a world-wide presence, we include foreign designers who give us an outsider view of the marque. We have access to the Citroën *Conservatoire*, which includes an example of nearly every Citroën car produced so we can more fully understand our history and draw upon it.

AY: What concept cars have been designed under your leadership?

J-P P: Osmose, C-Crosser, C-Airdream, C2 Sport, C-Airlounge, C4 Sport, C-Sportlounge, C-Airplay, C-Buggy, and C-Métisse.

AY: C-Métisse is a very strong statement. Is it a precursor of what we can expect from Citroën in the future, or is it just a one off?

J-P P: We will be quite mainstream in our image, but will create some special designs like the C-Métisse to increase our styling strength.

AY: The Peugeot and Citroën styling departments share the huge white ADN building (the acronym stands for Automotive Design Network, but also means DNA in French) near Paris. What is separate and what is combined?

J-P P: Peugeot and Citroën share platforms and volumes of course. The studios are completely separate so the solutions are unique to each brand. The competition and joint reviews improve the process and allow for talent to cross over from one brand to the other.

AY: Where do you get your inspiration?

J-P P: Nature, architecture, furniture and exhibitions.

AY: Finally, what are your all time favourite cars?

J-P P: The Bugatti Atlantic and the Talbot-Lago *Goutte d'Eau* (teardrop coupé), and today the Aston Martin Vantage designed by Henrik Fisker.

Concept cars are a useful instrument for manufacturers. They force a company to engage their design team into a dialogue with the future. The development process and the results themselves enable the rest of the company to rally around an idea and get a feeling for the way forward, a sense of direction that corporations often need. Design is perhaps the strongest rallying point for companies as a whole and concept cars continue to serve – internally and externally – as catalysts of corporate vision. Mission statements and CAD renderings do not match the reality of a full-scale working prototype. A prototype combines dreams with reality. Such is the power of a concept car.

Jean-Pierre Ploué's design leadership has been on quite a fast track considering the time to market in designing, developing and launching products. Out of Citroën's collection of recent concept cars the C-Métisse is a clear winner, confirming the company's commitment to the future, drawing inspiration from Citroën's rapidly evolving dreams, rather than past success or the work of competitors. The Louis Vuitton Classic Concept Award reaffirms Citroën's history of embracing the avant-garde.

OSMOSE

C4 SPORT

C-CROSSER

C-SPORTLOUNGE

C-AIRDREAM

C-AIRPLAY

C2 SPORT

C-BUGGY

C-AIRLOUNGE

C-METISSE

Mazda Nagare and Ryuga

The Nagare presented in LA, and the Ryuga – a progression of the Nagare design – that was presented soon after in Detroit, are the first designs to emerge from Mazda since Laurens van den Acker took over as General Manager of the Design Division in 2006.
In Japanese the Nagare name is formed of just one kanji (Japanese symbol) that expresses the concept of flowing – with a philosophical sense. As van den Acker said: "It's a bit like the concept of speed as racing drivers know it: the smoother you are, the faster you go."
Ryuga in Japanese uses two kanjis (the first of which is identical to Nagare) which together mean "gracious flow".
The concepts are the first proponents of the new "Flow Design" direction inspired by delicate natural forms and textures that will be developed further by subsequent show cars.
Sam Livingstone reports.

This is a sketch from Mazda's California Design Studio
where the Nagare and Ryuga originated. It shows
the core coupé style of the concept and some finalised
aspects of the rear, but not the side creases
or the similar four-part rear lights of the final design.

The flowing creases on both sides of the car are the most
explicit signature element of the "Flow Design" direction
that the Nagare introduced. These soft curves are sharply
defined and are very innovative in the way they consciously
introduce pattern and texture to an exterior form
– in automotive design this is a rare occurrence.

The final show model of the Nagare presented
in LA is nearly identical to the Ryuga that followed
in Detroit, but is an exterior model only; it has no
interior. With the front headlights and indicators
illuminated their two-part wave form can be seen
to clearly relate to the creases on the side of the car.

The Ryuga changed the colour and added an interior to the exterior form of the Nagare, as well as a 2.5-litre engine paired with an automatic transmission. Accessed through two huge 'gull-wing' doors, the Flow Design theme continues throughout the interior, most obviously in the door inners into which the rear seat sweeps to create a shape that contour lines then ripple out from. This theme is used also on the dashboard and, in different ways, on the front seat backs and on the seat coverings. More organic flowing lines are also used for the slim centre console, the two steering wheel spokes and even on the brake and accelerator pedals. The fairly monochromatic interior is then set off with thin strips of blue ambient lighting.

HYUNDAI HCD10 HELLION

Hyundai, like most foreign car brands selling in the U.S., has a California-based design studio. Chief Designer Joël Piaskowski heads an international team of designers based there, and the Hellion is the studio's most significant concept car to date. Taking inspiration from the original Oakley hard-shell backpack, the Hellion has what looks like ribs that push through the exterior surface as part of the car's structure. Between these ribs are surfaces that take the concave form of stretched fabric, and together these are the uniquely defining elements of the design. Squat crossover proportions, and some interesting detailing – like the motorbike-style pod rear lights, the camouflage roof and seat material, and the drinking water reservoirs integrated into the front seats – are also innovative aspects of the design.

HONDA REMIX

For America, the Honda Remix is a particularly small car. Whilst large cars and SUVs dominate the automotive landscape, the younger "MP3 generation" that the Remix is designed for are increasingly aspiring to small cars such as a Scion or Mini. This small 2+2 coupé was presented as an exterior design display model only with no interior. The design consciously mixes different forms such as the flat hood surface that contrasts with the rounded rear, and is full of interesting design features.

CHEVROLET VOLT

The Volt is one of the most significant GM
show cars ever as it shows the direction the
world's second largest car company intends
to take with environmentally friendly cars.
Using an "E-flex" driveline that consists
of electric motors, lithium battery and
small 3-cylinder petrol engine – powering
a battery generator only – the Volt is capable
of driving up to 40 miles on battery power
alone. Having no mechanical connection
between the engine and driving wheels,
along with relatively small driveline
elements, gave the designers the freedom
to give the Volt its compact and sporty
proportions, whilst still allowing room for
four. This dynamic design direction is also
new for an environmentally orientated car,
and it is particularly evident in the very
shallow cabin glazing, large wheels, minimal
overhangs and general lithe proportions.
Developed in strategic partnership
with General Electric, the Volt is also
particularly innovative in its use of advanced
plastics to reduce its total weight
and thus the energy it needs to accelerate.

The Interceptor underlines a shift in design direction for Ford in the U.S.. After several years of producing generally clean, almost European-style concept and production cars, the brand is taking a lead from Chrysler in its more classically American direction. Specifically, the Interceptor is Ford's riposte to the critically and commercially successful Chrysler 300C. It adopts much of the design identity of the Ford 427 concept from Detroit 2003, but does so in a more emphatically American way, with classic front engine, rear-wheel drive sporting proportions from its Mustang-based chassis, and with a prominent polished aluminium three-bar grille that runs full width across the front of the car and incorporates the headlights.

LINCOLN MKR

The MKR is the latest in a long line of Lincoln show cars that aims to define a future design direction for the brand. The shape of the side windows, near-flat clean side surfaces, classic notchback proportions and white interior are common with most previous Lincoln concepts, but the more dynamic feel from the pronounced front wings and diving shoulder is new for the brand. So too is the "bow-wave" double grille which is set to be used on future production Lincoln designs and is derived from the 1941 Lincoln Continental Cabriolet. The MKR is also notable for its "guilt-free luxury" theme evident in the re-engineered oak wood trim, chrome-free leather, mohair carpet, and also in its ethanol-powered twin-turbo 3.5-litre V6.

Developed in conjunction with Airstream – the caravan trailer company – this concept has been inspired by the spirit of adventure expressed by American space- and aircraft. The blue silver exterior paint finish and "2001: A Space Odyssey" inspired interior are literal testimonies to this. The simple MPV-like side profile is broken up with distinctive window shapes outlined in bright orange and different on each side. A two-piece gull-wing door on the right side and conventional smaller driver's door on the left side, continue the asymmetrical theme.

JEEP TRAILHAWK

The Trailhawk is based on the long-wheelbase platform of the relatively recent four-door Wrangler Unlimited. But it has a more premium, car-like Cherokee style to its design and a lower, faster profile than the rugged Wrangler. It also has no pillar between the front and rear door which, in combination with lowering the roof and side windows, gives a very large open cabin area. The Trailhawk not only shows a possible new type of production Jeep vehicle, but also develops the brand's front face to show a possible future direction for production designs.

CHRYSLER NASSAU

After the baroque Imperial concept of Detroit 2006, Chrysler is exploring with the Nassau a different and more contemporary direction for a large premium saloon. The most unusual aspect of the car is its short hatchback rear that bears some similarity with the Chrysler Crossfire coupé and would be very unusual in such a large car in the American market. Based on the production 300C platform, Chrysler claims the Nassau to be more of a four-door coupé than a saloon, and an emotional interpretation of what the brand means.

JAGUAR C-XF

The C-XF is a four-door coupé that shows the direction Jaguar intend to take with the forthcoming S-Type replacement. Like the Aston Martin Rapide concept shown a year ago at Detroit, the C-XF takes traditional British GT car design cues, and stretches them over a low four-door, four-seater saloon layout. It also introduces a new type of grille treatment and headlamp shapes for the brand. Inside the car is most remarkable for its almost austere design theme which gives it a totally different feel to the warm, ensconcing, but slightly old-fashioned Jaguar interiors of the past. This is done with simple, clean forms and the use of brushed aluminium, carbon-fibre and, uniquely, charred wood. Jaguar used to be renowned for their low slung, sporting luxury sedans, but Mercedes have stolen a march on them with the CLS, as have Maserati with the Quattroporte. With Aston Martin, BMW and Porsche also about to launch sporting, coupé-style four door saloons, Jaguar are using the C-XF to reassert themselves in this area, but they need to follow with a strong production design to do this fully.

ACURA ADVANCED SPORTS CAR

The main message behind the Acura Advanced Sports Car is that the forthcoming high-performance Acura (or Honda for markets outside of North America) will have a front engine, probably V10 in configuration, unlike its mid-engined NSX spiritual predecessor. The concept has a dramatic "sheer machine surface" exterior design language, but was displayed as an exterior model only, with no interior, like the Honda concepts shown two months earlier at the LA auto show.

KIA KUE

The Kue, like several concept cars that debuted at Detroit, was designed in California where many brands have their American design studios. As a large coupé-style SUV crossover similar in concept to the Infiniti FX, the Kue signals Kia's intention to move into this premium market sector within the next few years. It is also significant in being the first Kia announced after new Director of Design, Peter Schreyer, took up his position in 2006, although much of the design for the Kue had been completed prior to his arrival.

NISSAN BEVEL

The Bevel is specifically designed as a recreational vehicle for male "empty nesters" who would use the car mostly on their own for leisure activities with all of the other seats folded away flat to the floor.
The exterior is very simple and has a slightly retro quality in its brown colour and the way its front and rear extremities angle upwards away from the wheels. The interior features a kennel area behind the driver's seat, the door to which can be folded down when the tailgate is open as an outside seat.

LEXUS LF-A

The LF-A was originally shown
at the 2005 Detroit Auto Show, exactly two
years prior to this show car's debut. This new
LF-A is a progression of the original's
design and is a preview of the first Lexus
sports car that will soon be produced.
Just as the first Lexus car closely targeted
the top German luxury cars, the LF-A
targets the top high-performance sports cars:
its performance and proportions are very
close to the range-topping Ferrari 599,
and its design is equally dramatic.

TOYOTA FT-HS

The "HS" in the FT-HS stands
for Hybrid Sports, a new moniker from
Toyota that shows how petrol-electric
hybrid drivelines are becoming central
to high-performance Toyota cars.
The design uses an idea of "subtractive
mass" which means that much of the
exterior and interior has had volume
carved out of the overall core form to reduce
the bulk of the vehicle and emphasise
its lightweight construction. The interior
is arguably more extreme in its execution
than the exterior with a strong driver
focus to the cockpit, dramatic sweeping
forms, a hubless steering wheel
and exposed carbon-fibre structural elements.
This 2+2, front-engined coupé concept
preludes a high-performance production
coupé from Toyota that can be closely
compared to the Acura Advanced
Sports that also debuted at Detroit.

MERCEDES-BENZ CONCEPT OCEAN DRIVE

Over the last 10 years the range of Mercedes-Benz cars has grown dramatically. The Concept Ocean Drive previews another addition, although this time Mercedes are returning to a type they last produced 40 years ago: the large four-seater cabriolet based on their largest car, the S-class. With the Concept Ocean Drive, this cabriolet is a four-door, which would be very hard to engineer and unique in the market if produced. The design is also notable for its classic sweeping feature lines running back from both front and rear wheel-arches that are reminiscent of the great pre-war Mercedes cabriolets. Four individual seats, a very large and freshly-treated Mercedes-Benz grille, subtle use of colours, and C-shaped LED lights at the front and rear are also notable.

VOLVO XC60

The XC60 concept is a close preview of a production Volvo SUV that will be announced in about a year. It showcases the next evolution of the brand's exterior styling and, particularly, more distinctive lights front and rear – more notable on a Volvo than most brands as they run in many markets with their side lights permanently on. This aspect of night-time brand recognition is set to become a big trend area as new lamp technology allows for more variety of light cluster shapes to be designed. The interior is more conceptual and features an interesting development of the "pony tail" seat slot first seen on the Volvo YCC concept three years earlier that was designed exclusively by a female team. In this new application the slot was conceived primarily to aid air circulation for comfort.

INFINITI EX CONCEPT

The EX is a production preview of the new Infiniti (Nissan's North American market up-scale brand, the equivalent to Toyota's Lexus) SUV. Taking a lead from the successful FX design, the EX is smaller, slightly more mainstream and less masculine in its design image in order to appeal to the huge "soccer mom" market. The design is also notable for its short front overhang which helps give it a more sporting feel, and for its glass roof which can be adjusted from opaque through translucent to transparent.

CHEVROLET BEAT, GROOVE & TRAX

This trio of Chevrolet concept cars are designed to illustrate the spread of small car types that could be produced from the same platform. They were all designed by GM Asia Pacific Design in Inchon, South Korea, which means that although these were Chevrolets debuting in New York, they could have been Daewoos debuting in Seoul as these brands share models depending on sales territory. The Trax concept is a small crossover with petrol engine-driven front wheels and electric powered rear wheels, and some neat detailing, particularly its unique and elegant door handles. The more aggressive Groove has an upright windscreen and SUV profile, whilst the "vertigo green" Beat is more car-like and dynamic, and is the only one with an interior.

Hyundai QarmaQ

The Hyundai QarmaQ was the most significant concept car presented at Geneva,
reports **Sam Livingstone**. That is a particularly impressive result as it comes from a brand that,
last year's Hellion apart, has rarely delivered truly innovative or impressive concept cars.
QarmaQ is one of a growing number of coupé SUV crossovers that include the Mazda
Hakaze that also debuted at Geneva. It has seats for four accessed through two large
conventionally-opening front doors and two small rearward-hinged rear doors.
Developed in Hyundai's European design centre and in partnership with GE Plastics,
it features numerous advanced plastics including the Lexan material used
for the side glazing. This element takes inspiration from the Lamborghini Marzal
concept of 1968 and is the car's most distinctive signature design feature.

A sketch showing how the rear window, and surrounding greenhouse area were more distinct at the early stage of the design process. Note also the less developed side glazing solution and two-door only concept at this stage.

The QarmaQ is clearly a coupé with SUV genes: it has a sports car-like face and dynamic stance, but also an elevated ground clearance and chunky tyres. But unlike conventional coupés it has four doors and – unlike conventional SUVs – it is designed for an urban environment as suggested by the car park location shown in these images from Hyundai.

This is the best view of the QarmaQ, as the form sweeping back from the bonnet and the adjacent windscreen surface, that runs into side glazing, can be clearly seen. The subtle colour break from white to beige metallic and the charcoal under-body that sweeps up into the rear screen, can also be best seen from this angle, as can the unique glimpse of the interior that the side glazing gives.

The interior form reflects the exterior in the interplay of the charcoal and cream colours, and particularly in the forms that sweep down from the front into the door side and the unusual side glazing. Several unique design innovations can also be seen, such as the way the centre console is connected to the driver's seat, the use of metal in the seat, and the way the window seal is integral with the glazing.

The front of the car features innovative use of the latest GE plastics to improve the pedestrian impact performance of the car. With European legislation now demanding that new passenger cars meet pre-described parameters of design to reduce the often lethal damage caused to pedestrians in collisions, the QarmaQ shows new ways in which plastics can be used to achieve this.

OPEL GTC

In Opel's native Germany the classic Opel four-seat coupés such as the Kadett C, Commodore, Manta and even Calibra are working-class heroes and represent some of the strongest parts of the brand's design heritage. The GTC concept, like its namesake from four years ago, makes deliberate reference to its spiritual predecessors to suggest that Opel might soon legitimately make a production coupé. As well as suggesting that there may be a GTC-style coupé coming, the mission of the concept presented at Geneva was to introduce the next steps of the Opel design direction that will be seen in the forthcoming Vectra upper-medium saloon. The deep vertical shapes that incorporate lights and air intakes at the front of the car. and a slightly more sculptural exterior design appear to be the core proponents of this new language.

DODGE DEMON

The Demon is a show car preview of a soon-to-be-announced production Dodge sports car that will go head to head with twin rivals from General Motors: the Pontiac Solstice and Saturn Sky. The Demon will sit below the extreme Viper in the Dodge sports car line-up. The design owes something to the BMW Z4 in is crisp-edged, dramatic body side sweep and in its classic front-engine, rear-wheel drive proportions. Even the quality in the concept's detail and the way the design was resolved was more typical of German production designs. One of the most impressive concepts at Geneva, the Demon featured signature styling elements in the Dodge grille and headlamp design, along with exquisite door handles and an attractive retro interior.

MAZDA HAKAZE

The Hakaze was designed in Mazda's German design studio near Frankfurt and is the second of a trilogy of concept cars that show the direction newly incumbent design director Laurens van den Acker is taking. It follows the Californian studio's Nagare displayed in LA that became the Ryuga at Detroit, and precedes the Hiroshima-designed concept due to be announced at the 2007 Tokyo show. Although part of the new order at Mazda, the Hakaza takes cues from Sassou concept from Frankfurt two years earlier in its proportions and three-door compact hatchback style, and in some of its detail solutions. But it also embraces the new "Flow" design theme that the Ryuga introduced, with organic ridges rippling across the lower door sides and similar flowing lines breaking up the grille area and forming the rear lights. The interior is dominated by turquoise seats that are suspended off the centre cockpit tunnel, with the rear ones innovatively sliding forwards to cup closely the front seats and thus increase the load area.

TOYOTA HYBRID X

With the production Prius now in its tenth year and second incarnation, Toyota dominates the market and public awareness of petrol electric hybrid-powered cars. With the Hybrid X concept they are exploring how the unique technical qualities and environmental credentials of their hybrid-powered cars might be more uniquely represented through design. Created in Toyota's European design centre in the south of France, the Hybrid X has a simple but advanced exterior and interior that puts much of its emphasis on the calming experience it would provide for its occupants.

HONDA SMALL HYBRID SPORTS

Designed in Honda's European design studio based in Germany, the Hybrid Sports Concept (HSC) explores how aerodynamics and sports car styling cues could be combined to express the theme of this model's hybrid petrol and electric power. Honda's production Insight clearly influenced the proportions of this concept design, and inspiration has also been taken from the latest Civic and even the Honda Formula One car.

BERTONE BARCHETTA

Barchetta means "little boat" in Italian and is a word that has long been used by Italian car makers, including Ferrari, for their smaller roadster designs. Based on the mechanics of the current smallest Fiat, the Panda, this concept from Bertone is full of innovative design solutions, from the separate polished aluminium exterior surface that sits over a black composite structure, to the small opening blister on top of the trunk that contains a fitted leather case. The interior is accessed via rearward-hinging scissor doors, and is dominated by a retro theme with exposed gear-shift linkages in cast aluminium, square-shaped instrument pods with rounded edges, squashed steering wheel, and the use of glossy white and matte brown finishes.

RINSPEED EXASIS

Rinspeed is a Swiss coachbuilder and manufacture of car accessories, that every year produces one of the most unusual concepts of Geneva Motor Show. The Exasis concept is just such a proposal, but arguably one of their most impressive. It is a simple tandem-seat sports car with a vibrant translucent yellow body through which its aluminium structure can be seen. The Exasis is also notable for its application of several new materials including those used in the unusual seats.

KTM X-BOW

KTM is a company that produces a range
of focused sports off-road motorbikes.
With the X-Bow they are about to produce
their first car, although it was only after
a large amount of interest amongst potential
buyers at the Geneva show that its final
production plans were formalised.
The design takes the "naked" motorbike
aesthetic and applies it to a compact
mid-engine sports car proportion
for a powerful and very non-automotive look.
Although missing roof, doors
and even windscreen, the quality
of the design is evident in the finish
of its carbon fibre structure and details
such as the headlamps and mirrors.

SPYKER C12 ZAGATO

This is Italian design house Zagato's
take on the mid-engined Spyker C12.
The design has a uniquely sensual and
slightly classical quality that differentiates
it from the typical brutal aesthetics of many
other contemporary super-cars – note
the way that the character line sweeping up
from the front over the wheel arch is then
echoed in the way a similar line sweeps up
over the rear wheel arch. Classic Zagato
"double-bubble" roof, instrument dials
for the passenger, and an extreme polished
aluminium rear are other design highlights
of this unusual Dutch-Italian design.

RENAULT CLIO GRAND TOUR CONCEPT

The Grand Tour is a lightly disguised production variant of the current Renault Clio. Its three-door, tall estate car body style is both unique and yet conservative, but there are many interesting subtle innovations in the interior. The way the steering wheel spokes connect to the rim, the iris-like air vents, and the clear delineation of the seat sides are just a few examples.

PEUGEOT 207 SW OUTDOOR

This is a show car preview of the upcoming 207 SW production car that will replace the pioneering 206 SW. With SW standing for Station Wagon, Peugeot are unique in having such a small estate car in their range, although the Clio Grand Tour concept suggests Renault will soon launch a similar product. The 207 SW Outdoor concept has a separate opening window in the tailgate and one-touch folding rear seats which will make it to production, while complex rear lights, orange roof rack and parachute silk seats probably won't.

SEAT ALTEA FREETRACK

The Altea Freetrack previews a production four-wheel drive derivative of the Altea with more ground clearance than the standard car, new bumpers and wheelarches, and a spare wheel carried on the tailgate to give the car more of an SUV flavour. The most notable design elements of the car are its matte white exterior paint and the four individual seats with large apertures in the centre covered only by a fine mesh.

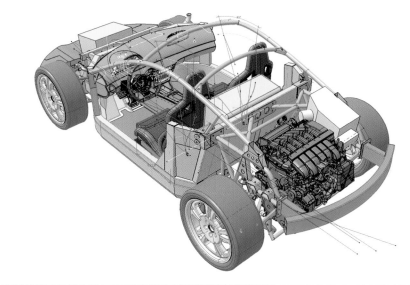

ARTEGA GT

This is a concept car preview
of a forthcoming production design from
this new company headed up by, amongst
others, ex-Alfa Romeo and Maserati CEO,
Karl-Heinz Kalbfell. The GT is a compact
mid-engined sports car, comparable in
concept to the Porsche Cayman, but smaller
and with a Volkswagen derived 3.5-litre V6.
The exterior design is particularly
interesting for the way in which the front
and side air intakes and rear end are
so decisively cut into the bodywork.

DIATTO OTTOVÙ ZAGATO

Diatto is an old Italian car brand that Zagato
have brought back to life 100 years after it
was originally established and 84 years since
it last produced a car. Conceptually the
Diatto is similar to Zagato's Ferrari 575 GTZ
(of which two were built), and its Maserati
GS that followed the Diatto's Geneva
debut. It is a front-engined premium GT,
with distinctive "eyebrows" that run over
its wheel-arches, tall slim headlamps, and
an attractively classical general form. With
enough interest from buyers, Zagato may
turn this concept into a production reality.

Concept cars from Shanghai & Seoul

As the Chinese market continues its vertiginous progression, international interest has arisen around its foremost motor show, held in Shanghai. The surest sign of this recognition came in the form of meaningful research vehicles from Western manufacturers Audi, BMW and Buick. **Sam Livingstone** describes the most significant concept cars unveiled in Shanghai and Seoul.

AUDI CROSS COUPÉ QUATTRO

The Cross Coupé is a preview of a soon-to-be-launched production Audi SUV crossover and follows on closely in its design from the Audi Roadjet concept of Detroit 2006. Despite the name, and unlike the coupé-style Hyundai QarmaQ from the preceding Geneva show, the Cross Coupé is more SUV than coupé – it has five doors, lots of cabin space and a large boot. The car was designed in Audi's main design studio in Ingolstadt, Germany with details created specifically to appeal to China – significant, given that Audi outsells both BMW and Mercedes-Benz in this fast growing market. These include the off-white interior, extensive exterior bright-work, an integrated ceramic tea cup between the front seats, and Chinese patterns on some minor controls.

BMW CONCEPT CS

To underscore how seriously BMW takes the Chinese car market, it chose Shanghai to announce this most luxurious of BMW concepts and, with it, a new design direction for the brand. Eschewing the sheer surfaces and discontinuous forms of the current BMW design direction called "flame surfacing", the design of the CS is dominated by its long (5.10 m), low (1.36 m) and wide (2.22 m) proportions. But it is the sports car style front of the car, its more fluid forms, and its strong broken side feature line that are the most obvious elements of this new BMW styling theme. As well as heralding in a new aesthetic direction for the brand, the CS shows that BMW are set to produce a large coupé-style saloon that follows on from the successful Mercedes CLS and will go head to head with Porsche's Panamera and Aston Martin's Rapide.

BUICK RIVIERA CONCEPT

Launched in Shanghai with the slogan
"It's Not East, Not West… It's Buick",
the Riviera is significant because it was
not styled particularly to appeal to the
Chinese market, despite having been
designed locally and Buick being a popular
brand in China, but to be the new leading
image design for the Buick brand.
The car is a large four-seater coupé like
famous Riviera designs of the past,
and is quite classical in its proportions
and its clean flowing form which gives
the car a relaxed but powerful feel. But
in its details, such as the sweeping-back
headlamps and windscreen, and the blue
fabrics and jade-coloured lighting inside
the car, the Riviera is more innovative.

CHERY SHOOTING SPORT CONCEPT

Although the Shooting Sport was the best
concept shown by a domestic Chinese
car brand in Shanghai, it was designed
in Italy by Torino Design, a new Italian
design house set up by ex-General Manager
of Stile Bertone, Roberto Piatti.
Based on production car mechanicals,
the Shooting Sport is a European-style,
compact, sporty three-door hatchback.
Whilst relatively conventional, the
Shooting Sport is very well resolved with
subtly innovative detailing around the
rear pillar area and in the front and rear
wheel arches, and a high-quality feel
from its consistently refined execution.
The white of the exterior carries
through to the interior and is joined
by a strident and unusual gloss green
on the doors and dashboard.

HYUNDAI HND-3 VELOSTER

The Veloster is a compact four-seater coupé that aims to appeal to Generation-Y just as the Scion Tc does in the North American market. Although not a preview of a production car, the Veloster (from Velocity and Roadster) does suggest that Hyundai will soon produce a similar type of coupé which would then complement the Hyundai Coupe/Tiburon which is set to grow in size. The Veloster shares a similar front grille shape as Hyundai's impressive QarmaQ concept car shown a month earlier at Geneva. It is also notable for having a more masculine, simple, Western style than previous Hyundai concept designs, and for some great design details: the red inserts in the wheel spokes, integrated central exhaust, and grille cross beam that runs into the wings.

KIA KND-4

This acid-green crossover concept takes a lead from the Kia Kue concept shown in Detroit four months earlier and also gives an indication of the theme that the forthcoming Kia Sportage production design will take.
The design is characterised by a Honda-style single front "graphic" (the simple shape defined by headlamps and grille in combination), estate-car-like up-right rear tailgate and adjacent thick roof pillars, and by the overall Western style of the design that sister brand Hyundai also had in Seoul with the Veloster. The KND-4 also had some impressive design details such as the unusual rear lights, the way the rear window extends to incorporate these, and the multifaceted interior theme that can be best seen on the doors.

Nissan Mixim

The Mixim shows how Nissan are looking at new types of vehicles to appeal to future
generations of driver; "people who currently find it difficult to love the car"
according to Shiro Nakamura, Senior Vice President and Head of Design.
Mixim is a small electric-powered coupé that also fits within the Nissan Green Programme,
the company's publicly stated desire to create a sustainable mobile society.
Central to both the car's environmental credentials and relevance with future generations
of driver, are its two "Super Motor" electric engines that have dual rotors which provide
output to two driveshafts – one for each wheel. These are powered by state-of-the-art laminated
Lithium-ion cell batteries that are so thin they are packaged in the floor to lower the centre of gravity.
Unusually perhaps for a debut at Europe's largest motor show, and one that precedes
the Tokyo show by only a few weeks, the Mixim was designed in Nissan's main Tokyo
Design Centre, reports **Sam Livingstone** from the Frankfurt IAA Motor Show.

This sketch clearly shows the "butterfly" doors which, along with the central driving position flanked by two passengers, is similar to the McLaren F1 supercar. The shear, machined metal surfaced wheels and dynamic lines are also shown off to good effect in this view.

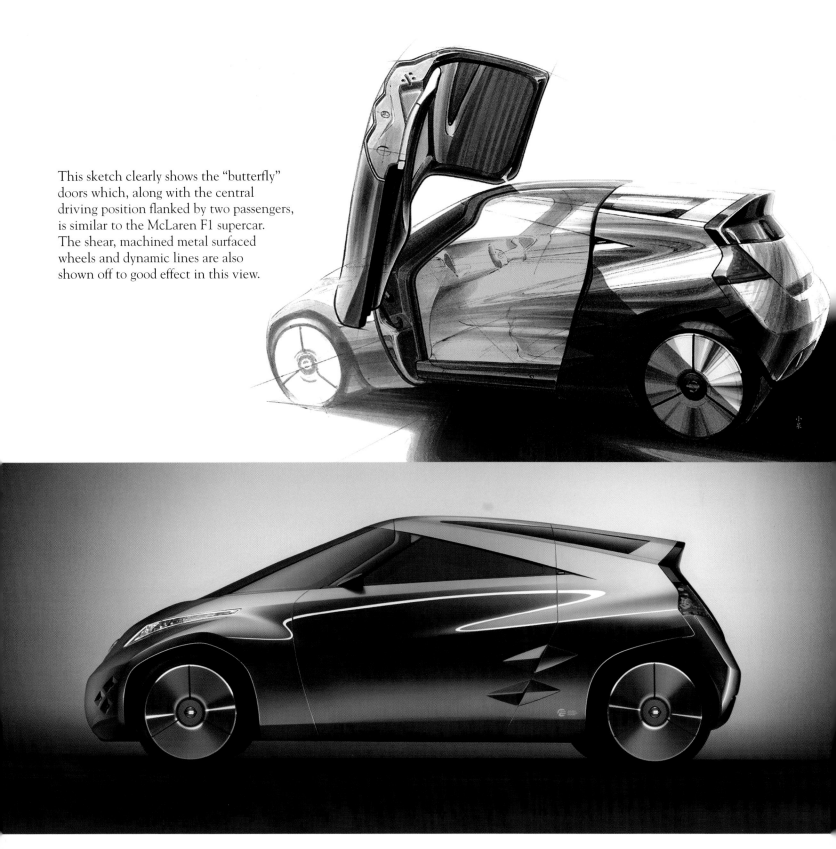

Although only 3.7 metres long, the Mixim is a very dynamic design thanks to a wrap-around windscreen and steeply angled side feature lines. From this view the way the wing visually extends the dynamism of the side into the frontal aspect of the design can also be seen. Rhombus-shaped lower front lights as a motif can also be seen in the vestigial side air intakes at the trailing edge of the door.

In side view the steeply raked windscreen and sharply tapering side window shape can clearly be seen, as can the unusual wheelarch shapes that are reminiscent of a Marcel Gandini design, such as the Lamborghini Countach. Two other interesting design features are the upper side/roof windows in the top section of the scissor doors and roof, and the alloy wheels – the antithesis of the classic spoke wheel of petrol powered coupés perhaps?

47

The dashboard is an unusual shape as it wraps around the centrally-positioned driver and U-shaped steering wheel. Digital displays dominate, with an advanced navigation system that integrates images from a forward-facing camera to give the driver a "real-time" view of the road and traffic ahead. And displays on the periphery of the dashboard show a virtual representation of the front wheels to give a single-seater racing car feel to the driving experience!

Uniquely the seats of Mixim are configured in a diamond shape: central forward-positioned driver flanked by two passengers slightly behind, and a smaller "occasional" seat centrally positioned to the rear – just out of view in this image. This layout is afforded by the car's particular electric power that means there is no large and heavy combustion engine impinging on space in front of the driver or behind the rear-most passenger.

TOYOTA IQ

The IQ was one of several Frankfurt show cars that previews a soon to be announced super compact production car with strong environmental credentials. Designed in Toyota's European studio near Nice, the IQ has a design theme inspired by a Manta-ray fish which can be seen inside and out in the way the gently flowing surfaces butt up to each other at finely defined creases. Despite the car's three metre length, only a little longer than the Smart ForTwo, there is seating inside for up to four.

VOLKSWAGEN UP!

With a tiny rear engine, short overall length of 3.5 metres, and simple design, the Up! was billed by Volkswagen as a potential icon car, although as a simple four-seater hatchback design it arguably lacks the character of the classic Beetle and Camper van. But the Up! has some intriguing details such as the way the bumpers appear to float within grille areas front and rear, circular door mirrors, and an exceptionally finely crafted purist interior. Overall the Up! had a lot of appeal.

FORD VERVE

The Verve is the first of three similar-sized concept cars from Ford that will ready the market for the next generation European market Fiesta. At Frankfurt the Verve made a particularly strong impact with its magenta exterior, a rare colour for a show car but one that suited the design well. The design is both dynamic without being overly "racy" and was notable for well integrated elements such as the side feature crease, trapezoidal grille, and both front and rear tail lamps. The exterior colour and polished aluminium multi-spoke wheels, as well as the overall form of the car, are designed to appeal well to a young female target customer.

RENAULT KANGOO COMPACT

Launched at the same time as the new
second-generation production Kangoo,
the concept extends the bold character
of Kangoo almost into a cartoon caricature
of itself. The design is very playful with
bright contrasting colours inside and out,
lots of simple large radius curves, and wheels
that feature transparent elements within
the spokes. Overall, the design theme and
details like roller blades integrated into
the fold down rear, underscores the leisure
lifestyle role Kangoo could play for many
young car buyers set to visit the show.

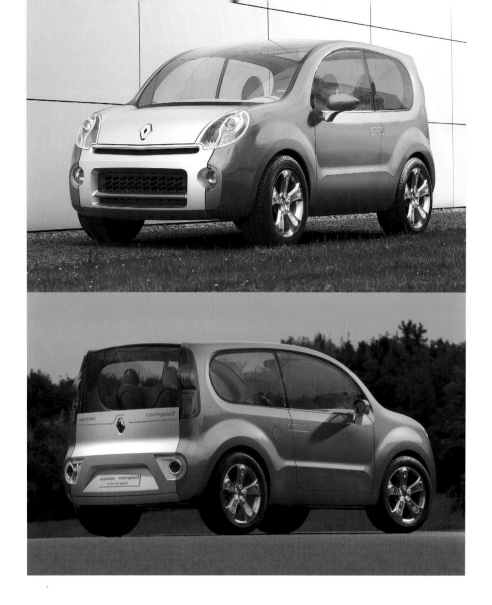

SEAT TRIBU

The Tribu is a compact European style
SUV concept, that suggests that Seat may
soon be entering this market sector.
The design also gives us the first taste
of a new Seat "face" with the lamps
integrated into the same graphical
element at the front as two side grille
elements. One of the most innovative
features on the car is its single-piece
transparent plastic tailgate that hinges up
on a parallelogram mechanism, and the
way the metallic orange brown colour
is carried through to parts of the interior.

CITROËN C-CACTUS

The C-Cactus is not the most beautiful of designs, but that is not its intention. Instead it explores a new low-cost, environmentally sensitive aesthetic design direction, that will inform (if not be directly translated into) a future low-cost Citroën car. Although the exterior is striking, it is the interior that truly shines: climb in onto painted foam seats, close a felt-lined door, and touch the cork covered air vents that have an exposed glass phial of perfume on top! This was the most innovative show car design at Frankfurt.

OPEL FLEXTREME

Following on from the GTC concept shown earlier in the year at Geneva, the Flextreme is another hybrid electric-powered "green" show car unveiled at Frankfurt. The design is notable for its unusual front lights that curve all the way to the base of the car, for having clear covers over grille and wheels, and for the two Segway human transporters it has integrated below its rear tailgate. The overall simple form inside and out is faultlessly executed and likely gives some indication of what to expect in forthcoming production Opels in Europe and Saturns in North America.

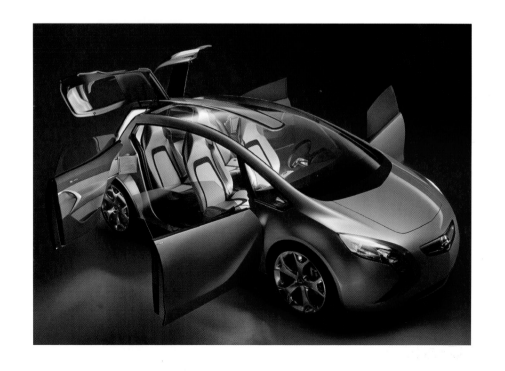

PEUGEOT 308 RC Z

This concept car is based on the production 308 hatchback that also debuted in Frankfurt, but from the windscreen rearward is quite different, with a coupé profile reminiscent of the Volkswagen Karmann Ghia in silhouette and in its "hips" over the rear wheel. Although unconfirmed, this concept may be produced and sit above the relatively large 207 and below the 407 coupé to be Peugeot's sporting flagship.

KIA KEE

The Kee was designed just outside Frankfurt at Kia's European design studio that has since moved to within a mile of the Frankfurt Motor Show location. With Kia now headed up by ex-Audi designer Peter Schreyer, it is arguable that this was one of the most German designs at the show. The concept is a 2+2 seat sports coupé, that whilst conventionally proportioned, has some innovative design features. These include a clamshell hood and tailgate, a new Kia grille, and a "keystone panel" window in the side pillar. But the design is most notable for its faultless execution and its subtle forms and detailing – archetypal German design qualities!

HYUNDAI I-BLUE

The i-Blue is an SUV crossover style car that showcases Hyundai's new fuel cell technology that is located under the floor of the car. The design is characterised by its rakish side window shape, the dynamic side feature lines below it, and the swept-back LED front lamps that all combine to give the car an athletic feel. The interior also has a dynamic feel, but ultimately the design does not have the distinction of other Hyundai show cars that have debuted over the last twelve months.

SUZUKI KIZASHI

The Kizashi is an unusually large concept car from a brand famous for its motorbikes and small cars. The core design of the car is a relatively normal mid-size fastback, albeit a rakishly handsome one. But with its glossy red paint, very low ground clearance, large polished aluminium wheels, deep black grille and imposing LED lights, the car makes quite an impact. The Kizashi, just a model for now, is probably a preview of a forthcoming production car, which after the impressive Swift is likely to be a very appealing design.

MERCEDES-BENZ F700

Mercedes-Benz use the "F" prefix for
the names of their show cars that are
essentially technically-driven experimental
cars. As such, most of these designs lack
the visual harmony of other Mercedes
concepts and the F700 is no exception.
The three most pronounced exterior design
elements are the very long wheelbase,
the way the side window dives down towards
the front of the car, and the low set nose with
tall headlamps. The soft form of the exterior
and the poor detail resolution are at odds
with the Mercedes production range, but
the core idea of a "new touring 5-door of the
future" with a very long cabin has relevance.
The F700 has a hybrid electric power-train,
the internal combustion part being a high-
tech 'diesotto' engine (combining the
economy of a diesel with the lightweight
construction of a petrol unit), active 'forward
reading' suspension, and numerous other
technical highlights within the cabin.

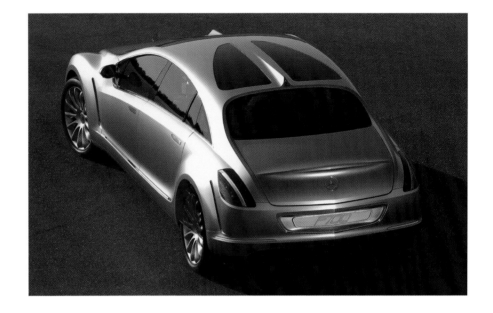

MITSUBISHI CONCEPT CX

The cX concept features the new, aggressive front design that the brand is rolling out on several of its core models. The leaning forward front surface and frowning headlamps define the core character of this compact, SUV crossover type concept and the deep black grille is echoed in the unusual full-height black tailgate glazing at the rear of the car. Along with the Ford Kuga concept and Volkswagen Tiguan production car that also debuted at Frankfurt, the cX is another European style compact SUV crossover. It is powered by a 1.8 diesel engine.

FORD KUGA

The Kuga is a near-to-production concept car that will introduce the first compact SUV crossover to the Ford Europe car range. It is also the latest proponent of the "Kinetic Design" strategy that Martin Smith, Executive Director of Design, introduced first with the Iosis concept car in 2005. The Kuga takes its cues specifically from the Iosis X concept that debuted a year ago at the Paris motor show, and although far less extreme than that design, is the most expressive Ford and perhaps also the most expressive compact European market SUV. A 2-litre diesel engine powers the concept.

BMW X6

This concept car is very close to the final production car design of the forthcoming SUV-coupé crossover based on the BMW X5, which is set to be the first car of this type to enter the market. The sloping rear tailgate and dynamic side window shape of a coupé is uniquely combined with SUV ground clearance and generally rugged SUV design cues. Significantly, one of the two X6 models shown at Frankfurt was a petrol-electric hybrid-powered version which suggests BMW are close to offering this on production cars and also keen to send the right message about this car's environmental credentials.

RENAULT LAGUNA COUPÉ

Renault announced their production
Laguna design at Frankfurt along with
this study for a coupé of a similar size. The
pearlescent white paint and calmly elegant
exterior may not be attention grabbing,
but this was one of the most handsome show
cars of the year. It also had an exquisitely
detailed interior: chocolate leather seats that
spilled out over the side sills, polished billet
aluminium minor controls, and an overall
svelte, modern and very high quality feel.

CITROËN C5 AIRSCAPE

The C5 Airscape is a close indication
of what the forthcoming production C5
will look like, in detail if not overall concept.
It also shows how Citroën can add a more
premium dimension with the use of bright-
work, LED lamp technology and good
detail design. As a four-seater convertible,
the Airscape could be a preview of a type
of production C5 variant that has not been
seen in the Citroën range since the classic
DS Décapotable nearly half a century ago.

GM ECOJET

Announced at the ever-growing SEMA
show in Las Vegas in November 2006,
the Ecojet is unique in being conceived
by a car enthusiast, the famous US chat show
host Jay Leno, and developed by a large
automotive manufacturer, in this case GM.
Based on a 650-horsepower bio-diesel
powered jet turbine engine and Corvette
chassis, the exterior design is by Juho Suh,
with the interior still under development.
The design is characterized by its large roof
mounted air intake, short front overhang,
tapering cabin, fin-like rear fenders and
Cadillac-style vertical front and rear lights.

MASERATI GS ZAGATO

Created "in homage to the tradition
of the gentlemen drivers who asked
Zagato to transform the bodywork of their
cars…" this is the one-off Maserati GS
Zagato commissioned by the entrepreneur
Paolo Boffi that debuted at the Italian
Concorso d'Eleganza Villa d'Este in April.
Although aluminium-bodied, the car
is based on the outgoing Maserati Spyder,
and in character pays homage to the classic
Maserati A6 G Zagato of 1954. Compared
to the Spyder it has shorter overhangs to
give it a more sporty look, while the unusual
hatchback rear and classic Zagato "double-
bubble" roof – like the Spyker C12 Zagato –
give the car a very distinct appeal.

CASTAGNA AZNOM

Castagna is an Italian coachbuilder that designed
the one-off Aznom over the current Corvette
sports car chassis. The design has an American
feel notably in the "egg-crate" grille with inset
torpedo-shaped driving lamps that recall classic
1950s American cars such as the original Corvette.
The 800bhp concept has multiple air inlets and
outlets to cool brakes and engine, extensive use
of carbon-fibre to reduce weight, and a prominent
front splitter (the low leading edge at the base
of the front) and rear diffuser (the area directly
below the quad exhaust pipes at the rear of
the car) to improve aerodynamic down-force.

Italdesign looks ahead

The time when the coachbuilder's art was merely aesthetic is long gone. Designers have today taken over from the stylists of the past, and they can no longer simply create attractive bodywork, but have to rise up to the challenge of addressing what the future of the automobile holds. With the VAD.HO project presented here by **Serge Bellu**, Italdesign-Giugiaro affronts the theme of sustainable mobility with optimism, experimenting with a revolutionary engine powering a concept for a sports car. Proof that responsibility does not necessarily equate with austerity. Giorgetto Giugiaro and his son Fabrizio have constantly sought to question the future of transportation, reinventing the car's architecture, rethinking its use while maintaining intact its intrinsic appeal.

The name chosen by Italdesign-Giugiaro for its 2007 Geneva Show car was eloquent: "vado" in Italian means "I go". The "H" that found its way into the model name stands for the hydrogen power that lies at the heart of the project. VAD.HO is thus quite a dynamic and visionary name for a grand tourer for the future. Incidentally, Vadò also happens to be the name of the industrial area in Moncalieri, just outside Turin, where Italdesign has been based since 1974.

The VAD.HO is a low, sporty-looking coupé, with its two seats in a tandem arrangement. Its styling is not a million miles away from the Aztec project of the late 1980s. Its not inconsiderable size (4.55 metres long) is in line with modern-day GTs. The tandem seating lay-out was a deliberate reference to the world of motorbikes and planes, and that theme is carried over to the steering wheel which has been replaced by two joysticks, something younger video-game users will identify easily with. The instrument panel is LCD, and communications between the driver and the passenger are based on a game console!

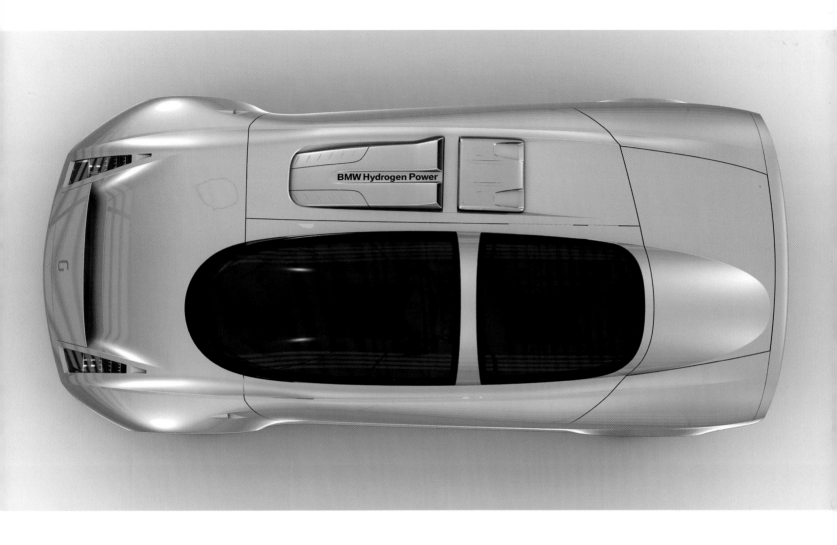

The long upper cockpit section lifts to allow access and inside the dominating colour is grey in a harmonious mix of shades varying from shiny to matte, underlining the technological feeling of the whole model. BMW's input in the project is implicit thanks to the use of the running gear used for the hydrogen-powered V12 Series 7 prototype. Hydrogen is often said to be the fuel of the future because its only by-product is water vapour. Rather than use hydrogen to feed an electric motor via a fuel cell BMW, like some other manufacturers, see hydrogen replacing petrol, enabling them to maintain the internal combustion engine in its present guise. In fact BMW launched the first fleet of Series 7 saloons in May 2000. In the VAD.HO the engine unit is fitted on the right-hand side of the body, counterbalancing the passenger cell.

While this lay-out may not be a feasible proposition going forward, hats off to Giugiaro for taking a lateral look at traditional automotive architecture to back up the new technology. Many manufacturers are working on alternative sources of energy or on unusual engine technology, but the majority apply these to conventional vehicle types. It is evident that the transformation in technology we are witnessing will require a serious rethinking about positioning mechanical parts and ancillaries. Fitting electric engines, hydrogen tanks, batteries and even the increasing use of electric controls will all call for changes in traditional architecture.

Giorgetto Giugiaro (left) and Fabrizio: father and son are working together to perpetuate the tradition of design excellence through innovation which has been an Italdesign-Giugiaro trademark since the company's creation four decades ago.

GIUGIARO'S OTHER INNOVATIVE CONCEPT CARS

Under the banner of Italdesign, the company he co-founded in 1968, Giorgetto Giugiaro quickly imposed himself as a formidable innovator in the automotive sector. After the Taxi, which was presented at the Museum of Modern Art in New York (1976), and the Megagamma (1978) which laid down the basis for modern compact MPVs, Giugiaro set out to define new types of vehicle, optimising the relationship between exterior dimensions and interior packaging.

The MPV concept was declined into multiple forms, breaking away from the limitations of a family-car approach. There was the Capsula (1982), a very functional concept car boasting an interior that featured various storage spaces for luggage, tools or spare parts. The other extreme was the Asgard (1988) which was a sporting evolution of the MPV with a streamlined form. The Structura (1998) was an architectonic interpretation of an automobile with the very deliberate use of visible structural elements in its aesthetic expression.

With the Buran, a proposal for a Maserati model in 2000, Italdesign demonstrated that an MPV could match the appeal of a GT car for driving pleasure. Before that,

the company had also explored urban vehicle design with the minimalist Biga (1992). At the same time, and in a deliberately paradoxical move, they also presented the Columbus, an enormous and luxurious touring MPV that could seat seven in immense comfort.

In the last few years, Italdesign-Giugiaro's research has concentrated on the integration of new technology. With the Alessandro Volta project (2004), Italdesign introduced an interesting large hybrid GT *berlinetta* concept, collaborating with Toyota, no less. A 3.3-litre V6 was linked up to two electric motors to give a total of 400 hp, sufficient to take the car to 100 km/h in just 4 seconds. When the petrol engine ran, a part of its power was routed through a generator to recharge the batteries or to drive the electric motors without the driver feeling any change in the power delivery. The Nessie sport-utility vehicle (2005) instead resorted to a hydrogen-fed engine.

Italian design houses can only survive by committing in this very manner to researching creative and realistic answers to the concerns of our modern society.

NEW YORK
TAXI

COLUMBUS

MEGAGAMMA

STRUCTURA

CAPSULA

BURAN

ASGARD

ALESSANDRO VOLTA

BIGA

NESSIE

Design trends in 2007

For manufacturers, concept cars are a means of propagating their image as leading designers and proposing something out of the ordinary. They also provide an opportunity for presenting ideas in embryonic form, with a view to gauging public reaction before going into production. In 2007, the latter approach seemed to predominate. **Anne Asensio**, who until recently was Head of Advanced Design at GM, and for whom the highlights of the year were the Hummer O$_2$, the KTM X-Bow, the BMW Concept CS and the Hyundai QarmaQ presented elsewhere in this volume, gives us her take on current trends.

The automotive world is still under pressure: with a looming energy crisis and growing concerns over pollution and safety, the private car is embattled on all fronts. But despite the hostile climate, opportunities exist on an unprecedented scale. The key lies in creativity, in tailoring solutions to fit problems and in deploying multiple strategies – because the days of one-size-fits-all are gone. Attack is the best form of defence, so cars are emphasising their masculinity. Competition is governed by the law of the jungle, where the most aggressive beast wins. The drive to differentiate, which manufacturers have embarked upon with their teams of designers, has spawned a profusion of concept cars.

THE ENVIRONMENTAL MESSAGE

The broad trend emerging in 2007 is the growing need for car brands to convey a responsible image and send out the right environmental message, in the face of fears about sustainable development, global warming and the emergence of a possible energy crisis. So the hybrid has become an essential feature of automotive strategy. While this may not be the best solution to environmental problems and oil dependence, it has certainly become the leitmotif of communication. Designers have thus come up with a new paradigm of style, that can be defined as "green" or "eco" design. This is manifesting itself in long-term visions of complete systems, taking the form of futuristic offerings such as the Hummer O$_2$ virtual concept, medium-term solutions, such as the Chevrolet Volt – an electric vehicle with the captivating contours of a sports coupé – and more immediate, style-driven initiatives applied by designers to give visual emphasis to the environmental credentials of existing vehicles. Green design is cool! Signs of it were already apparent, but the aggression with which manufacturers have pursued it in 2007 has given a big boost to the creative adventure of ecologically designed vehicles, which are technological items in substance, but presented under the guise of head-turning design. Green vehicle design is diversifying, and rather than distancing itself from the core values of motoring, appears to be re-appropriating them. The image of the outmoded, passionless ecowagon has been turned on its head. The latest expression of these concepts can be intellectual, as in the Nissan Cube with its emphasis on functionality, or specific, as in the Toyota Hybrid X, whose simplified design points to a conscious ecological choice by the customer. Preference is often given to one-box architecture, with aerodynamic shapes and fully integrated, flush surfaces, distinguished by non-aggressive facial features that provide a stark contrast with the rapacious grilles of traditional motors. High-performance green vehicles are also in the ascendant: with their athletic proportions and sports-car styling left intact, they offer the kind of sexy, desirable design that's in evidence on the Toyota FT-HS. So ecological driving with no compromises is an option.

General Motors' California-based Advanced Design studio came up with a refreshing view of environment-friendly vehicles, both conceptually and stylistically, with its Hummer O$_2$.

The Tesla and Venturi adventures, in California and Monaco respectively, are also redefining the sports car.

GLOBAL DESIGN

In a shrinking world, the time-honoured benchmarks of what we, in the West, call "good taste" in automotive design, are facing extinction.
The values and expectations of new consumers in emerging markets such as India and China, of which the latter alone reported sales of 6 million units in 2006, are challenging our established frames of reference. A minor revolution is under way, as a competition of preferences unfolds between European customers and their Asian counterparts, by whom demand is being driven. Clinic tests (involving anonymous presentations of projects to a targeted selection of buyers) are affecting design even more. The distinguishing features of Chinese design are influencing European and American creations. The decorative aspect of interiors is acquiring greater importance, as appearances become overstated, inserts in a wide variety of materials take centre stage, and wood, in all its forms, makes a comeback. Designers are also drawing inspiration from kitsch. Technical, ergonomic and practical considerations, meanwhile, seem to have dropped down the list of priorities.
After 10 years of hard work adapting and customising western products, the big emerging economies aren't going to settle for copying anymore. The emergence of original creativity has given rise to a number of design studios whose clear ambition is not only to offer consumers an expression of local design, but to throw down the gauntlet to western markets too. In other fields, such as fashion, the link-up of "good design" with culture has been very swift. The Brilliance range of vehicles, made in China and presented at the Geneva Motor Show, have all the hallmarks of attractive design and luxury styling. A lack of overall coherence and build quality still raises doubts about their potential to challenge European manufacturers in the short term; but how much longer can that go on? The response of western manufacturers has been to assert the identity of their brands and set up a network of design studios around the world so as to draw upon local skills and expertise. In 2007, several of these, including BMW, GM and Renault Nissan, to name but a few, stepped up their global design strategy.

BRAND REINFORCEMENT

While the brands with a dominant identity still have the upper hand, the mass market is beginning to show signs of dilution. In the top-end and luxury markets, reinvention is the order of the day. A blurring of the boundaries between different interpretations of style is driving the need for differentiation to further extremes. Sophistication is increasing constantly.

*Answering the growing demand for niche vehicles
intended for pure driving pleasure, KTM put
its long experience as a motorcycle manufacturer
to good use in creating the X-Bow. Its transversal
design language reflects current trends for sources
of inspiration drawn outside the automotive world.*

Aggressive, hyper-expressive design seems to be the strategy
of the day for brand reinforcement, giving rise to a frantic
race, which intensifies distinguishing features, accelerates
the search for personalisation and pushes design to extremes.
Front ends – which contribute most to brand identity –
are aggressive; emblems are oversized. Headlight lenses
– the technological showcase of a vehicle – are wrapped
around the bonnet, and rear lights are three-dimensional.
The result? An unprecedented show of luxury, as the classic,
discreet luxury of the past is pushed aside. The trick is to
reinvent in keeping with the values of the brand. BMW
and its CS Concept provide a good example of this.
American manufacturers, meanwhile, differentiate their
products by extending the offering of rear-wheel drive
platforms and playing upon a masculine expression,
a muscular look and the advantageous proportions favoured
by designers, namely long bonnet, short front overhang and
rear-set cabin to evoke performance. Even in Europe, these
dream proportions are gaining ground. The American brands
started the "tough look" by accentuating signs of virility and
bodies built on steroids, to evoke solidity. This monolithic
look engendered by smaller side windows, high waistlines,
lowered roofs, vertical windscreens and large wheels, gives
an impression of power and safety that is not far removed
from the most appreciated qualities of SUVs and crossovers.
The trend also derives from the constraints imposed by side-
impact and pedestrian impact requirements, which have led

to an increase in bonnet height, and a consequent rise
in waistline height in order to keep proportions balanced.
Styling is often reinforced by associating retro design
features with a modern expression, for example,
by re-using details such as side air vents on the
front wings, to symbolise power and luxury.

NICHE MARKETS

As markets fragment with increasing pace, cars are
breaking free from the constraints of segmentation
and convention, with the result that niches evoking
heritage, sport and leisure are gaining strength.
As the use of RWD platforms increases, the Americans
are harnessing the design heritage of muscle cars such
as the Chevrolet Camaro, Dodge Challenger and
Ford Mustang, to free themselves from the tenets
of European design, which favour the clean, aerodynamic
lines that are sometimes perceived as boring.
The Europeans, meanwhile, are still shaping their designs
around sporting values and the saloon-in-coupé-clothing
look coined by the Mercedes CLS, with lowered greenhouses,
hollowed out flanks and accentuated wings, especially
round the wheel arches, all combining to give a suggestion
of power: just take a look at the Opel GTC Concept.
Urbanisation is spawning an increasing number of small,
fun cars with character and low emissions, as a creative

69

Introduced in Shanghai, the BMW Concept CS appears to hold the seeds of BMW's new design language for the near future. Many thought the often controversial design direction promoted by Chief Designer Chris Bangle was coming of age with this sleek saloon offering.

response to the demands of consumers with a variety of lifestyles all revolving around city use. What's surprising is that American city cars are winning hearts in their homeland, as witness Chevrolet's triplets, the Beat, Trax and Groove. The trend for individualisation, which is clearly visible in Europe, continues in the States, as the success of the Mini and its derivatives has shown. Conversely, the need to feel safe amid an ocean of SUVs, like in the States, has found its way to Europe! The styling cues of SUVs, in the form of upright volumes, large wheels and a high driving position for improved visibility, are thus finding their way into smaller cars, such as the Dodge Hornet, which are small but tough. And the mutations continue… The return of the iconic Fiat 500 with its cute, retro design and period-style gadgets cannot fail to win hearts. But manufacturers are also offering roadsters and hard-top cabriolets in all sizes, and extreme sports cars. The search for automotive pleasure goes on, the passion still burns and we are now witnessing a convergence of influences from other arenas, such as motorcycling, with the KTM X-Bow naked car; Formula 1 with the Caparo, and aviation and marine sport, with the Bertone Barchetta and the Audi TT clubsport quattro. Every aspect of design is made to bear fruit. Details, such as wheels, have become powerful means of differentiation. The graphics and décor from the world of mangas, and graffiti drawn from underground culture are bursting into

the world of cars and accessories. One example is the sudden profusion of matte paintwork on display at the 2007 motor shows, combined with technical colours. The SEMA show in Las Vegas is becoming a trend-setting event that certain brands can no longer ignore. While the product remains central, the detour towards increasingly targeted experiences prevails.

THE FUSION OF TECHNOLOGY AND DESIGN

Instead of glass – which is too heavy – the Chevrolet Volt and Hyundai QarmaQ use a plastic supplied by General Electric, as one of a raft of measures aimed at reducing weight. New materials are thus giving rise to fruitful partnerships between manufacturers and equipment suppliers, while preserving the identity of each. What we are witnessing is a fusion of technology and design. Interior design is taking on new, emotive values too. Vehicle interiors are becoming a stationary centre of experience, with a more natural atmosphere than in the past, due to the emergence of natural materials with unusual and appealing qualities. Light is provided in countless ways, and its increasingly adventurous use is widely exploited as a distinguishing feature, involving natural light, sliding glass roofs, hard tops, artificial ambient light, diffused, coloured and indirect light, and so on.

Hyundai and its parent company Kia have recruited many designers in the past five years to strengthen their design studios worldwide. Their aggressive quest for a brighter image was well supported by the QarmaQ coupé off-roader, one of the nicest new concepts at the Geneva Show in March.

In the longer term, the deployment and original integration of technology within the framework of an intelligent man/machine interface will become the only real differentiators. The high-tech and low-tech schools of thought, meanwhile, are becoming increasingly polarised. The high-tech trend, with its "Star Wars"-style multi-functional screens, draws upon the world of video games: elaborate graphics, visual overstatement, personalisable lighting and flashy colours take their cues from the new icons of the moment, mobile phones, MP3 players and other mass devices. At the opposite end of the spectrum, the low-tech trend based on the cognitive logic of not putting an excess of resources at the disposal of the driver, uses design as a means of integrating functions. This is the path taken by Renault and Volvo. Lastly, we are witnessing the emergence of virtual concept cars such as the Mazda Hakaze, which made its debut on Second Life before appearing at the Geneva Motor Show, and the Hummer O_2, in a new departure that's set to become a must for the unveiling of concept cars in the future.

Design is fulfilling its role as a trend-setter and an indicator of fashions and developments in society. But it is also a new arena for expressing the globalisation of our lifestyles, which it reflects. In the hands of designers, as well as eliciting passion, cars become an interface for interaction with our environment. For decades, the car has been an expression of our freedom. What it now needs to become, is an expression of our responsibility.

Designers will be the dedicated craftsmen of this expression, and the winners will be those who recognise the key aspects of its reinvention – a reinvention that is essential for its survival.

The automotive industry tomorrow

Bob Lutz is Vice Chairman, Global Product Development, at General Motors. He is also one of the few top executives in the industry to be known as a true 'car-guy'. In the lines that follow, he tells us in a very concrete way how a global manufacturer is preparing for the future.

When the editors of this prestigious publication asked me to write an essay about the future of the automotive industry, I had the same reaction I always do when someone queries me on the topic. I defer to the wisdom of the American baseball legend Yogi Berra, who once said, "It's hard to make predictions, especially about the future." I will say this about the future: it will be here before you know it. It will arrive quickly, and it will look vastly different. This industry is in for some big changes, not only in propulsion technology, but also in vehicle-to-vehicle communications, that will directly affect the way we'll drive. Despite a steady stream of technical advances, today's automobiles share the same DNA as the first ones ever built. The basics haven't changed much in 100 years. The automobile is still powered by an internal combustion engine, fueled by petroleum and controlled by mechanical linkages. That said, we have seen great improvement in the formula over the years. Emissions of hydrocarbons, CO_2 and NOx have been reduced significantly in the past few decades. Traffic fatalities have dropped by two-thirds since 1965. Vehicles have become more affordable to all since the early days. And since 1974, in the United States, fuel economy has improved 130 per cent in cars and 75 per cent in trucks.

ADVANCED TECHNOLOGY STRATEGY

All automakers have clearly made steady gains in fuel economy in recent years. At GM, we have a comprehensive short-, mid- and long-term advanced technology strategy:

- we are working to improve the efficiency of our internal combustion engines in the short term, and also plan wider availability of diesel powerplants
- mid-term, we will increase our hybrid offerings
- and long-term, we feel the future of automotive propulsion will be electrically-driven vehicles, ultimately powered by hydrogen-powered fuel cells.

Let me stress why this plan is so important. The numbers say that by the year 2020, there could be as many as 1.1 billion vehicles on the planet, enough to circle the earth 125 times! And more than half of them will be in urban areas. So it's pretty clear we must find solutions to the energy, environmental, safety and congestion impacts of automobiles. All the while, we must enhance the passion, fun and affordability they offer. Our goal is simple: get this new mode of propulsion developed to the point that it provides the same performance, range and cost as today's internal combustion engine. And when we do, we have a real chance to reduce and ultimately eliminate our oil dependency.

MANY CHOICES

As stated above, we can begin to do that by increasing the efficiency of our internal combustion engines and diesel powerplants, and also increasing our roster of ethanol-capable FlexFuel vehicles, which we're doing. We'll have 2.5 million on the road this year in North America. We're also actively promoting the use of ethanol and the opening of more refueling stations that offer it. In Europe, when running on bioethanol, our Saab BioPower emits 70-80 per cent less CO_2, while delivering 17 per cent more horsepower. Saab now offers "eco-friendly" variants in all models of its European line-up. And hybrids? We have over 12 models approved for production. By the end of 2007 we'll have five on the market, and by the end of 2008 we'll have nine, including full-size SUVs and pickups. Down the road, we're developing several new technologies, including a "plug-in" version of our Saturn Vue Green Line hybrid. Drivers will be able to recharge their plug-in Vue, which is similar to an Opel Antara, at a standard electrical outlet, and get up to double the fuel economy of any SUV on the road today. We've also shown our latest fuel cell advances with a media drive of the Sequel concept car, which can travel 300 emissions-free miles on a single tank of hydrogen. This year we'll have the world's largest customer-driven demonstration fleet of 100 Chevy Equinox Fuel Cell vehicles. That's a lot of different methods of fuel-saving technology… because that's what we believe is required. We believe that no one solution is right for every part of the world, or even every consumer in any given market. So our approach is simple: offer as many choices as possible, to as many consumers as possible, everywhere we do business.

E-FLEX

As we've said a lot this year, we really feel the future of the automobile is electrification. We have a company-wide commitment to production of the Chevrolet Volt, which I'm personally as excited about as anything I've ever done. The Volt, introduced in January 2007 as a concept car at the North American International

The Volt is the first example of an innovative GM propulsion system called "E-Flex". All E-Flex vehicles will run on electricity, which can come from many different sources, such as a small motor running on bio-fuel, a hydrogen fuel cell, or even directly from the power grid.

Auto Show in Detroit, combines many of these technologies I've described in one vehicle. It's the first example of an innovative new GM propulsion system called "E-Flex." The E-Flex system is a family of electric vehicle propulsion systems built into a common chassis. An on-board engine or fuel cell creates electricity and extends the range of the vehicle. As you would surmise, the "E" stands for "electric," because, no matter their configuration, all E-Flex vehicles will run on electricity. And E-Flex is "flexible" because the electricity can come from many different sources, such as a small motor running on bio-fuel, a hydrogen fuel cell, or even directly from the power grid. By offering a system that drives vehicles with any of these fuels, E-Flex will provide our customers around the globe with a single elegant solution to tomorrow's energy issues. For most daily commutes, the Volt could nearly eliminate going to the gas station altogether and greatly reduce tailpipe emissions. For a 40-mile (65 km) daily driving pattern, the Volt will use no petrol and have zero emissions. For 60 miles (nearly 100 km), drivers would average about 150 miles per gallon (close to 65 km per litre), and save 570 gallons (2,150 litres) of gasoline annually compared to a similarly sized vehicle that gets 30 mpg (equal to a consumption of about 8 l/100 km). On longer road trips, the Chevrolet Volt's range-extending power source will continuously recharge the vehicle's battery for the duration of the trip to help drivers get the driving range they expect from today's vehicles. Before vehicles using the E-Flex system become a reality, we need further advancement in battery technology. We're making great progress in that area, together with our research partners, and I suspect it won't be long before we have E-Flex on the road.

ELECTRONICS

While we're on the subject of future technology, there's one last area I'd like to get into that goes a step beyond the propulsion discussion.
There's no question the area of technology in which automobiles have evolved the most is electronics. In the last 15 years, we have witnessed a reduction by a factor of 3,000 in the cost of computer memory and processing power – even as capability is increasing. That has allowed for advances like anti-lock brakes, traction and electronic stability control, semi-active suspension, adaptive steering and cruise control, obstacle detection, and others.
This advanced technology "ladder", enhancing the safety of the vehicles and helping reduce traffic congestion, would include such elements as lane departure warnings, collision avoidance, and vehicle-to-vehicle communications.
It will all be possible through Global Positioning System satellites, and transponder technology that will revolutionize vehicle-to-vehicle communications.
This isn't wacky stuff of the future… it's happening now; I have *driven* it. In fact, it's little different than transponder systems already in use in aviation, but with one less dimension. It starts with collision avoidance and goes from there.
The key difference between these new systems and current adaptive cruise control systems is in the communication. Today's systems are active. They send out a signal – whether radar, laser, sonar or whatever it uses – and the signal bounces back to it. Sensors determine the speed and location of the vehicle ahead and direct the car accordingly. The next-generation transponder systems are *passive*, and far superior to today's active systems. Each vehicle would be outfitted with

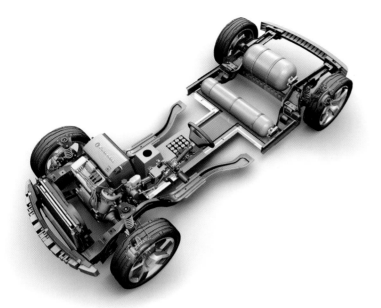
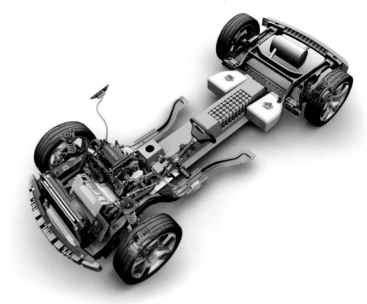

a transponder that just transmits and never gets anything back from *itself*, but it senses other vehicles' transponders. Sending an active signal and receiving it back limits you to exactly as far as the signal can go before it hits something. The passive transponders offer 360-degree "vision" or coverage, for up to 250 meters ahead or 150 meters behind. So, if six cars ahead somebody in a transponder-equipped vehicle steps on the brakes, your transponder immediately knows that. The computer starts going into brake alert, and starts slowing down the car before you're even aware you need to stop. It could also begin evasive steering, or seatbelt tensioning, or whatever it deems necessary. You would have no visual contact to know you need to slow down. And even if you had today's advanced adaptive cruise control, the radar would never get past the car in front of you. But the transponder would pick that up. It will know. I have driven this type of system at our proving ground, and we have already demonstrated an application using four communicating vehicles. During my test-drive, I heard the warning tone in the car that let me know somebody had slowed down to 20 mph far ahead of me, not just in my lane but in the lanes on either side of me as well. I saw the warning lamp light in my mirror if a vehicle moved into my blind spot. If a transponder-equipped car approached mine from the rear at a high rate of speed, my car sensed it, and activated my reverse lights and centre-high-mounted stop light, to alert to the fact that I was there.

AUTOMATED DRIVING EXPERIENCE

This type of technology, unheard of 10 or 15 years ago, is real. And it's coming. It's just another step toward the fully-automated, autonomous driving experience. Once you have transponders, radar, GPS and the rest, it will be possible to programme your vehicle for a Paris address before leaving Zürich, and then lean back and have the car take you there without any human intervention. That's something that is anathema to those of us who are keen drivers, and highly susceptible to the thrill of controlling a speed machine. But that's why people like us will always have motorcycles… Highway accidents and fatalities would be greatly reduced, and snarling traffic jams would be a thing of the past. That may seem far-fetched now, but so did the idea of a horseless carriage, once. Now we're working on transportation powered not by horse but by hydrogen. And suddenly, nothing seems so far-fetched anymore. So, as I said, we are working on many solutions to the same problems, all at once. Whether we're talking vehicle-to-vehicle communications or hydrogen-powered electric cars, in the über-competitive environment this industry faces, the companies that succeed will be those that take this sort of approach. They'll be the companies that are leveraging their resources the best, on a global scale, whether via acquisition or alliance, or, in our case, in maximizing our efficiency using what we already have. We have a long way to go yet, but we're harnessing our global talent in a way that we never have before and I think we've made some pretty significant progress thus far.

Again, the future of the automotive industry, which is fast approaching, will look radically different than what we know today. And I personally can't wait to get there.

Surface calm masks turbulent undercurrents

Europe's automotive sector appears to be a sea of tranquillity, with sales figures almost unchanged. But as **Xavier Chimits** explains, significant movement is afoot within the marketplace, and it might be a case of the calm before the storm.

To all appearances, it's been a quiet year, and judging by the slight upturn reported in the first eight months (up 1 per cent), Europe's car market should close 2007 with just over 16 million new car registrations. So apparently there is little to concern manufacturers. But they should not be deceived, because beneath the surface, three powerful undercurrents are at work.

Firstly, a closer look shows that Europe's car market is now made up of two distinct blocks. In historic strongholds, car sales were stable or dwindled slightly. In these markets the number of vehicles per household is high, while demographic growth is weak. These countries take the lion's share of European car market pie charts. Between them Germany, Italy, the United Kingdom, France and Spain account for almost 80 per cent of sales on the Old Continent. Which doesn't leave much for the other 23 member states. Nonetheless, the breeze that's fanning the flames of Europe's modest increase in sales is blowing from this latter direction and, generally speaking, it's an easterly. Suffice it to say that there was a 21 per cent rise in new car sales in Bulgaria, 25 per cent in Poland, 29 per cent in Romania and Estonia, 42 per cent in Lithuania and 47 per cent in Latvia. While impressive enough on first sight, the true impact on the overall trend is far lower because of the size of the markets in question. The largest – Romania – accounts for just 300,000 cars a year, or ten times fewer than the number sold in Germany, while the smallest – Estonia – equates to no more than 20,000!

The second undercurrent sweeping across the European car market in 2007 was more unexpected, and came in the form of a change in the make-up of the key players. Porsche, which now has a 30 per cent shareholding in the Volkswagen Group, is no longer coy about its intentions. What it wants is a controlling stake, and the only obstacle in its way is a curious point of Lower Saxon law. In Lower Saxony, no shareholder is entitled to more than 20 per cent of the voting rights in a company, regardless of the extent of their shareholding. Porsche reckons this is a breach of free-market principles and has taken its case to the European Court of Justice. Without even waiting for a verdict, Bernd Pischetsrieder decided that the game was up, and resigned his post as head of the VW Group in February 2007. This brings the patriarchal Ferdinand Piëch within a hair's breadth of realising his long-cherished dream of bringing VW and Porsche – the marques created by his ancestors – under the same roof. It looked like destiny that one day VW would swallow up Porsche. The disparity in size of the two companies left no alternative, with VW selling 5 million vehicles a year, against Porsche's 100,000. And yet the minnow is set to swallow the whale, as old-school industrial capitalism takes revenge on modern free-market economics, leaving the scattered shareholders of VW defenceless against the united, family shareholders of Porsche.

The other shift in the balance of power that's about to hit Europe has its origins in the United States: Ford has decided to focus more attention on its core business by lopping off some of its branches. For Aston Martin, the job's already done. But only half-done to tell the truth. Because the solution adopted can only be an interim measure. Ford sold Aston Martin to an investment consortium from the Gulf region, led by David Richards, a British industrialist who has built his reputation in motor sports. So far so good, but where are the engines and platforms for future Aston Martins going to come from? Eventually from a manufacturer with a profitable business, which has not yet shown its hand. In the meantime, Ford has put Jaguar and Land Rover up for sale, too, and is reflecting about the future fate of Volvo. Potential buyers are either established or emerging constructors (Indian conglomerate Tata is said to be interested), or private investment funds. But come what may, the cards are destined to change hands in Europe's car industry.

The third tendency affecting the globally flat European car market this year derives from the simple logic of one man's gain being another man's loss, in the same way that when a certain market segment slows, another will accelerate.

Volkswagen certainly lost a few points over the first eight months of 2007 (sales down 2.7 per cent over the same period in 2006), but remained comfortably ahead of its competitors, now that Renault is no longer a credible challenger. The French manufacturer's move to find strategic alliances outside its home territory in recent years (Nissan, Samsung and the construction of production plants for the Logan all over the world) will undoubtedly prove beneficial in the medium term. But the investment required came at a cost: almost two years had past before Renault rolled out new models in the shape of the Twingo II (June) and the Laguna III (September). The vacuum created left a considerable hole in Renault's European sales, which fell 11.7 per cent last year and a further 10.2 per cent in the first eight months of 2007, and Renault dropped two places in the manufacturers' league table, to the benefit of Opel and Ford.

Fiat, meanwhile, were heading in the opposite direction. In the space of three years, Sergio Marchionne has freed the Group from the influence of General Motors and brought it back into the spotlight by playing upon a distinctly Italian style. The Fiat brand is still a long way from the glories of its heyday, when it was Europe's biggest-selling brand, but it's making up for lost ground, and has gone one step up the league table again this year, to the detriment of Citroën. Fiat is still over-dependent on its home market, however, with Italy accounting for over 60 per cent of its European sales. And at 85 per cent, the equivalent figure for Lancia is even worse. The Fiat 500 will definitely make a positive contribution, but one country is no longer enough to ensure a manufacturer's survival, so Fiat needs to learn to cross borders.

A surprise emerged from the ranks of the three premium German brands, as Audi pushed BMW out of Europe's top ten by just over 400 units. Yet Audi has a less comprehensive range than either Mercedes–Benz or BMW, providing the company with untapped reserves at its disposal for further growth.

Lower down the list, Skoda (up 4.2 per cent), Honda (up 15.2 per cent) and Suzuki (up 5.9 per cent) predictably benefited from the renewal or extension of their ranges, in the same way as the C30 put a spring in Volvo's step (up 10.2 per cent). The outlook for Saab, meanwhile, is less rosy (down 9.1 per cent), as the brand gradually disappears from the European landscape. GM is clearly at a loss as to what to do with the Swedish manufacturer.

BEST SELLERS IN EUROPE

	Make	Sales 2007*	Variation	Market share
1	Volkswagen	1,099,143	-2.7%	10.2%
2	Opel	916,917	0.9%	8.5%
3	Ford	877,658	1.3%	8.1%
4	Renault	821,516	-10.2%	7.6%
5	Peugeot	765,893	0.5%	7.1%
6	Fiat	671,089	8.8%	6.2%
7	Citroën	653,820	2.3%	6.0%
8	Toyota	620,958	5.3%	5.7%
9	Mercedes	488,390	0.1%	4.5%
10	Audi	452,854	5.1%	4.2%
11	BMW	452,412	2.5%	4.2%
12	Skoda	317,555	4.2%	2.9%
13	Seat	267,000	-0.5%	2.5%
14	Honda	211,852	15.4%	2.0%
15	Hyundai	208,322	-6.4%	1.9%
16	Nissan	202,028	-10.6%	1.9%
17	Suzuki	190,386	5.9%	1.8%
18	Volvo	174,164	10.2%	1.6%
19	Mazda	161,687	-9.4%	1.5%
20	Kia	150,349	-5.4%	1.4%
21	Chevrolet	134,607	13.8%	1.2%
22	Dacia	114,487	20.9%	1.1%
23	Alfa Romeo	102,783	1.8%	0.9%
24	Mitsubishi	97,219	3.5%	0.9%
25	Mini	91,865	18.8%	0.8%
26	Lancia	88,188	6.7%	0.8%
27	Chrysler	70,264	4.2%	0.7%
28	Land Rover	59,834	4.1%	0.6%
29	Smart	56,213	-22.4%	0.5%
30	Saab	55,110	-9.1%	0.5%
	Europe	**10,823,680**	**+1%**	

* private vehicles registered between January and August 2007 in 28 European countries: Germany, Austria, Belgium, Bulgaria, Denmark, Spain, Estonia, Hungary, Finland, France, Greece, Ireland, Italy, Iceland, Latonia, Lithuania, Luxemburg, Norway, Netherlands, Poland, Portugal, Czech Republic, Romania, United Kingdom, Slovakia, Slovenia, Sweden and Switzerland.

While 2006 was a relatively quiet year on the saloon-car front, 2007 saw European manufacturers come up with a raft of new models in the family and luxury car segments, including the Renault Laguna, Ford Mondeo, Audi A4, Jaguar XF, Mercedes-Benz C-Class and Volvo V70 estate. **Xavier Chimits** reviews these and other new entries.

SMART FORTWO

Viewed from a distance, nothing has changed. But get up closer and you'll see that the new Smart (2.70 m) is 20 cm longer than its predecessor, to the benefit of interior and boot space (220 l). You can't park two Smarts in a single parking space any more, but the essence of the vehicle remains unchanged: with its trendy looks, nice two-tone effect and pocket-size format, the Smart clears every hurdle in the urban jungle. With its extended range of engines (with 61-, 71- and 84-hp versions of the little 1-litre), you'll even feel a frisson of speed: 145 km/h to be precise, which is 10 more than before.

OPEL AGILA

This model looks destined to provide a bridgehead into Europe for solutions developed by Suzuki: first there was the Wagon R (1990), then the Splash which only differed in the front-end treatment. The main difference is that it is a lot bigger – 3.74 m long – 20 cm more than the outgoing model. Ride comfort has improved with the adoption of a semi-independent rear suspension set-up. Its main selling point remains the boot capacity – 1,250 litres with the rear bench lowered.

FIAT 500

"The people's Mini": in just three words, Fiat boss Sergio Marchionne said it all. The new Fiat 500 was launched on 14 July, 50 years to the day since the launch of the original. The stylistic link is clear, with its curvy shape, ultra-short overhangs, three doors and diminutive size. But unlike its illustrious forebear, the Fiat 500 is not designed to mobilise the masses. Rather, like the Mini but one notch down (measuring just 3.55 m), it's designed to fill a "premium" niche in its class. There's no Twingo-style modularity either; just two rear seats, which fold to add a bit of extra space to the small boot (185 l). But its lines are irresistible, the interior design is minimalist "neo-retro" and there's a catalogue of options that can send prices soaring. Over and above the two basic petrol engines (a 69-hp 1.2 and a 100-hp 1.4), there's a frugal diesel (75-hp 1.3), and the Abarth version has already been presented which should guarantee plenty of attitude, courtesy of a 135-hp 1.4-litre turbo. Estate and cabriolet variants are also in the pipeline. So this 500 looks set to become an icon right from the word go.

RENAULT TWINGO

By not taking any of its styling cues from the much-loved Twingo I, the new Twingo generated a sense of betrayal among many of the original car's French fans. But according to Carlos Ghosn, the feminine features of the Twingo I hampered its international career. The Twingo II subscribes to the prevailing trend in the dynamic city car class (C2, Swift). This 3-door hatchback has gained 17 cm in length (3.60 m), in the name of improved safety, but the wheelbase and boot (165 l) remain pretty much unchanged. Apart from its shape, the new car remains essentially Twingo, and now features two separate sliding rear seats, with an adjustment range of 22 cm, in place of the old bench seat. Two more major changes complete the picture: firstly the Twingo II gets a diesel engine (65-hp 1.5 dCi) to join the petrol line-up (60-, 75- and 100-hp versions of the 1.2-litre), and secondly, it will make its UK debut in right-hand drive form.

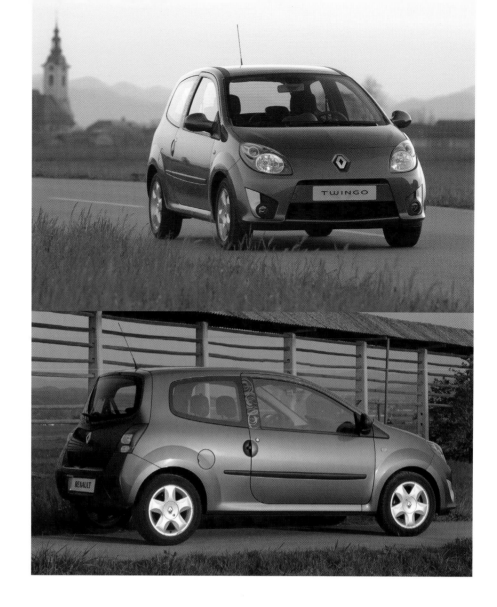

SKODA FABIA

With the face of the Roomster, a high waist-line and a Mini-like top half, the new Fabia has more presence than its predecessor, launched in 1999. Although a shade longer (3.99 m), it retains the chief quality of the latter, namely hospitality, thanks to a large boot (300 l) and a spacious, well-finished interior. It's only available in 5-door hatchback and Combi estate versions, which are very popular with customers. There's also a generous line-up of engines, with petrol variants from the 60-hp 1.2 to the 105-hp 1.6, and no less than three diesels – a 70- or 80-hp 1.4, and a 105-hp 1.9. This much-improved Fabia is further evidence of Skoda's revival.

FIAT BRAVO

With the characterless Stilo already forgotten, the Bravo epitomises Fiat's very Latin, very sensual new style. With its steeply raked waistline, the Bravo makes a foray into Alfa territory, but the vitality of its styling is not matched by its lacklustre performance. True to Fiat tradition, the Bravo (4.34 m) offers a roomy interior and spacious boot (400 l). Peculiarly, the range is built around just two engines, a 1.4 petrol and a 1.9 turbodiesel, tuned to deliver different power outputs. A steroid-enhanced version wearing the Abarth badge is also in the pipeline.

PEUGEOT 308

The 308 echoes the tall lines of the outgoing 307. It's the same height (1.5 m), but at 4.28 m in length it's 7 cm longer. That increase is concentrated exclusively in the overhangs, as the 308 is built on the 307's platform and thus maintains the same wheelbase. Like the 207, the 308 can be ordered with one of two different front grilles. The biggest improvement over the 307 comes in the assembly quality and a more complete specification.

RENAULT LAGUNA

The Laguna's predecessor, launched in the autumn of 2000, was ambitious in style and technology, but the latter proved not to be entirely flawless. The new Laguna takes the opposite approach: discreet styling and a sworn commitment from Renault to totally trouble-free electronics! But its interior design is strong and pure, with a wave-shaped dashboard. Interior quality gives the impression that the Laguna belongs in the next class up, while its size (4.69 m) places it in the large family segment. On the engine front there's a choice of diesels, starting with a 110-hp 1.5-litre and topping out with a 175-hp 2.litre. The Laguna's petrol engine range includes a 110-hp 1.6, while the 2-litre's output has been upped to 145 hp. A V6 will join the range later.

FORD MONDEO

The motoring public is barely on speaking terms with mainstream family cars at present, so to rekindle the flame, Ford brought forward the release of its new Mondeo to replace the car launched in 2001. Built on the same platform as the S-Max MPV, the Mondeo III inherits the dynamic styling of the latter. Now 5 cm longer (4.78 m), it takes over the title of Class Giant from the Passat. But more importantly, it's now 7 cm wider, hence the cavernous boot (540 l). A fine long-distance cruiser, the Mondeo is still designed to offer the best price-to-usable-space ratio in its class, although this tactic bore little fruit for its predecessor. The Mondeo debuts with a new engine line-up, with petrol offerings from 110-hp 1.6 up to 220-hp 2.5 turbo, while the diesel range includes a 100-hp 1.8 and a 140-hp 2.0.

AUDI A4

Elegance remains one of the A4's strong points, but discretion is no longer part of the appeal. With this latest incarnation, Audi continues its march towards a design language with a hint of underlying aggression. To the point that the new A4 appears rather like a four-door version of the A5 coupé, with which it shares the nose treatment and the dash, with its driver-oriented central console. But it is a lot bigger – at 4.7 m in length, it's 12 cm longer than the previous generation A4. That's to the benefit of the rear passenger knee room as the wheelbase has stretched by 18 cm. Petrol engines available at launch range from a 4-cylinder 1.8 to a 6-cylinder 3.2 (265 hp), while diesel offerings go from 2.0 to 3.0 (the latter developing 240 hp).

JAGUAR XF

More than a new model, the XF is a break with tradition. It replaces the S-Type which took design cues from the classic Mk II for its neo-retro styling. With taught lines, a distinctive honeycomb radiator grille and sophisticated cabin, the XF looks forwards, not back. And with an eye on the BMW M, Mercedes AMG and Audi S series, because the future XF-R will be powered by a turbo-charged 5-litre V8 which will break the 500-bhp barrier. Other engines include a 3-litre V6, 4.2-litre V8 and a diesel-powered 2.7-litre V6. A tad longer (4.96 m) than the outgoing S-Type, the XF also stands out for the aluminium knob on the central tunnel. An IDrive like BMW's? No, rather the automatic gearbox command.

MERCEDES-BENZ C-CLASS

The sharp, modern styling of the new C Class (4.58 m) brings it closer to its big brother, the S Class. The design brief was to "enhance driving pleasure without compromising comfort". Mission accomplished thanks to the Agility Control system, fitted as standard, which constantly adapts the degree of steering assistance and suspension damping to the road surface and driving style. The C Class thus takes a step in the direction of the BMW 3 Series and Audi A3, while retaining a higher price, of course. There are four petrol engines available right away (from 156-hp 1.8-litre to a 272-hp 3.5 V6), and three diesels (136- or 170-hp 2.2-litre and a 224-hp 3-litre).

VOLVO V70 AND XC70

The previous version was over-cautious, and lost sales to the A6 Avant as a result. But Volvo has learnt the lesson, so its new V70 estate is based on the S80 platform rather than the S60 platform as before, and the engines move up a notch too, with a range of six-cylinder powerplants backing up the traditional five-cylinder unit. The V70 is now 11 cm longer (4.82 m), thus combining ample boot space (540 l) with elegant contours, in keeping with the new paradigm of the estate car, which has been a Volvo institution since 1953. And for the rough stuff, there's still the XC70 variant, complete with four-wheel drive and 21 cm of ground clearance.

CITROËN C-CROSSER AND PEUGEOT 4007

There's no shame in looking outside for missing know-how. So Citroën and Peugeot join the SUV club by re-badging the Mitsubishi Outlander, to which they will add their own engines, starting with the 160-hp 2.2 HDi for now. Measuring 4.64 m, the C-Crosser and 4007 will take you along dirt tracks but not far beyond, with ground clearance of 17 cm.
The dynamic styling and backward-sloping roof don't benefit boot space (510 l), but these 4x4s offer modularity in the form of a sliding rear bench and a third row of two stowable seats. If nothing else, they provide a valid alternative to Citroën's Picasso.

VOLKSWAGEN TIGUAN

The Tiguan offers what's expected of new 4x4s – it's available in both two-wheel and four-wheel drive versions, although VW expects the latter to be the best seller. At 4.40 m in length, this is a compact SUV and it's based on the Golf platform, so expect more a road-plugger than a mud-plugger. The lines closely recall those of the Touareg and are both elegant and reassuring at the same time. With an almost vertical tailgate and rear seats that can be folded 2/3 or a 1/3, the Tiguan can swallow a lot of luggage.

AUDI A5

After an 11-year absence, the length (4.62 m), fluid style, and huge boot (455 l) of the A5 mark Audi's return to the four-seater coupé segment, or more precisely the 2+2 segment, given the plunging roofline. Agile and well-balanced, what the A5 loses in vitality it gains in serenity, with the Quattro drive system complementing the three best engines, the 3.2 V6, the 4.2 V8 and the 3.0 V6 diesel. The range has yet to be completed: a 1.8 will bring the entry-level price to around €31,000, while an RS5 (4.2 V8 uprated to 430 hp) will make its debut in 2008, with an altogether different mission…

BMW M3

The M5 has shifted up to a V10, so the fourth generation M3 has moved up a notch accordingly. The first V8 in the car's history is carefully chosen, and delivers 105-hp per litre from its 3,999 cc capacity. In other words, by sheer coincidence, it has the same number of cylinders and same power (420-hp) as the Audi RS4 4.2… But the carbon-fibre roofed M3 coupé has watched its weight, which stands at a modest 1,655 kg. As such, it regains the leadership, with a 0 to 100 km/h time of just 4.8 seconds. As usual, the coupé has blazed the trail, with the rest of the family following swiftly behind.

MASERATI GRANTURISMO

A large Italian 2+2 coupé with a lengthy bonnet and a gaping front grille. How can one's thoughts not turn to the Ferrari 612, when the GranTurismo rivals its cousin for size? At 4.88 m long it is just 2 cm shy of the Ferrari. For its size alone, the new Maserati coupé has distanced itself from the outgoing Gran Sport (4.30 m). Its close parentage with the Quattroporte puts it very much at the high end of the GT segment: equipped with the same 405-hp 4.2-litre V8, it has also dropped the paddle-shift Cambiocorsa 6-speed in favour of a ZF automatic. The price should remain below €115,000. The powerful, fluid styling is courtesy of Pininfarina – 50 years after the Maserati A6 1500… which says it all.

ASTON MARTIN DBS

Maybe it should have been called the Vanquish, because the DBS is the maximum expression of the Aston Martin DB9. It shares the same sober yet magnetic styling that typifies Aston, with large air vents on the wings and bonnet. It doesn't shout power, it just hints, with 20" wheels, lower overall height (2 cm lower at 1.28 m), all-aluminium chassis, carbon-fibre body, carbon-ceramic brakes, weight reduced by 100 kg over the DB9 and a hike in power to 517-hp, a 62-hp increase. That's enough to see the DBS reach a top speed of over 300 km/h, and cover the 0-100 km/h sprint in 4.3 seconds with a manual gearbox. Is it brutal? A car for purists, rather.

BENTLEY BROOKLANDS

Bentley is divided into two families these days: the modern one, under the Continental name, with German engines and chassis; and the classic, 100 per cent British one, with its hallmark wide grille and bespoke price tag. Lined up beneath this banner are the Arnage, the Azure convertible and the new Brooklands coupé, fitted with the most powerful engine ever to come out of Crewe, which is a 537-bhp bi-turbo version of the venerable 6.7-litre V8 that drives the Arnage. The Brooklands coupé will have a strictly limited production run of just 550 cars.

ROLLS-ROYCE PHANTOM DROPHEAD COUPÉ

While the Maybach remains discreetly covered, the New Phantom goes topless. By virtue of a purely Rolls subtlety, the convertible is not known as the Corniche, as tradition would demand, but as the "Drophead Coupé". With a five-layer fabric top and teak deck, the Drophead is 22 cm shorter than the limousine, measuring 5.61 m. It's also lower (1.58 m), but 135 kg heavier, weighing in at 2,630 kg.

An industry on the move

Slumping sales, particularly in profit-heavy trucks, continue to bedevil the American market, **Matt DeLorenzo** reports. While all manufacturers are relying on incentives to keep the iron moving across showroom floors, the industry's real drama is playing out in boardrooms coast-to-coast with unprecedented restructuring of the business.

Perhaps the biggest single change on the American automotive scene is the arrival of private equity at the industry's highest level as Cerberus Capital Management purchased the Chrysler Group from DaimlerChrysler to form Chrysler LLC. While these privately funded firms have had a strong presence among Tier 1 suppliers, this move to take over a member of the Big Three is a first; one that was greeted with mixed emotions. Although Stephen Feinberg, the reclusive principal of Cerberus, promised that he was doing this out of a sense of patriotism, others harboured fears that he would merely clean up the books slightly, then slice and dice the company selling it off for more than the $7.4 billion it paid for the lesser half of what was billed as a merger of equals just 10 years earlier.

Fears that it would be more of the latter than the former were fueled when Cerberus hired Robert Nardelli, a hard-nosed cost cutter from GE and Home Depot, to run the company instead of Chrysler alumni Wolfgang Bernhard who, since his departure from Volkswagen, was advising the equity group on the acquisition. Tom Lasorda, Chrysler chairman, was forced into a vice chairman role with responsibilities limited to manufacturing, while a huge bombshell was dropped when Jim Press, freshly minted as the first non-Japanese board member for Toyota, stepped down to share the vice chairman spot to oversee sales and marketing.

This came at a time when Chrysler, Ford and General Motors were engaged in contract negotiations with the United Auto Workers, in which the Big Three were expecting significant concessions to regain their competitive footing with import nameplates, which for the first time ever, saw their combined market share pass the 50 per cent mark. Fortunately for Chrysler and Ford, the UAW picked GM as its strike target, since that company showed improved sales through 2007 and could least afford a lengthy strike. GM's newfound vigour is the result of an aggressive product offensive that included all-new full-size pickups and SUVs, new mid-size entries from Saturn in the form of Aura and the Chevy Malibu, a redesigned Cadillac CTS and a new family of purpose-built crossovers – the Buick Enclave, Saturn Outlook and GMC Acadia.

Ford, on the other hand, continues to struggle with its line-up of dated vehicles, facelifting its poorly received Five Hundred sedan and Freestyle crossover as the Taurus and Taurus X. Outsider Alan Mullaly, brought in from Boeing, promised a more global approach to product development and is looking for the European product line to turn things around in the U.S., but it will take some years before those cars come on stream. In the meantime, cost cutting in the form of plant closures and lay-offs continued apace. And rumours swirl that the next victim of downsizing will be the elimination of the Mercury line of vehicles. Also at the top of Mullaly's list, after the sale of Aston Martin to a consortium led by David Richards, were the divestiture of Jaguar and Land Rover and possibly of Volvo. Indian auto company Tata is said to be ready to take over Jaguar and Land Rover, which would free up assets and allow Ford to concentrate resources to reinvigorate Lincoln as its premiere luxury brand.

Toyota marked its 50th year in America by opening its San Antonio, Texas assembly plant to introduce the Tundra, a full-sized pickup aimed at the heart of a domestic industry stronghold. While boasting impressive specifications, it also carried a sticker price to match. The improvements to the truck over the previous generation weren't enough to make significant inroads in the market. Sales got off to a slow start and only when the new truck received incentives and the product line broadened sufficiently to have lower-priced models, did the needle begin to move for the Japanese maker. Although Toyota is looking for first years sales of somewhere in the neighborhood of 200,000 units, the plant itself is capable of producing twice that.

Archrival Nissan, which has already seen how difficult it is to compete in the full-size truck market, completed its transition from its Southern California home to a new headquarters in Nashville, Tennessee, ostensibly to be closer to the American heartland and its mid-South manufacturing base, although some observers believe it was a calculated move on the part of Nissan/Renault Chairman Carlos Ghosn to move the company out of the shadow of Toyota as well as a way to reduce head count and overheads.

Also on the move are the offices of Volkswagen of America, as well as the Audi and Bentley brands, which announced plans to decamp from its suburban Detroit home of Auburn Hills to Herndon, Virginia, a suburb west of Washington, D.C. Like Nissan, the VW move is considered one way to move out of the shadow of the troubled Big Three in an effort to jump start its sales. In addition to moving its headquarters, VW is promising an aggressive product assault specifically aimed at the U.S. market which would include a new mid-size saloon and SUV developed specifically for American tastes. VW officials also wouldn't rule out the possibility of eventually reestablishing a U.S. manufacturing base.

All the manufacturers will be spending considerably more time in Washington, D.C. as a consensus has developed that it is a matter of not if, but when and how much fuel economy standards will be increased. Fears of global warming and a desire for less dependence on foreign oil have fueled legislation raising the standards from the current 27.5 mpg to upwards of 35 mpg. Although the manufacturers agree that standards can and should be raised, they are wary of automatic annual increases written into the legislation and the prospect that lower truck requirements will be combined with the higher car standards. It's a debate that will likely rage into 2008 and be part of next year's Presidential elections.

BEST SELLERS IN THE USA

	Make	Sales 2007*	Variation
1	General Motors	2,599,119	-7.4%
2	Toyota (inc. Lexus)	1,788,603	4.9%
3	Ford Motor Co.	1,782,545	-12.5%
4	Chrysler Motors	1,419,024	-2.7%
5	Honda (inc. Acura)	1,066,320	2.1%
6	Nissan (inc. Infiniti)	718,781	4.5%
7	Hyundai (inc. Kia)	533,149	1.7%
8	BMW Group	223,613	8.1%
9	VW Group	219,455	0.2%
10	Mazda	203,298	7.6%
11	Daimler AG	157,958	0.4%
12	Subaru	122,165	-8.0%
13	Mitsubishi	93,724	17.4%
14	Suzuki	74,347	1.3%
15	Porsche	23,637	-2.3%
16	Isuzu	4,969	-17.8%
-	others**	4,974	5.6%
	USA	**11,036,119**	**-2.8%**

* sales January through August
** including estimates for Ferrari, Lamborghini and Lotus
Source: Automotive News Data Center

Faced with strong competition from imports – and several important new models from foreign manufacturers built locally – the Big Three have taken steps to diversify their product range and even their brand portfolio. **Matt DeLorenzo** presents the most important new metal to hit the US market in 2007.

SCION XB AND XD

For 2008, Scion has revamped two-thirds of its product line-up with all-new xB and xD models (the tC coupé returns essentially unchanged). The boxy xB is 12-in. longer than the previous model and sports more rounded edges. Power comes from a 2.4-litre four producing 158 bhp, a gain of 55 bhp. Likewise, the xD is larger and more powerful than the xA model it replaces. The xD, however, is boxier than the hatchback it succeeds and sports a rounded nose that wouldn't look out of place on a locomotive. Only slightly larger than the xA, the xD has a 1.8-litre four-cylinder engine that produces 128 bhp, a gain of 25 bhp over the xA's 1.5-litre unit.

SATURN ASTRA

General Motors continues its drive to revitalize its Saturn division by melding its product line with Opel. The next step in the process is adapting the 3- and 5-door Astra to the U.S. market. The 2008 Astra is offered in two trim levels, a base XE on the five-door and a more upscale version called the XR in both three- and five-door body styles. Power comes from a 1.8-litre four producing 140 bhp mated to a choice of five-speed manual or four-speed automatic. The Astra, which will be imported from Belgium, rides on a 103-in. wheelbase.

FORD FOCUS

Evidently Ford believes the conventional wisdom that hatchbacks don't sell in America by axing its three- and five-door body styles (as well as the estate) in favour of adding a coupé to the Focus line-up. Rather than adapting the successful C1-based European Focus for the U.S. market, the manufacturer has opted to facelift the current CT170 version with styling that looks more Asian than European. The new Focus, which carries over its 2.0-litre four-cylinder engine, introduces Ford's new Sync system developed with Microsoft to provide Bluetooth connectivity to phones and music players.

DODGE AVENGER

With muscle car looks lifted from the larger, rear-drive Charger, the Avenger is Dodge's front-drive stable-mate to the Chrysler Sebring. Offered in three trim levels, the Avenger's engine choices include a 173-bhp 2.4-litre four, an E85-fueled 2.7-litre V6 rated at 189 bhp and a top spec 235-bhp 3.5-litre V6. The latter is offered with a six-speed automatic, while the other two engines get a four-speed auto. All-wheel drive is expected to be offered as an option midway through the '08 model year.

FORD TAURUS

Responding to lagging sales of the Five
Hundred, Ford ordered a quickie facelift
incorporating the Fusion's three-bar grille
theme and rechristened this full-size family
saloon with the legendary Taurus name.
In addition to the makeover and name
change, the Taurus also benefits from a
significant upgrade beneath the bonnet -
the 3.0-litre V6, which made just 203 bhp,
has been replaced by a 3.5-litre V6 rated at
260 bhp. The CVT is gone and all models,
whether front- or all-wheel drive, now
have a six-speed automatic transmission.

HONDA ACCORD

The 8th generation Honda Accord saloon
bows in with much bolder styling, a longer
overall length and wheelbase and an
upgraded interior that rivals the offerings
from its sister Acura division. The Accord
is offered with a base 2.4-liter four-cylinder
engine in two states of tune, 180 or 200 bhp.
Buyers can opt for a 5-speed manual or
automatic transmission. The optional V6,
which comes with a 5-speed automatic only,
has been increased in displacement from
3.0 to 3.5 litres and now makes 273 bhp.
Honda has further refined its fuel-saving
cylinder deactivation system, which
operated on either three or six cylinders
to include a new four-cylinder mode.

CADILLAC CTS

In its first major redesign since it was introduced in 2003, the CTS still retains its sharp-edged styling. The grille is bolder and the CTS now sports a front wing vent that is a new signature for all Cadillacs. The interior has been completely reworked with a new dash, hand-sewn leather on the dash, doors and thin-back bucket seats, and more luxurious wood and chrome trim pieces. Power comes from a 3.6-litre V6 that will be offered in two states of tune, a 255-bhp base engine and a direct injection variant rated at 300 bhp. All models come with a six-speed automatic transmission. A year later, Cadillac is expected to launch a successor to the V8-powered CTS-V.

CHEVROLET MALIBU

Based on the Epsilon architecture used by the Saturn Aura, the 2008 Chevy Malibu represents a significant upgrade in exterior and interior styling on the five-passenger mid-size saloon. The richer looks are complimented by the optional 255-bhp 3.6-litre V6, which is mated to a six-speed automatic. The base engine remains the 164-bhp 2.4-litre four, which is also equipped with the six-speed automatic. The Malibu is offered in just one body style, as the five-door Maxx model has been dropped from the line-up, and in three trim levels, LS, LT and LTZ.

PONTIAC G8

The Pontiac division is again turning to GM's Holden subsidiary in Australia to provide it with another rear-drive entry, this time a Commodore saloon called the G8. The saloon essentially replaces the GTO, a Monaro-based coupé that met with limited success. The G8, which rides on a 114.3-in. wheelbase, offers a choice of two engines, a base 3.6-litre V6 rated at 261 bhp and a 360-bhp 6.0-litre V8. The former comes with a five-speed automatic, while the V8 can be equipped with either a six-speed manual or automatic transmission. There will be no G8 coupé.

CHRYSLER TOWN & COUNTRY AND DODGE GRAND CARAVAN

The revamped Chrysler Town & Country and Dodge Grand Caravan are squared off to increase interior space and allow for such features as drop-down glass in the sliding rear doors. Chrysler has added the option of second row captain's chairs that swivel instead of stowing. These minivans have now a limousine-like interior. Along with the new shape, Chrysler is offering three engine choices, a 170-bhp 3.3-litre V6 base engine, a 3.8-litre V6 making 198 bhp and a 4.0-litre six rated at 240 bhp.

SATURN VUE

With styling similar to the Opel Antara, the Saturn Vue is offered in four trim levels, XE, XR, Red Line and hybrid Green Line. Base front-drive XE and hybrid Green Line models are equipped with a 164-bhp 2.4-litre four, while the XE all-wheel drive has an ohv 3.5-litre V6, which produces 215 bhp. XR and the performance-tuned Red Line model have a 250-bhp 3.6-litre V6. All V6 models come with a six-speed automatic transmission, while a five-speed manual will become available mid-model year. The five-passenger Vue is based on GM's Theta architecture, which is also used on the Chevy Equinox and Pontiac Torrent crossovers.

NISSAN ROGUE

Instead of selling the Mexican-built X-Trail to compete with the likes of Toyota's RAV4 and Honda CR-V, Nissan has developed the 182.5-in. long Rogue, a 5-passenger front- or all-wheel drive crossover that borrows styling cues from the much larger Murano. Like the Murano, the Rogue is offered with a CVT that can be equipped with an optional manual shift mode that provides 6 steps in the transmission. The Rogue, which rides on a 105.9-in. wheelbase, is powered by a 2.5-litre in-line four that produces 170 bhp and 175 lb ft of torque. Among the standard features are traction and vehicle stability control systems.

LEXUS LX 570/470

Toyota reworked its full-size Lexus SUV with new styling, added electro-hydraulic suspension to improve on-road ride and equipped the vehicle with a new crawl mode to benefit its off-road capabilities. The base 470 model carries over the previous model's 4.7-litre V8 engine. The range topping LX 570 has an all-new 5.7-litre V8, which makes 381 bhp, mated to a six-speed automatic. This full-size SUV's brother in the Toyota line, the Land Cruiser, received a similar makeover for the model year.

TOYOTA HIGHLANDER

The brand new Toyota Highlander boasts a roomier back seat and more rugged SUV styling inspired by the company's legendary Land Cruiser. In addition to a more spacious cabin that features a new second row captain's chair option, there's more power under the bonnet – the vehicle gains 55 bhp over the previous model and now extracts 270 bhp from its standard 3.5-litre V6. A rearview camera for backing up is standard equipment. Offered in base, sport and limited models, the Highlander is also available in a hybrid version.

JEEP LIBERTY

Riding on a 106.1-in. wheelbase and measuring 176.4 in. overall, the redesigned Jeep Liberty is larger and more rugged-looking than its predecessor. The squared-off looks and rectangular headlamps reinforce the family look of the full-size Jeep Commander, which moves this SUV from the compact to the mid-size segment. The Liberty is offered with a choice of either part- or full-time four-wheel drive and a sole 210-bhp 3.7-litre V6. 2008 will bring an all-new rack-and-pinion steering system as well as a revised independent front and five-link rear suspension.

NISSAN ALTIMA COUPE

Think of it as a G37 for those on a budget. The new Altima Coupe, which is priced in the $20,000-$30,000 bracket, is a more stylish alternative to the standard Altima saloon. The coupé rides on a four-inch shorter wheelbase that contributes to an overall length seven inches shorter than the saloon. Unlike the rear-drive Infiniti, however, the Altima is front-drive and is offered with a choice of a 170-bhp 2.5-litre four-cylinder engine or an optional 3.5-litre V6, which produces 270 horsepower. The Altima also comes with a choice of six-speed manual or CVT transmission.

INFINITI G37 COUPE

Although it looks similar to the G35 it replaces, the new Infiniti G37 Coupe has all new body panels and much higher quality interior materials and finish. The rear-drive G37 is equipped with a V6 engine that now displaces 3.7 litres and produces 330 bhp. The car, which is aimed squarely at the BMW 3-Series coupé, uses the increased displacement, variable valve timing and a higher compression ratio to achieve its higher performance. Other technological improvements include electronically controlled four-wheel steering, which Infiniti says improves the car's handling.

HONDA ACCORD COUPE

Recognizing that coupés may be making a comeback in the U.S., Honda has tooled up a new two-door version of its all-new Accord. The coupé features styling distinct from the saloon, with narrower headlamp openings, a more aggressive grille and nose treatment and a steeply raked rear window. The coupé rides on a shortened wheelbase and comes with a 200-bhp 2.4-litre four-cylinder engine. The optional 3.5-litre V6 produces 273 bhp and dispenses with the saloon's cylinder deactivation system in order to have a fatter torque band. The V6 coupé is offered with a choice of 6-speed manual or 5-speed automatic.

DODGE VIPER SRT10

Thanks to variable cam timing and a slight bump up in displacement and compression, the Dodge Viper SRT10 now boasts 600 bhp – a gain of 90 bhp over the previous model. The V10 engine displaces 8.4 litres, up from the previous models 8.3, and utilizes a unique cam-within-a-cam design to change valve timing, which not only allows the engine to rev higher, but produce much more power. Although the basic design of the Viper remains unchanged, the larger vents and intakes on the front fascia and bonnet announce the fact that there is much more muscle in the engine bay. Dodge estimates that the Viper can accelerate to 60 mph in less than four seconds.

CALLAWAY C16

Specialist tuner Reeves Callaway is offering both bespoke bodywork and significant power upgrades to Corvette aficionados with his new C16 conversion. In addition to the revised exterior panels and upgraded interior, the C16 package includes a supercharger fitted to the 6.0-litre LS2 V8, which bumps horsepower up from 400 to 616 bhp. Callaway estimates that the car can accelerate to 60 mph in 3.5 seconds, run the quarter mile in 11.2 seconds and hit a top speed of 200 mph. Available in coupé and convertible form, the Callaway C16 starts at about $120,000.

Japanese exports soar

If anyone doubted the strength of the Japanese auto industry, the figures for 2006
– or some of them, at least – should have easily changed most opinions. However,
as **Fred Varcoe** tells us, there were still some conflicting signs within the industry
– some real, some imagined – but the health of the industry is hardly in doubt.

Japanese automakers produced a total of 11.48 million vehicles in 2006, up a healthy 6.3 per cent from 2005 and outpacing production of U.S. manufacturers by 220,000 vehicles. Production in the U.S. declined 5.7 per cent by comparison. Almost equally as startling were China's production figures, which leapt 25.9 per cent to 7.19 million vehicles, shoving Germany down into fourth place in the "rankings." South Korea came in fifth with a total of 3.94 million units, up 4.3 per cent from 2005.

Toyota continued to dominate Japanese automakers and it was reported that the auto giant is aiming to grab 14 per cent of the global market by 2010. For now, it can bask in the glow of becoming the No. 1 automaker in the world, overtaking the sales of General Motors from the first quarter of 2007, a trend likely to continue throughout the year and beyond. Toyota's financial performance overseas reached record levels for the company (early 2007), with net revenues growing 13.8 per cent, operating income 19.2 per cent, and net income 19.8 per cent – all records for the company. While vehicle sales in Japan and Asia dropped (by more than 10 per cent in Asia and a surprising 3.9 per cent in Japan), Toyota posted rises of 15.1 per cent in North America and 19.6 per cent in Europe.

Japan's automotive exports continued unabated, rising a stunning 19.7 per cent to 16.2 trillion yen (about 140 billion U.S. dollars). Exports of passenger cars rose 21.4 per cent to 5.3 million units, with 41.7 per cent of them heading to North America. Production of vehicles overseas also continued the upward trend as Japanese automakers expanded their overseas manufacturing bases, particularly in China and south-east Asia. The number of vehicles produced in Asia (outside Japan) by Japanese manufacturers breached the 4 million-unit mark for the first time. The total number of vehicles manufactured overseas rose by 366,086 to 10,972,243 units.

While the number of new vehicle registrations remained static in Japan at 5.85 million units, China saw a massive leap of 13.5 per cent to a figure – 5.76 million units – almost equal to that of Japan. India and South Korea also showed a healthy increase in the number of new cars registered with rises of 6.3 per cent (to 1.43 million units) and 4.9 per cent (to 1.17 million units), respectively. On the flipside of these statistics, automotive imports into Japan fell 2.3 per cent in terms of numbers (to 262,000) but increased 7.9 per cent to 1.4 trillion yen in terms of money spent, reflecting an increase in sales of high-end vehicles rather than a more universal appeal towards buying foreign vehicles. BMW (together with its Mini brand) continued to set the pace with a 6 per cent increase in sales to a very creditable 62,000 vehicles. In fact, the domestic market saw a decline in most categories with only the minicar (K-Car) section on the rise. Sales in this section breached the 2 million-unit mark for the first time, with Daihatsu accounting for nearly a third of sales in Japan.

The number of so-called "green" vehicles continued to rise as Japanese manufacturers sought ways to improve fuel efficiency, reduce exhaust emissions and find alternatives to petrol-based fuels. Mercedes-Benz added a diesel car to their line-up in 2006, while Nissan has been working with partner Renault in the same field and will introduce a diesel version of the Dualis into Japan in 2008. The Japanese government has taken the lead in providing incentives for eco-friendly cars with legislation that reduces the annual automobile tax by up to 50 per cent and the purchase price of vehicles by up to 300,000 yen (about 2,600 U.S. dollars).

China is expected to see continued growth in the coming years, but there are signs that the frenzied pace of expansion is slowing down slightly. Luxury cars are attracting substantially more buyers and the market tends to prefer saloons rather than hatchbacks. Competition for the major players – nearly all Japanese as far as manufacturing goes – is growing from within with the result that prices are edging down. There have been concerns over patent infringements with some foreign car companies claiming that local rivals are stealing their designs.

In South Korea, local manufacturers dominate but the high-end brands of Japan's major manufacturers have made a surprising dent in the market, with Infiniti and Lexus competing with Mercedes-Benz and BMW.

The political situation in Thailand has caused some waves, but is unlikely to affect long-term investment and production by the major manufacturers. All the Japanese companies have invested heavily in Thailand, particularly in the pick-up market, the second largest in the world after the United States.

India is booming but the focus is on affordability. Tata will launch their "1 lakh" (equivalent to 100,000 rupees or $2,500) car next year, which could turn the whole industry upside down. The market is set for growth in the future and will be a mix of super-affordable products and the inevitable increase in the upper-end, albeit with relatively low volumes. Most people in India who can afford a car can also afford a driver. The super cheap cars will change that.

BEST SELLERS IN JAPAN

	Make	Sales 2007*	Variation
1	Toyota	939,165	-10.6%
2	Nissan	452,027	-9.0%
3	Suzuki	421,244	-4.0%
4	Daihatsu	398,058	+3.8%
5	Honda	368,076	-9.7%
6	Mazda	157,463	-8.1%
7	Subaru	141,963	-4.9%
8	Mitsubishi	139,145	-16.1%
-	Isuzu	41,095	-22.6%
-	Mitsubishi Fuso	30,427	-21.7%
-	Hino	27,211	-14.8%
-	Lexus	21,722	+67.7%
-	Nissan Diesel	8,582	-28.2%
-	Others**	135,280	-9.2%
	Japan	**3,281,458**	**-7.9%**

* sales January through July
** including import brands

The historical competition between Subaru's Impreza and Mitsubishi's Lancer (known as the Galant Fortis in Japan) was further emphasized as both ranges were entirely renewed in 2007. **Fred Varcoe** reviews these and other significant new entries – whether domestic or export – from Japanese and Korean manufacturers.

DAIHATSU MIRA / CUORE

The Mira may not be the most fashionable car in Japan, but you can pick up a two-door "Van" version for just 582,750 yen. That's less than $5,000. At the top of the range (1.186 million yen), you at least get double the number of doors, but probably not double the value as the benefits are mainly cosmetic. Outside Japan, Malaysian automaker Perodua is now producing a version known as the Viva with engine sizes ranging from the standard (in Japan) 660cc unit to 1,000cc, which produces 60 hp.

NISSAN PINO

With the K-Car market topping 2 million units in Japan in 2006, Nissan is obliged to put K-Cars on the market – but is not obliged to make them. Instead, in the case of the Pino and its sister car the Moco, they buy them in from Suzuki. The Pino is aimed at the lower end of the market (specifically for "girls who don't live in the city," according to Nissan) and comes with a three-cylinder DOHC 12-valve unit mated to either five-speed manual or automatic transmission. A four-wheel drive version is also available. Prices for the Pino (the name is derived from Pinocchio), which comes with its own range of cute accessories, start at 861,000 yen.

SUBARU JUSTY

Japanese automakers are quite happy to rebadge the vehicles of their competitors under their own brand – the idea being to keep loyal customers in the family – especially in Japan where brand loyalty remains strong. For Subaru, it seems like a step up in ambition, and you have to wonder if the new Daihatsu-produced Justy is going to do the job. It's a relatively cheap and cheerful small four-door hatchback powered by 1.0- and 1.3-litre engines, but it's hardly likely to start a dynasty.

SUZUKI SPLASH

Suzuki takes aim at the European compact market with the new Splash, based on the Swift chassis and offering newly developed 3-cylinder/65-hp 1.0-litre and 4-cylinder/86-hp 1.2-litre petrol engines alongside Suzuki's tried-and-tested 1.3-litre/75-hp diesel unit. While the length (3.7 metres) and width (1.7 metres) are similar to the Swift's measurements, the Splash is significantly taller at 1.7 metres to accommodate bigger European drivers and passengers. The Splash will be manufactured by the Magyar Suzuki Corporation in Hungary and there are currently no plans to market it in Japan.

MAZDA2 / DEMIO

Mazda has been shifting around 60,000 units of the Demio each year in Japan and the Hiroshima-based firm will be hoping to boost that with the all-new version introduced in July 2007. What was a boxy workhorse is now a lean and considerably more stylish sub-compact. Mazda has trimmed 40 mm off the length, 55 mm from the top and 100 kg in weight, and plugged in CVT transmission alongside 1.3- and 1.5-litre engines, giving the car a healthy 23.0 km/l fuel economy. It will also be manufactured and sold in China as the Mazda 2.

TOYOTA BLADE

Based on the Auris, the stylish Blade speeds into territory occupied by other hot hatches such as Mazda's 2.3-litre turbo-charged 3 series, Alfa Romeo's 147 GTA and VW's Golf R32. Introduced with significantly modified suspension and a 2.4-litre engine, the Blade was upgraded mid-2007 with a road-burning 3.5-litre version to offer serious competition to the best of Europe (apart from the Mazda, there's little competition in Japan).

HYUNDAI I30

The i30 was intended to help Hyundai in the European market, but has been a surprising success in Korea, where hatchbacks have previously been regarded as "lower class" by status-conscious South Koreans. While there has been criticism of its pricing range in Korea, in Europe the i30 significantly undercuts rivals such as the Ford Focus and Volkswagen Golf. Power ranges from an 89-hp diesel to 138-hp 2.0 diesel and petrol engines. Its biggest rival will probably be the Cee'd, made by sister company Kia.

KIA CEE'D

With the Cee'd, Kia has opted to attack Europe from within. The stylish hatchback was designed in Germany and is made in Slovakia (it is not sold in South Korea). Whether or not that will be enough to convince buyers to "go Korean" rather than opt for the Cee'd's many European competitors remains to be seen, but Kia is rapidly expanding the range and engine options, so there is now an estate version, there will soon be a three-door option (the Pro-cee'd) and 2008 will see a convertible. Engine sizes range from 1.6-litre to 2.0-litre petrol units and a 1.6-litre diesel. The Pro-ceed will also have a 1.4-litre option.

TOYOTA ALLION

Originally built to replace the Carina and Corona, the Allion received a facelift in mid-2007 but remains a classic "middle-of-the-road" vehicle – conservative in design (four-door saloon), price (1.74-2.33 million yen) and engine size (1.5-litre/1.8-litre). This is the car for middle Japan. Giving it CVT makes sense, but quite why they needed to add four-wheel drive remains a mystery. Toyota says the Allion is aimed at older drivers looking to downsize.

MITSUBISHI DELICA D:5

Following on from the brilliant i, Mitsubishi's road to recovery and pursuit of "cool" continues with the D:5 – with a colon –, the latest in the Delica line of people carriers. This one has "Hummer" written all over it, especially the serrated grille at the front. Where the old Delica was very tall and narrow, the D:5 is flat and fat. Inside, it's still largely just a people carrier, but it does have the options of all-wheel drive and CVT linked to its rather lightweight 2.4-litre petrol engine.

HONDA CROSSROAD

Honda says the Crossroad "transcends categories," but that claim doesn't really hold water as the chunky, scaled-down SUV seems to be trespassing on Nissan X-Trail/Dualis and Toyota RAV4 territory. You do get seven seats in what is fairly limited space inside, with 1.8- and 2.0-litre power units.

NISSAN GRAND LIVINA

After only selling 4,000 vehicles in Indonesia in 2006, some thought Nissan were being optimistic in their 12,000-per-year sales forecast for the three-row Grand Livina. In fact, they received more than 8,000 orders in the first three months for the economical, 1.5-litre people carrier, based on Nissan's B platform. MPVs sell well in Indonesia, the Philippines and Malaysia, where the Grand Livina is also on sale, as well as in China where it is known as the Livina Geniss.

TOYOTA VANGUARD

Launched in Japan under the slogan "Touch & Gentle 7-Seater," Toyota's replacement for the Kluger is all-new, but is a surprisingly more restrained design than its predecessor (despite being based on the trendier RAV4 platform). Toyota will offer the Vanguard with 2.4-litre/168-bhp and 3.5-litre/276-bhp engines and in five- and seven-seat versions. The 2.4-litre engine is linked to a seven-speed CVT transmission system, while the 3.5-litre version will get a five-speed automatic. Prices range from 2.65 million to 3.35 million yen.

NISSAN X-TRAIL

Nissan's first redesign (after seven years) of its popular X-Trail SUV is more about extending the capabilities of the vehicle rather than transforming it into something else. Even the cosmetic changes have been introduced with practicality in mind, such as increased visibility and roof-mounted spotlights. The X-Trail remains a cheap and practical SUV aimed at the young and active, and has increased its street cred with a six-speed gearbox, intelligent four-wheel drive, hill descent control, and both a variable and locked power distribution system. Engine sizes in Japan are currently limited to 2.0-litre and 2.5-litre, but in the autumn of 2008, Japanese owners will have the option of a diesel engine.

SUBARU IMPREZA

Subaru likes to impress upon people
the sporting pedigree of the Impreza,
and when they shove their flat-four 2.5-litre,
227-hp turbo-charged engine into the family
runabout, it really delivers. The car's already
stunning performance and handling have
been refined further (added torque, modified
transmission, greater rigidity) and the sleek
new design (at least, of the hatchback
version) means drivers no longer have
to wear paper bags over their heads
when they take one out for a spin.

MITSUBISHI LANCER / GALANT FORTIS

Known as the Lancer to the outside world, this Mitsubishi has been subject to a less extrovert remodelling, but the company has still sought to add a certain "funk" to its small four-door saloon. In fact, it now markets the Galant Fortis as a "sports sedan" and highlights the brand's sporting pedigree (particularly its suspension). Still, you're only going to get a 2.0-litre engine, which will send 152 horses to 2WD or 4WD setups with paddle-shift CVT transmission (you can have five-speed manual in the Sport option). Mitsubishi has obviously paid a lot of attention to customer opinion and at prices ranging from just 1.78 million yen to 2.26 million yen, it will certainly get noticed by those looking for a thrifty saloon. Those looking for greater thrills will have to wait for the Lancer Evolution X.

MAZDA6 / ATENZA

Mazda unveiled its new 6 Series (Atenza in Japan) at the Frankfurt Motor Show and really it was more of the same. Perhaps no bad thing. Mazda is far more adventurous than its Japanese counterparts when it comes to design but has lost out in the power stakes. The new model will be powered by a 170-horsepower, 2.5-litre petrol engine, so maybe it will have to rely on style again. The new 6 Series is slightly longer, taller and wider, but is also lighter, more aerodynamic and greener.

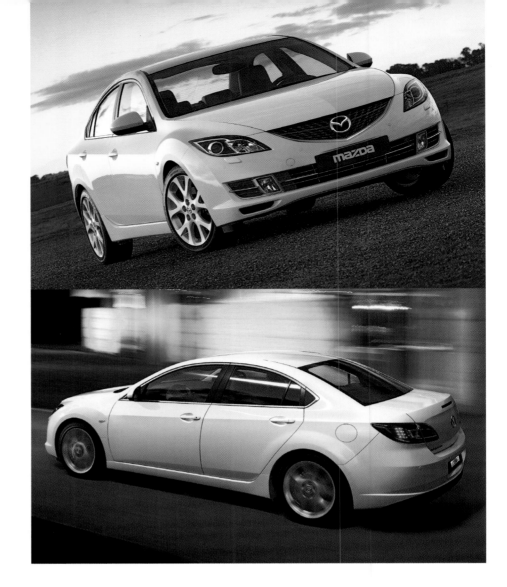

SUBARU LEGACY

Subaru's ambition of producing a limited number of models with almost infinite variations reaches its apotheosis with the Legacy, which comes as a cheap 2.0-litre family saloon, a practical all-wheel drive estate, a road-burning 280-horsepower, 2.0-litre four-door sports car, or as a 3.0-litre executive car. All within a price range of 2 million yen to 4 million yen (with a lot of bells and whistles). You won't find Subaru lacking for cars (at least in the Legacy range); all they need now is a little more recognition.

NISSAN GT-R

If any car is going to pull Nissan out of the doldrums, it will be the all-new GT-R. No longer based on the Skyline, this rare Japanese sports car (did someone say supercar?) will be released world-wide – unlike its predecessors – and Nissan hopes the V6, 3.3-litre twin-turbo coupé will give the company a badly needed PR shot in the arm. The car is similar to the prototype unveiled at the 2005 Tokyo Motor Show and its 480 horses will take less than 5 seconds to propel the GT-R to 100 km/h; not bad for a car that is likely to cost considerably less than some of its more prestigious rivals.

Moving towards an integrated approach to road safety

Challenge Bibendum (the latest round of which took place in Shanghai as we went to press) is dedicated to sustainable mobility. For Michelin, sustainable mobility encompasses the provision of energy, reducing pollution and improving traffic flow and safety. The safety aspect, and particularly the technology behind it, is reviewed here by **Laurent Meillaud**.

CHALLENGE **BIBENDUM** SHANGHAI 2007
Rallying together towards sustainable road mobility

According to World Health Organisation (WHO) statistics, there are 1.2 million road deaths worldwide each year (2.1 per cent of all deaths) – 85 per cent of which occur in developing countries – and 20 to 50 million injuries are caused in road accidents. In total, accidents cost an estimated $518 billion worldwide. Without drastic measures being taken, mortality on the roads will increase by another 80 per cent in developing countries in the next 10 years, in line with the rising number of motor vehicles, while it is likely to decrease by 30 per cent in wealthy countries over the same period. The WHO also predicts that the road will become the third-largest cause of deaths in the world by 2020, while it is currently only the ninth. But awareness is beginning to dawn. Thus the first United Nations Global Road Safety Week was held last June, arousing debates and demonstrations under the aegis of private companies and public bodies.

A DIFFERENT CULTURAL APPROACH

In emerging countries, it is not drivers who pay the heaviest toll in road accidents. The victims are mostly vulnerable categories like pedestrians and cyclists (most of whom are children). Excessive speed is easily presented as one of the major root cause of these accidents. However speed remains limited by the absence of infrastructures and the dilapidated condition of vehicles. Instead, high-risk driving is responsible for more of the carnage. In these countries it is important to raise awareness on wearing seat belts and helmets and the dangers of alcohol, not forgetting the importance of respecting basic rules of safety! Effort must also be brought to bear on infrastructure design and the introduction of emergency services, in order to be able to help injured people more quickly. Challenge Bibendum,

which has already travelled to China (where some 90,000 road deaths occur per year) and is once again in Shanghai, puts across positive messages on safety and shows how technology saves lives, whilst still preserving the pleasure of driving. After having devoted itself to the lessons brought by the industrialised countries, this year it is turning its attention towards the challenges confronting developing countries.

A VOLUNTARY POLICY IN EUROPE

In Europe, the efforts of governments have borne their fruit. The introduction of speed limits and the mandatory wearing of seat belts in both front and back seats have resulted in a significant reduction in the number of deaths. Reducing the legal alcohol level (0.5 g/l in the EU, 0 g in eastern European countries), has also played a role. Some manufacturers (Saab, Volvo) are already testing an onboard breath test aimed at preventing drink driving: drivers will need to blow into a sensor linked to their car key in order to be able to start their vehicle. In 1990, Europe had 60,000 road deaths per year but has now succeeded in bringing this number down below the 40,000 mark and is aiming at 25,000 by 2012 (source: European Conference of Transport Ministers), a further reduction of 40 per cent. While the Americans have invested massively in passive safety (seat belts, front and side airbags), European manufacturers have both increased the protection of occupants and improved roadholding (tyre grip, braking) in order to prevent – and if possible avoid – accidents. More recently, all countries have recognised the concept of pedestrian shock, with more "accommodating" car bonnets. The approach is now an integrated one, with links between the road, tyres, vehicle sensors and restraint systems.

*New forms of crash-tests are appearing, such as this
40 km/h pedestrian collision undertaken by EuroNCAP
on a dummy. Manufacturers (such as Nissan, seen testing
here) are introducing systems such as bonnets that lift
automatically to cushion impact and reduce injuries.*

And before, during and after an accident with the emergency call: this is an overall strategy taking shape for the future.

THE IMPORTANCE OF ACCIDENT STUDIES

Manufacturers use in-depth studies of real cases to best reflect the reality of the road. In 1970, Volvo was the first in the world to introduce a team specialising in accident analysis. French manufacturers have a structure called the LAB (*Laboratoire d'Accidentologie et de Biomecanique* – Accidentology and Biomechanics Laboratory). Financed jointly by Renault and PSA Peugeot Citroën, this laboratory has compiled a register of 50,000 real accidents. Each case has been studied by experts in order to better understand the circumstances under which it occurred. Their expertise also relates to the human body. Like all manufacturers, Renault and PSA use biologically faithful dummies in crash tests. They reproduce the characteristics of the human body better than articulated dummies and are packed with sensors to simulate the lesions that would be suffered by a real driver. Post mortem tests are also carried out by medical staff on real accident victims. All these efforts help to provide relevant responses to safety issues and to improve the protection of vehicle occupants by reducing lesions.

THE IMPACT OF 5-STAR CRASH TESTS

Who could have foreseen that the 5 stars awarded by EuroNCAP* for the vehicles best resisting head-on shocks would one day become a selling point? Renault was the first to achieve this, first for the Laguna in 2001, then for almost its entire range, being followed shortly afterwards by most European, American and Japanese marques. "For us, the 5 stars

was telling, validating the very stringent tests we had introduced to better reflect reality," declared Jean-Yves Le Coz, Director of the Renault Group's road safety policy. To achieve excellence in passive safety, manufacturers have worked on the materials and design of vehicles. The kinetic energy generated by a shock is absorbed by the structure of the vehicle, which deforms at the front whilst still protecting the passenger compartment. The formula is widely known nowadays, but the French have unique expertise. They also developed seat belt pre-tensioners, belts with anchor points that are integral with the seat, and above all the famous effort limiter, which reduces the effect of a shock by causing the seat belt to exercise less pressure on the thorax. Renault also focuses on submarining, an important safety aspect, but one that is not recognised in legislation: it prevents the occupant of a car from sliding under a seat belt by restraining the abdomen.

European New Car Assessment Programme: an independent association based in Brussels supported by the Commission, the F.I.A. and consumer organisations, which carries out more stringent crash tests than those demanded by European legislation (frontal crash tests at 64 km/h, lateral crash tests at 50 km/h and pedestrian collisions at 40 km/h). Australia has since aligned itself on EuroNCAP's tests. The United States performs its tests under the aegis of NHTSA, the National Highway Traffic Safety Administration.

OTHER EQUIPMENT THAT IMPROVES SAFETY

Amongst other vehicle equipment with a role in improving road safety is lighting, which has already made such progress with Xenon headlamps (producing 2.5 times more light than halogen bulbs), swivelling headlamps that light the inside

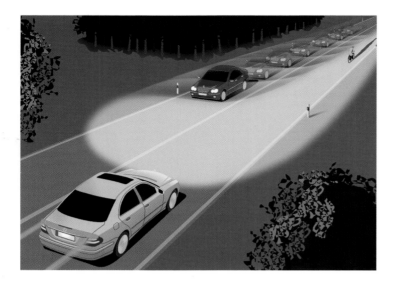

Integrating headlights with an on-board camera (a study undertaken also by Mercedes-Benz as in the image) enables the beam to be directed on the basis of the traffic flow. This helps to prevent dazzling on-coming drivers and yet ensures sufficient illumination in the direction of travel.

of bends, and also infrared vision on some upmarket models (BMW and Mercedes), enabling drivers to see better at night and in fog. Equipment manufacturers are preparing for the arrival of LED lights, which are even more effective and last longer whilst consuming less energy. Coupling headlights with a video camera will make it possible to use high beams more at night and adapt luminosity to traffic in order to avoid dazzling oncoming road users.

ACTIVE SAFETY AS A PRIORITY

The trend is now focused on avoiding accidents, particularly through the use of electronics. In agreement with European manufacturers, the European Commission has decided to launch the "E-Safety" programme, rolling out systems to help driving. The first step was to make ABS braking standard on all models sold in Europe from 2004. Remember that anti-locking on wheels can be accompanied by braking control on bends and a system that amplifies emergency braking, even when the driver releases the pressure under the effect of panic. More recently, Brussels launched a campaign aimed at promoting stability control programmes (ESP, developed by Bosch), which it has renamed ESC (Electronic Stability Control). The ambassador of the "Choose ESC!" message is none other than Michael Schumacher, seven-times F1 World Champion! Why this type of campaign? This system has a low profile in Europe, although it is fitted in over 40 per cent of new vehicles. Conversely, 80 per cent of motorists who have the benefits of this safety equipment explained to them would like to see it in their next vehicle. Europe is also keen to catch up with the United States, where ESP has spread more rapidly and will even be mandatory from 2009 for new models, and in 2012 for all new vehicles.

ELECTRONIC STABILITY CONTROL

Invented by Bosch in 1995, ESP is a complex system integrating an ABS braking and anti-skid module, wheel rotation speed sensors, an angle sensor in the steering wheel and a yaw sensor to determine both the vehicle trajectory and the manoeuvre desired by the driver. By comparing the direction taken by a car as opposed to the direction being steered by its driver (and this up to 25 times per second), ESP is able to brake the wheels individually and restore balance. Put simply, it is as if a driver had four brake pedals, but they would still need to be activated correctly, and in a fraction of a second! This is precisely what ESP does. In a situation where the driver swerves violently then corrects, going into a skid, the system kicks in to correct the trajectory and re-establish control of the vehicle. Adopted by all manufacturers, ESP is continually being improved. For example it acts on electric power steering in such a way as to naturally make corrections on a surface with differences in grip, so that the car continues to brake in a straight line. The advantages of such a system are demonstrable. Various studies carried out by manufacturers (Toyota, Volkswagen) and specialist institutes indicate that ESP could contribute to reducing the number of fatal accidents by 25-50 per cent if it were to become more widespread.

THE TYRE REMAINS AN ESSENTIAL ELEMENT

The development of on-board electronics in no way excludes the tyre, which remains the only point of contact between the vehicle and the road. Moreover, Michelin and Bosch are working together on the theme of braking, proof – if proof be required – that rubber still has a part to play. "We must provide both grip and longevity of performance,"

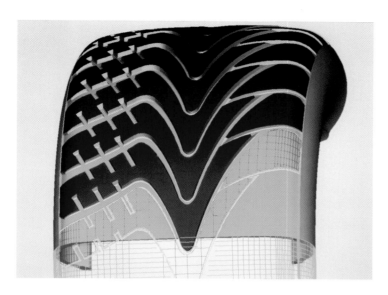

As the first point of contact with the road, tyres remain a fundamental element of road safety. Research and development continues apace on materials and treads to improve tyre grip in all weather conditions, with tyre manufacturers like Michelin working in close collaboration with the car makers themselves.

says Pierre Menendes, who is in charge of technical communication at Michelin. To arrive at this result, the Clermont-Ferrand manufacturer's R&D teams work on both materials and treads. Tyres must be able to provide good grip in dry conditions, but also in the wet and snow for some markets (Germany for example), whilst still giving good stability. Tyres must be progressive, to make a car "predictable" in a dangerous situation. It is worth mentioning here that Michelin has increased driver safety by equipping heavy trucks with "anti-splash" tyres, which limit the amount of water thrown up in rainy weather. Bibendum is also working on pressure loss and sensors in tyres, both with component manufacturers (like TRW, with whom it has a joint venture) and vehicle manufacturers. It is also developing tyres that can continue to be driven after a puncture such as the "Pax" or "ZP" (zero pressure) tyres which allow a car to be driven with a puncture for 200 km at a speed of 80 km/h, thus doing away with the spare wheel.

THE ROLE OF INFRASTRUCTURE

And where does the road come in? As with EuroNCAP for crash tests, so an association named EuroRAP (European Road Assessment Programme) has been created to assess the road network in Europe and draw attention to the role infrastructure can play in safety. Its task is to inspect roundabouts, crash barriers and the state of road surfaces. This point has not escaped road constructors. Eurovia, which belongs to French group Vinci, is thus developing a higher-grip road surface called Viagrip. Performance is considerably increased by the use of a high-power glue and a resin combining bitumen and epoxy to aggregate the gravel. Under braking, the saving is 2 m at 30 km/h,

4.5 m at 50 km/h and even 16 m at 90 km/h. This type of surface is spectacularly effective, but also more expensive. Another solution is to slow down vehicles in towns by using narrower roads or urban development. Roads may become more intelligent with luminous markings, variable message panels and paints that are more sensitive to frost, giving warning when salting is required. But, for many countries, the priorities are to improve signage, provide better surfaces and to be able to separate carriageways as on motorways.

PREVENTING ACCIDENTS

In conjunction with the road, cars can anticipate accidents. The Americans have the VII (Vehicle Infrastructure Integration). Several models from Citroën and the Lexus LS460 have infrared sensors which detect when white lines are crossed. If a driver changes lane without indicating, the car calls this to their attention. Another approach consists of detecting signs of tiredness in drivers by using a camera that films blinking and correlates this data with the way the driver is steering. Using GPS navigation with more precise mapping can help to warn of dangerous bends or high-risk areas. To avoid being taken by surprise by a vehicle arriving in a driver's blind spot, Audi is vaunting a radar to monitor the rear of the car (Side Assist system in the Q7). Volvo prefers cameras placed on each side below the wing mirrors (BLIS system), which analyse danger by processing images. If a car or motorcycle is preparing to overtake, the system displays a luminous alert on the relevant side in the event of danger. "BLIS helps drivers to make the right decisions and helps to maintain their attention," stresses Ingrid Skogsmo, Director of Volvo's Security Centre. The Swedish manufacturer also

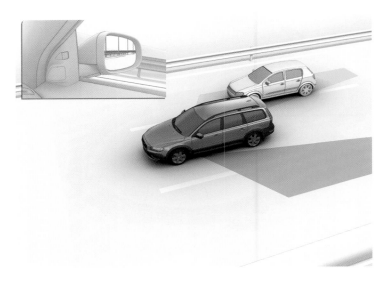

A number of car manufacturers, such as Citroën, are already producing models with infrared sensors which detect when a car crosses the white lines. If the driver changes lanes without signalling, the car advises them with a warning sound.

Volvo has approached the problem of blind spots with its BLIS system. Cameras set under the rear view mirrors process images to predict danger and light up a warning signal on the side where the danger is.

offers a system that can brake a car in the event of sudden deceleration by acting on the brakes and the engine, thus keeping a safe distance between it and the one in front. This is what is known as an ACC (Adaptive Cruise Control) radar. Component manufacturer TRW specialises in this system, which it supplies to Volkswagen amongst others. The radar detects obstacles at a distance of up to 250m and can manage braking to the point of bringing the vehicle to a total standstill. "We can provide radars capable of detecting what is going on right around the vehicle, both in urban traffic and on motorways," says Claude Gonzales, in charge of innovation at TRW for Renault and Nissan. "In future, we will have one or more radars for comfort and safety. But I think mostly that the radar will be coupled to a camera to tell the difference between pedestrians and fixed obstacles such as walls. The system could also possibly be applied to airbags".

VEHICLE-TO-VEHICLE COMMUNICATION

And to be able to anticipate collisions even better in the future, vehicles will be able to communicate with one another. The Car2Car consortium has been formed in Europe on the initiative of Audi, BMW, DaimlerChrysler, Volkswagen, Fiat, Honda, Opel and Renault. The purpose is to develop a form of wireless communication, similar to WiFi and with a range of several hundred metres, so that cars equipped with this type of transmitter-receiver can send information to one another about tailbacks, accidents or even the presence of black ice or a patch of oil. The information will be relayed and analysed by the vehicles' electronic systems. Once they can communicate, cars could signal their presence at a crossroads to one another. They could give warning that they are about to undertake emergency braking by

transmitting information directly from the sensors. An initial Car2Car forum has just been held by Audi to accelerate the introduction of a European standard. This type of approach also exists in Japan, where Honda has developed the ASV (Advanced Safety Vehicle) concept with a car and a motorcycle that are capable of communicating remotely. Drivers are warned of danger by a series of visual and audio signals, but also by vibrations in the steering wheel and the accelerator pedal to get them to brake or change their path.

PRE-CRASH

Several manufacturers (including Mercedes, Lexus and Honda for example) are now offering a function that enables restraint systems to be prepared as soon as an accident is judged to be unavoidable. This is known as "Pre-crash". Once an obstacle is detected by the radar or a camera, the seat belts tighten, sun-roofs are closed, seats move into the upright position and the airbags are deployed several fractions of a second before the shock. Systems supplier Bosch has given the name of CAPS (Combined Active and Passive Safety) to this concept, which is structured around their electronic stability programme. Systems combining ESP and ACC radar are already on the market. Eventually, information from wheel and airbag sensors will be used jointly to better protect vehicle occupants.

THE EMERGENCY CALL

The integrated emergency call, usually linked to a vehicle's navigation system, is a pinnacle of progress. The idea is to be able to make more rapid contact with the emergency services in the event of a crash via an automatic call, and to be able to locate the vehicle using GPS. Historically,

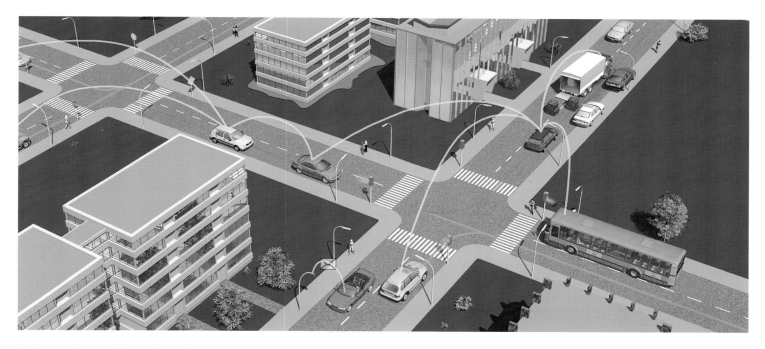

In the near future vehicles will be able communicate between themselves, automatically exchanging information regarding traffic jams, accidents or even the presence of ice or oil patches on the road ahead.

General Motors was the first to offer this service in the United States in 1996, under the name of On Star. In Europe, several manufacturers (BMW, PSA Peugeot Citroën, Volvo) are developing a similar service, with varying degrees of success. There is no doubt that PSA is the most active, having offered an emergency call in the seven main European countries (and soon nine with Portugal and Austria) since 2003, and with 400,000 vehicles equipped. To date, the French manufacturer has processed more than 1,500 calls and its customers have often passed on alerts about accidents they have seen. "In the event of an accident, survival is influenced by the first hour. This is what is called the *Golden Hour*," says Franck Batocchi, who is responsible for road safety at PSA Peugeot Citroën. It is estimated that 2,500 lives could be saved per year in Europe once the integral emergency call is more widely rolled out. This is the reason why the European Commission would like to make the emergency call mandatory in new cars by 2010, linking the service to the emergency number 112 (whereas manufacturers have set up a private service with operators who then transfer the calls), even if that poses organisational problems within 25 countries. Be that as it may, the emergency call is set to expand. In future, it will be possible to determine a driver's chance of survival statistically according to the nature of the accident. Honda even envisages a video link with vehicles, and sensors capable of measuring heartbeat and respiration. Last but not least, manufacturers can help the emergency services to react faster and better. For example, PSA provides instruction sheets to the Emergency Services to help them cut victims free safely and efficiently. Because there is an unexpected consequence of technical progress: car bodies that are more resistant to shocks are also more difficult to cut into.

The objective of "zero deaths" may perhaps one day become a reality. The continued improvement of road safety through technical progress and driver education is in any case inextricably linked to sustainable mobility, and Michelin, by periodically bringing all the interested parties together in its Challenge Bibendum, is making an essential contribution to it.

1000 hp per ton ...on the road

Power-to-weight ratio has fascinated automotive designers and drivers for over one hundred
years and, of course, it is the automotive Holy Grail for the racing car designer.
Professor Gordon Murray recounts his experience with Caparo's T1, the latest project he helped devise.

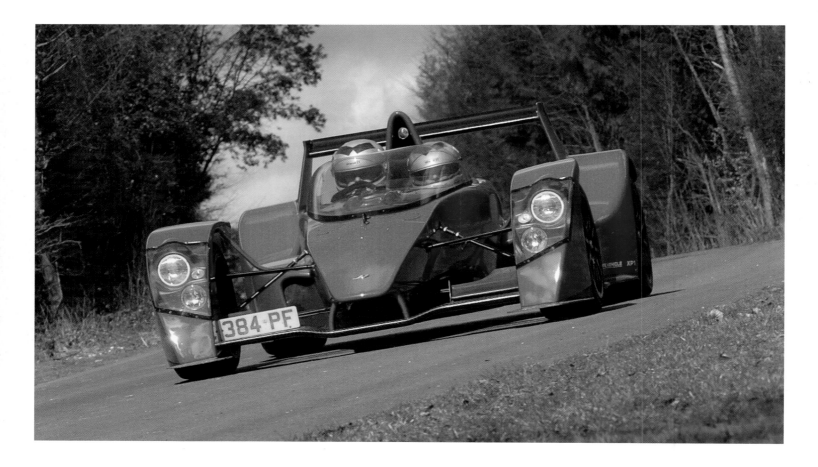

One simple variation of the power-to-weight equation
is often overlooked by car constructors and users alike.
There are two ways of achieving the same figure with two
completely different results. For example 500 hp per ton can
be achieved in a 2-ton car with 1000 hp or it can be achieved
in a 1-ton car with 500 hp. The two resultant vehicles
couldn't be more different as, obviously,
the 1000-hp car will have a much higher top speed,
but the vehicle dynamics with double the weight will not be
in the same league as the lightweight car. Weight is the
performance car designers' arch enemy and is the only
factor in car design equations which counts against you
100 per cent of the time that the vehicle is moving
– acceleration, braking, steering, cornering and ride.

When looking back through car design history we can often
see how certain aspects of engineering have developed through
phases. Power-to-weight ratio is certainly one of these areas.
During the first 20 years or so the car constructors did not
have many options available to them, so performance was
achieved almost exclusively by increasing the size of the engine
and thereby the power.
During the middle years of car design, certain segments of the
industry did try and design for light vehicle weight in order to
achieve performance. Motor racing helped push the philosophy
along, and designers such as Colin Chapman were instrumental
in transferring this approach from racing to road cars. I finally
beat Colin Chapman's record for the world's lightest road car
– the Lotus Seven – when I designed the 370 kg Rocket in 1990,

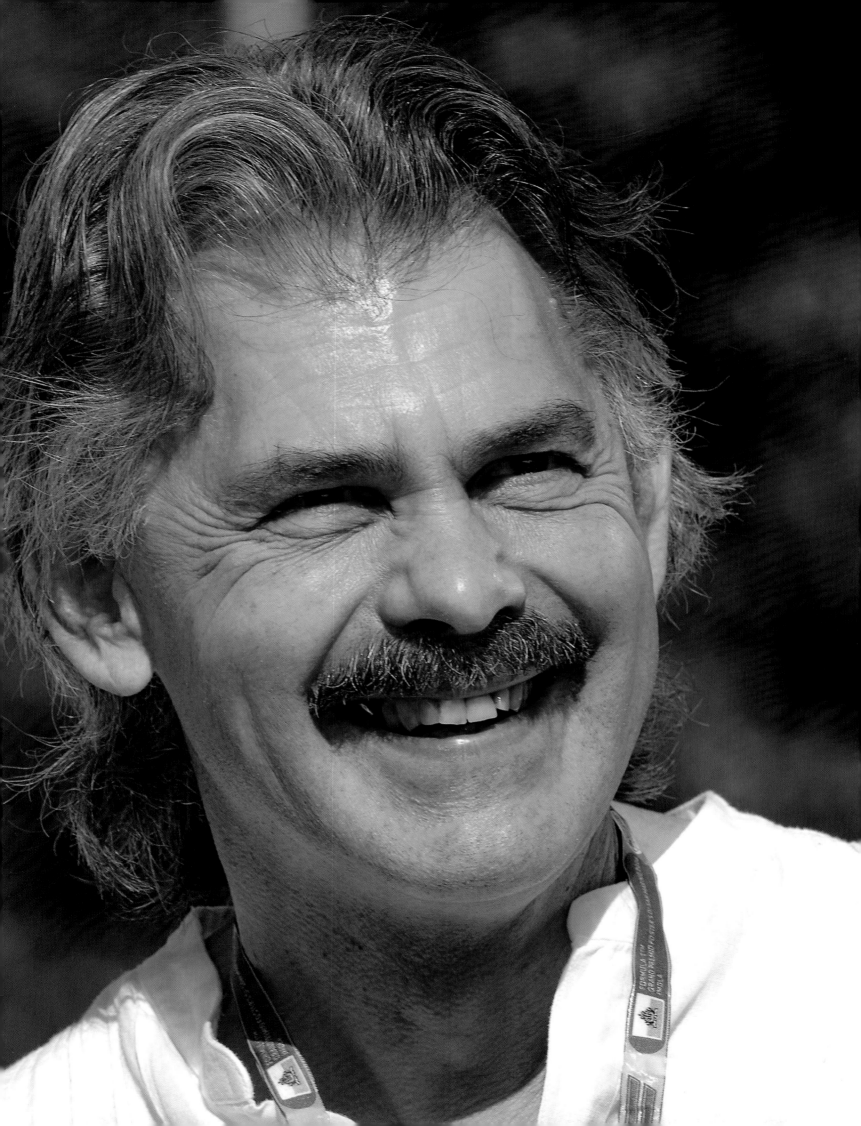

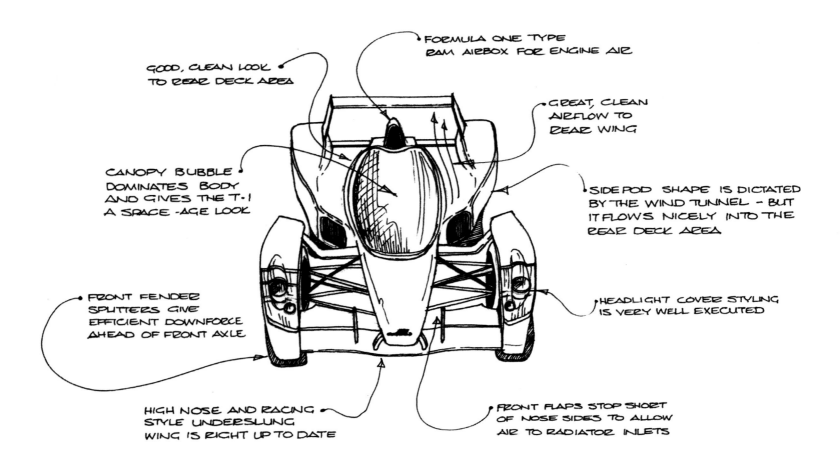

GOOD, CLEAN LOOK TO REAR DECK AREA

FORMULA ONE TYPE RAM AIRBOX FOR ENGINE AIR

GREAT, CLEAN AIRFLOW TO REAR WING

CANOPY BUBBLE DOMINATES BODY AND GIVES THE T-1 A SPACE-AGE LOOK

SIDE POD SHAPE IS DICTATED BY THE WIND TUNNEL - BUT IT FLOWS NICELY INTO THE REAR DECK AREA

FRONT FENDER SPLITTERS GIVE EFFICIENT DOWNFORCE AHEAD OF FRONT AXLE

HEADLIGHT COVER STYLING IS VERY WELL EXECUTED

HIGH NOSE AND RACING STYLE UNDERSLUNG WING IS RIGHT UP TO DATE

FRONT FLAPS STOP SHORT OF NOSE SIDES TO ALLOW AIR TO RADIATOR INLETS

but that was only achieved by designing a rather radical vehicle and using a fanatical approach to lightweight design! The last 10 years have seen a return to the old-fashioned approach to power-to-weight ratio figures with more constructors and tuners turning to ever larger engine capacities and even greater horsepower outputs in heavy cars. I think we are on the cusp of another change where environmental pressures will drive car engineers to look for performance from a more intelligent approach to materials selection and design.

A FORMULA 1 FOR TWO

No automobile illustrates this better than the wildly extreme Caparo T1. Admittedly this car is designed to be a track vehicle, but it is also capable of being road registered. Technically the car benefits from the team's in-depth knowledge of Formula 1 design, materials and technology, but conceptually it benefits from a fresh start, a lateral look at performance cars and a completely clean piece of paper. The T1 is fundamentally a two-seater F1 car with a carbon-fibre monocoque and body, ground-effect venturis, combined with conventional wings and a 3.5-litre V8 engine. The shape of the Caparo is straight

out of the "form follows function" book dictated mainly by packaging requirements and wind-tunnel results, while material selection is definitely "fit for purpose". To keep the large parts of the car's structure as light as possible, pre-preg carbon-fibre has been used for the monocoque, nose box, body panels, wings, aerodynamic wings and underbody parts. The chassis itself is a sandwich construction using the ½-in. honeycomb aluminium core and 2 mm thick skins from a mixture of high-strength woven and unidirectional fibres in an epoxy resin matrix. The monocoque is moulded in one piece with no cold bonding necessary. The chassis packaging is interesting with the passenger slightly behind the driver to take advantage of the shoulder to hip differential, to achieve close-coupled seating and limit the chassis/body width, rather like two thirds of a McLaren F1. Point loads inserts are all integral in the sandwich construction in true Formula 1 fashion. The chassis weighs just 32 kg. The primary structure is completed with a high-strength steel engine frame. Rollover protection comes from a high-strength steel roll hoop mounted to the carbon tub. Body panels are, unusually, also sandwich construction with 0.2 mm carbon skins and a Nomex honeycomb core. The cored construction principle continues with the front crash box and "floors" or underbody panels.

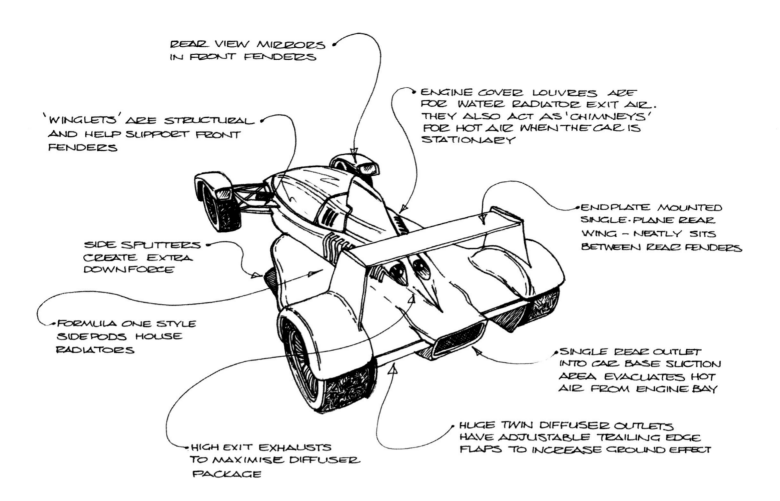

REAR VIEW MIRRORS IN FRONT FENDERS

'WINGLETS' ARE STRUCTURAL AND HELP SUPPORT FRONT FENDERS

ENGINE COVER LOUVRES ARE FOR WATER RADIATOR EXIT AIR. THEY ALSO ACT AS 'CHIMNEYS' FOR HOT AIR WHEN THE CAR IS STATIONARY

ENDPLATE MOUNTED SINGLE-PLANE REAR WING – NEATLY SITS BETWEEN REAR FENDERS

SIDE SPLITTERS CREATE EXTRA DOWNFORCE

FORMULA ONE STYLE SIDEPODS HOUSE RADIATORS

SINGLE REAR OUTLET INTO CAR BASE SUCTION AREA EVACUATES HOT AIR FROM ENGINE BAY

HIGH EXIT EXHAUSTS TO MAXIMISE DIFFUSER PACKAGE

HUGE TWIN DIFFUSER OUTLETS HAVE ADJUSTABLE TRAILING EDGE FLAPS TO INCREASE GROUND EFFECT

The shape of the T1 was happily not conceived under the oppressive shadow of F1 regulations, so the designers could optimize the major component placement and packaging to achieve the required weight distribution and optimum aerodynamic shape. The aerodynamic work was conducted using a sophisticated 30 per cent model. A target of 3g cornering capability meant that the underbody airflow tests included a massive programme on diffuser shapes and sizes. There were many aero tests conducted on the moving ground belt to ensure a stable centre of aerodynamic pressure under all pitch conditions. The downforce on the vehicle comes from three major areas. The majority of the downforce comes from the underbody with the venturi and diffuser designs being wilder than those allowed in F1. Secondary downforce is achieved with two adjustable Fowler flaps on the trailing edge of the body, which can be adjusted to enhance the base suction bubble behind the car and thereby increase effectiveness of the aero load on the floor of the vehicle. The third major downforce element is a set of conventional wings. The front wing assembly is current racing car practice with a high-set nose carrying an underslung fixed mainplane with adjustable flap elements. The rear wing assembly is single-plane adjustable and is end-plate-mounted. Total downforce is of the order of a current

racing prototype and enough to "run off the ceiling" at 150 mph. Cornering and braking forces should be amazing. Chassis running gear is pure F1 with double-wishbone suspension linkages front and rear and pushrod-operated rockers driving concentric springs and dampers. The suspension components are all fabricated from heat-treated 4130 high-strength steel. The aluminium-bodied dampers are three-way adjustable with remote reservoirs on the rear. Most T1 owners will get as much pleasure just looking at the components of their machine as they will driving the car. Design engineering at this level with such attention to weight targets and pure load paths always results in wonderful works of art rather than just parts of a motorcar. The suspension uprights, hubs and quick-release wheel nuts are no exception to this theory.

600 HP AND 600 KG

The other big feature of the T1 and the other half of the power-to-weight figure is, of course, the engine, which is another jewel-like piece of engineering and packaging. This unit is a 90-degree twin-cam V8 with a displacement of 3.5 litres. The V8 is fully dry-sumped with a four-stage scavenge system and a racing-type windage collector

OVERALL STYLE IS HALF RACE CAR
- HALF JET FIGHTER PLANE

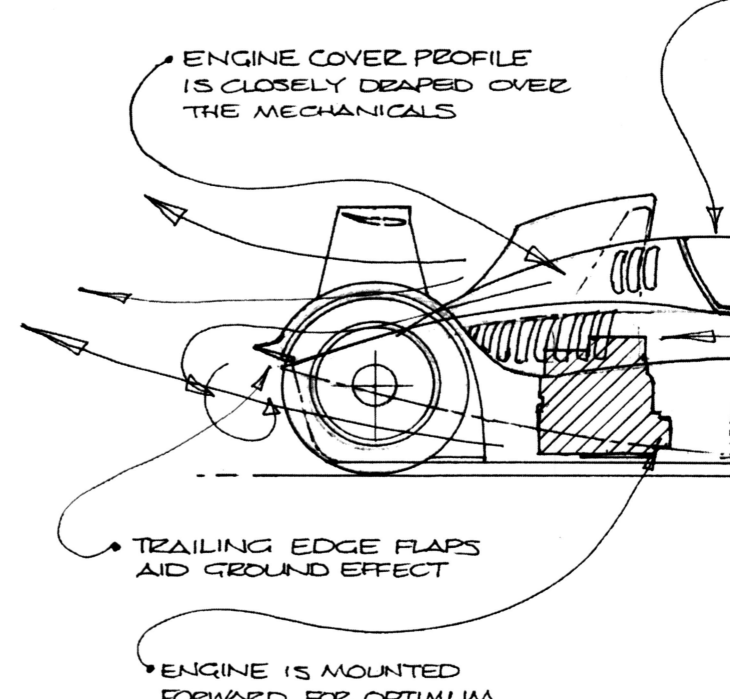

• ENGINE COVER PROFILE
IS CLOSELY DRAPED OVER
THE MECHANICALS

• TRAILING EDGE FLAPS
AID GROUND EFFECT

• ENGINE IS MOUNTED
FORWARD FOR OPTIMUM
WEIGHT DISTRIBUTION

CANOPY HAS GOOD, STRONG,
LINES . IT IS FORMED IN
ONE PIECE AND HINGES
FORWARD FOR ACCESS

NOSECONE HAS A
GREAT MIXTURE OF
CLASSIC AND MODERN
LINES

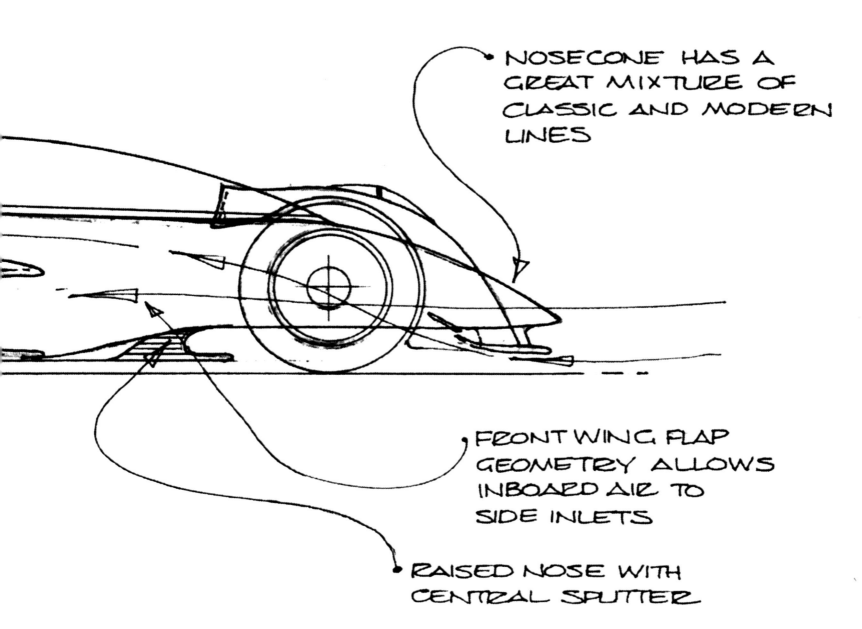

FRONT WING FLAP
GEOMETRY ALLOWS
INBOARD AIR TO
SIDE INLETS

RAISED NOSE WITH
CENTRAL SPLITTER

in the crankcase. The engine is normally aspirated and derived from one originally designed for Indy-car racing. The unit is a 4-valve design with a 93.0 mm bore and 64.3 mm stroke incorporating titanium valves and a finger-follower valve train system. The all-alloy engine has some interesting features – such as internal piston cooling, aluminium/Nikasil liners and gas-filled cylinder head sealing system. The crankshaft is flat-plane and the dry-sump system uses a ladder frame geometry for increased torsional rigidity. On the induction side, electronic sequential fuel injection operates via an 8-butterfly system and twin spray injectors. Fuel pressure is 5 bar (around 73 psi) and the engine-management system is a Pectel SQ6 ECU. The V8 weighs in at 256 lb. (116 kg) and produces 600 bhp at 10,200 rpm. Water cooling is supplied from twin single-core aluminium radiators with electric fans. Power transmission is through a 5½-in. diameter, triple-plate clutch and bespoke 6-speed sequential transmission with gearshift power coming from an engine-driven air pump. The transmission casing is aluminium but the bell-housing attachment to the engine is of carbon-fibre. Final drive is a hypoid bevel and Salisbury limited-slip differential. Driveshafts are gun-drilled for weight, and inboard tripod constant-velocity joints are integral with the drive flange.

The exhaust system has tapered primary pipes hand-crafted from 0.9 mm stainless steel, with the silencer made from titanium. Emissions control is by a closed-loop Lambda-sensor system. All the power is transmitted to the ground by wheel and tyre combinations to suit both road and track. Rims of 10 in. front and 11 in. rear are 18 in. forged magnesium units for the track and 19 in. forged aluminium for the road.

So the Caparo T1 looks like being a car which could break the 1,000 hp per ton barrier with around 600 hp and 600 kg. But this car is about performance above all else, and the trend towards optimum power-to-weight through lightweight design and engineering will begin to show itself in all types of cars in the next 20 years or so. And we, the motorists, will benefit from the lower running costs and improved vehicle dynamics that this direction will give us.

Motor Sports

Thrills and spills

Without doubt, reports **Pierre van Vliet**, the 2007 season was the closest and the most gripping in a decade, since the tumultuous final at Jerez between Michael Schumacher and Jacques Villeneuve. This year, just like in Adelaide in 1986, three drivers were still in with a chance for the title as they went into the last race of the season. At the start of the race at Interlagos, Brazil, McLaren's gifted 22-year-old novice, Lewis Hamilton, had the cards to win with four points over his team-mate Fernando Alonso and seven over Kimi Räikkönen. Faced with the challenge, and after having missed a first chance to claim the title in China two weeks earlier, the young Brit cracked under pressure, running wide during the first lap and then being slowed by a gearbox glitch that saw him relegated to the back of the pack. The way was clear for a tremendous one-two for Ferrari, with Räikkönen picking up the world title along with the race win. The outsider going into the race in Brazil, Kimi triumphed in a truly eventful season characterised by an internal feud within the McLaren team between Alonso, the reigning World Champion, and the young pretender, Hamilton. The Scuderia Ferrari demonstrated superior organisational consistency despite a bumpy start to the season, with the F2007 lacking reliability. But during the summer a decidedly unsporting affair threw clouds across the world of F1, when it was discovered that a disgruntled Ferrari engineer had given confidential information to his opposite number at McLaren. The British team paid a dear price as the FIA World Motor Sport Council voted to strip McLaren of its points in the Constructors' Championship and fine the team $100 million (a record amount). Ferrari won nine of the GPs to McLaren's eight.

The 2007 season kicked off in Australia, followed by Malaysia and Bahrain. From day one Ferrari and McLaren were the teams to beat. Pictured right is the start in Sepang – Massa (right) was on pole but was not fastest away from the lights.

Felipe Massa and Fernando Alonso tangle at the first corner in Barcelona. The Ferrari driver brushed aside the Spaniard's attack and went on to build up a gap, leaving the two-times World Champion to finish third behind his team-mate, Lewis Hamilton.

A spectacular fire envelops Massa's Ferrari during his pit-stop at the Spanish GP. But despite the fright he went on to win his second race of the season after Bahrain. With three victories in four races, Ferrari gave the impression of having the upper hand despite less than perfect reliability, as proved by the electrical fault that halted Räikkönen's F2007.

The McLarens dive into the Sainte-Dévote corner right after the start in Monaco. Alonso and Hamilton would finish in that order, even if Lewis later complained that the team had forced him to adopt a defensive strategy towards Fernando, and had made him pit early despite still having several more laps in his fuel tank. This was the first sign of frustration that said a lot about the burning ambition firing the young pretender. And it marked the start of a relentless internal feud that would undermine the atmosphere within the team.

Raced under a deluge, the European GP at the Nürburgring was the venue for a thrilling duel between Massa and Alonso, the McLaren driver muscling Felipe out of the way to take victory with just a few laps to go. And angry words were exchanged as they headed for the podium! This was also the first race of the season where Hamilton did not make it into the top three. He aquaplaned off at the first corner, like several others, and was helped back onto the track by a tractor to finish a distant 9th.

The first of a long series of victories! Hamilton was devastatingly effective in Montreal, demonstrating a skill beyond his years in a race that was chaotic (see Kubica's accident in the previous double page) in more than one way. Lewis pulled off a fine piece of driving while Fernando Alonso had to make do with a modest 7th place.

A week later at Indianapolis, Hamilton took home another win despite considerable resistance from his McLaren team-mate who tried to pass him on several occasions without succeeding. And the tension mounted between the two drivers.

When his engine stalled on the starting grid at Silverstone, Massa was forced to start from the pit lane, leaving his team-mate Kimi Räikkönen to beat Alonso and Hamilton on their home ground a week after he had dominated the French GP.

The return to the majestic Spa circuit for the Belgian GP saw another memorable duel between Alonso and Hamilton, who went side-by-side into the Eau Rouge at the start. Fernando got the upper hand, but Lewis kept his lead in the championship rankings thanks to a resounding one-two by the Ferraris. Coming, as it did, after the catastrophic verdict of the F.I.A. World Council against McLaren (all its points taken away and a fine of $100 million for its role in the espionage scandal), the title was now mathematically Ferrari's.

Bottleneck in the pit-lane at the Hungaroring. This incident cost Alonso his pole when the race directors decided to drop him back five places on the grid for having deliberately obstructed his team-mate, delaying him in the pits during qualifying.

In Turkey, a burst tyre saw Hamilton's championship hopes put back. Although Alonso only managed third place behind the Ferraris of Massa and Räikkönen, he was now within just five points of Lewis.

Although still very much in the shadow of McLaren and Ferrari, the BMWs regularly shone thanks to the efforts of Heidfeld and Kubica, 4th and 5th here at Monza. The team did better in the constructors' championship than Renault, well off the pace compared to their previous two title seasons.

Alonso tried to make the most of the appalling
weather conditions in Japan to put pressure on
Hamilton, but in the end it was Fernando who lost
out, crashing out of the race on lap 43 and leaving
Lewis to pick up his fourth victory of the year.

Eight days later and the Chinese GP got underway
in similar weather. This time it was Hamilton who paid
the price for staying out with the intermediate tyres
too long, running into the gravel in the deceleration
lane at the entrance to the pit lane. Räikkönen finished
ahead of Alonso and the two drivers reduced their gap
from Hamilton to seven and four points respectively.

For the first time since 1986, there were three drivers in the running for the championship going into the last race of the season in Brazil. Hamilton failed to make a clean getaway from his second place (behind Massa) on the grid at the start and was overtaken by both Räikkönen and Alonso going into the Senna switchback. As Lewis tried to out-brake his team-mate going into the corner at the end of the first straight, he overcooked it and went wide. Under pressure, the young Brit then had trouble finding the gears and fell back to 18th place before working his way back up to 7th at the chequered flag. Räikkönen managed to pass Massa after the second pit-stop and thus the Scuderia succeeded in snatching the Drivers' title from McLaren after Hamilton had led the rankings for six months!

Imagination and courage

Formula 1 is a paradoxical universe, a secretive world that likes to keep itself to itself – despite huge global media coverage. And that interest burgeoned throughout 2007, thanks to a series of headlines that didn't always relate to on-track affairs. **Pierre Dupasquier**, recently decorated with the French Legion of Honour, was head of Michelin's global motor sports operations until the end of 2005 and is intimately acquainted with the clandestine world of F1. Here he offers his own take on a hectic season.

The 2007 grand prix season was not the calmest on record. Formula One is an ultra-sensitive business at the best of times – it is, after all, the apotheosis of circuit racing – but all the recent political distractions highlighted in the media suggest that the sport needs to think carefully about its future.

Look, first of all, at how this season's leading lights have conducted themselves.

Fernando Alonso, a thoroughly deserving world champion in 2005 and 2006, found himself in the midst of considerable turmoil – as, indeed, did the whole McLaren team, for a variety of reasons. It was clear from the beginning of the campaign that McLaren had produced a very effective chassis – one that was good enough to allow its drivers to challenge for motor racing's ultimate accolade. But Alonso probably hadn't counted on the threat posed by a GP2 graduate with no F1 race experience, a newcomer who capitalised fully – and remarkably well – on both his team's and his team-mate's experience. I observed Lewis Hamilton in action during the 2005 GP2 Series. Things didn't go particularly well for him towards the end of that season, but his calm, rational approach impressed me greatly. The developing tension between Alonso and the young Englishman was palpable – and it stirred a bit of friction in the McLaren camp. It became one of those situations in which even the slightest incident could provoke mistrust, or accusations of favouritism, with predictable consequences…
We also had an illuminating episode when Ferrari accused McLaren of being in possession of confidential technical documents that had leaked from its own design office. The sporting headlines were soon full of serious allegations about renegade employees supplying such information and the motor racing authorities duly became involved. Some people consider that Ron Dennis must have been aware this was going on. That's possible, because he runs his business with a great deal of attention to detail, but I know him too well to believe for a moment that he would ever have conjured up a scheme such as this. The whole plot struck me as risky, inefficient and, above all, not very bright. And having to harness Alonso and Hamilton in the middle of all that? It wasn't an easy situation.

Ferrari had to work hard at the start of the year. Like McLaren, its two drivers proved to be evenly matched… and extremely talented with it. Perceived as the victim in the spy scandal that brought it into conflict with McLaren,

Jean Todt's team was not subjected to psychological blows from the outside world and knew exactly how to maintain its professional focus as it went about its duty, although it was no longer the byword for mechanical reliability that it had been at the start of the present decade.

On a personal note, I harbour very warm feelings towards both Ferrari drivers. I first became acquainted with Kimi Räikkönen during his McLaren days. I know many of his compatriots well – I adore Finland – and I quickly came to realise that, like most of them, he's not a man with whom long conversations are a necessity. He's bright, exceptionally gifted and his head is screwed on. He knows how to analyse problems and understands how to seek solutions. As for Felipe Massa, he has no further need to prove his speed. He has a good sense of humour and a very pleasant manner. I first met him at Sauber, where team owner Peter told me a little tale. When the team first switched to Michelins, Felipe wasn't sure it was the right thing to do. When he tested on our tyres for the first time, however, he called his boss as soon as he got out of the car to tell him that, actually, his judgment was sound.

Renault found itself in the middle of a downward spiral – two consecutive world titles can take their toll. It's a brilliant team – compact and competent – but, in this business, a little inertia can be costly, no matter how solid the infrastructure. It certainly isn't true that Heikki Kovalainen lacks talent. Carlos Ghosn's decision to hand the F1 reins to Bernard Rey, and to invest seriously in a new wind tunnel, were more than just a breath of fresh air for the Anglo-French team: it confirmed a long-term commitment to F1 – and that opened the door to negotiations with drivers, as well as ambitious sponsors. One can only assume that the company chairman can see the benefits in an F1 programme, especially as now is not a time to be losing visibility on the world stage. Two world titles represent an excellent return for Flavio Briatore's team, whose efforts might easily have been overshadowed by rival PSA's decision to commit to endurance racing and, especially, the Le Mans 24-Hours.

It was a pleasure to watch BMW Sauber's progress. Mario Theissen continued to deliver a masterclass in the art of team development and he now has all the resources he needs to fight at the front of the field for many years to come. There was a healthy rivalry between his two drivers throughout the season, and that doubtless helped boost team morale. During one of my recent visits to the Michelin

Ron Dennis and the McLaren-Mercedes team found themselves in the thick of a spy scandal over the summer. The F.I.A. World Council eventually settled the matter by inflicting the Anglo-German team with an unprecedented fine of $100 million and by stripping it of its constructors' points.

plant at Stomil, Poland, most of the questions I was asked were on the subject of Robert Kubica – everybody wanted to know whether he would become world champion.

I will deal with the Toyota-Williams duopoly as a single entity, albeit one that could furnish a book, such is the scope for philosophical, technical and sporting contemplation. The evidence suggests that the Japanese giant has not yet worked out how to put together a team capable of fighting for a slot at the front of the grid. You certainly need patience in F1, but the team members' vast ability, technical know-how and commendable hard work ought by now to have made the car much more competitive. To find a reason for this failure, which is how we must regard it for the moment at least, we have to look at the infrastructure.

There was nothing wrong with the World Rally Championship team Ove Andersson put together for Toyota. It ran smoothly, won the title and fulfilled expectations. The company was also competitive when it turned its attention to the Le Mans 24-Hours, where its André de Cortanze-designed chassis was the class of the field for two seasons, even if it didn't actually win the race. When the F1 project began, however, André's latest endeavours weren't to Tokyo's taste and things began to deteriorate. The team was left looking for a new technical director – a pivotal role in F1. Only a technical director can orchestrate the thousands of ideas put forward by the development team with an energy that's matched only by their imagination. Without such an authoritative figure at the helm, things can lose direction. And the Japanese need to realise that their efforts in this domain have not so far been successful. I felt sorry for Tsutomu Tomita, who has returned to Japan to take up a management role at Fuji Speedway, but I am encouraged by the arrival of Pascal Vasselon.

He has a fine knowledge of chassis dynamics – and tyres in particular – and such assets can but help the team's quest for victory. In the meantime, Sir Frank Williams has proved that there isn't much wrong with Toyota's engine.

Like Toyota, Honda has found it extremely difficult to put together the right kind of infrastructure. The management team that succeeded David Richards still seems to be some way from coming to terms with F1's demands. I have known the company's dynamic CEO, Fukui-san, since he ran the engine division. He is a great motor sports enthusiast, as well as a former competitor, and he must be finding that time is dragging on.

Aside from what's happening with the teams, one line of paddock conversation endured all season: the show needs to be improved and running costs must be slashed. In themselves, those are entirely reasonable propositions. But... the championship is designed to showcase the world's best driver and this is a mechanical sport.

A few months ago I heard a convincing and amusing explanation while chatting to some of American motor sports' true greats, such as Parnelli Jones, Johnny Rutherford and the Unser brothers. They were very wary of engineers whose exploits might deprive them of victory, or who might at least bring their ultimate driving talent into question by embellishing motor sports with parameters beyond their control!

The words "mechanical" and "sport" feature a number of inherent contradictions – most obviously that a driver's results hinge, to a degree, on the design, construction and operation of a machine. If you take into account the detailed fine-tuning that engineers carry out during test sessions, so that drivers can extract every last ounce of performance from their car,

As Pierre Dupasquier points out, it is high time the powers that be in F1 acted with determination and common sense to bring the action back to where it belongs: on the racetrack. And avoid that overtaking becomes confined to pit strategy.

it is glaringly obvious that the world title isn't just a matter of driving talent – it is also the consequence of a sophisticated technical team that consumes significant financial resources.

Is the spectacle all it might be? The answer, surely, must be yes, because Bernie Ecclestone's slick organisational machine generates huge audiences, both at the tracks and in front of TV screens – even when the racing is little more than a dull procession. Look at the situation in the GP2 Series, F1's official ante-chamber: the races there are frequently exciting, but it hardly stirs the general public's interest at all.

In 2005, a lady stuck her head into our working area in Monaco and asked me to sign a photograph, which she told me she'd taken in Barcelona. When I asked her what on earth fascinated her about F1, she replied, without hesitation: "What attracts people, I think, is the fact that everything in F1 is pushed to extremes."

There are many potential evolutionary courses in F1's sumptuous technical arena and two have particularly caught my attention this year: the lack of overtaking and pollution. Fair points, both. And it is impossible to discuss the topic of overtaking, or rather its absence, without mentioning pit stops and aerodynamics.

The former are part of each team's race strategy and cars generally stop once or twice per grand prix, but the pattern of racing has become predictable. For drivers, attempting a risky pass has come to be considered a professional *faux pas* when the alternative is a straightforward bout of place-swapping during the routine stops. Their task is thus to make as good a start as possible and then wait for the first and second stops. Barring major incident, that's when places can be gained. So let's get rid of pit stops! That would deprive the show of the mechanics'

well-rehearsed pit lane ballet, but drivers would be left with no option but to fight on the track from start to finish.

Aerodynamic pressure generates grip. The greater it becomes, the more important it is to maintain the car in a precise position in relation to airflow, which makes late braking manoeuvres ineffective. Thence, let's reduce downforce and make aerodynamic aids independent of the car's set-up! Technically, those are perfectly feasible solutions that wouldn't compromise safety.

As far as pollution is concerned, it might be a bit marginal but why not include it in the current round of ideas for future regulations? It is a must, if not an essential condition for survival. It is also quite easy. F1 is one of the world's best research laboratories in terms of human and technological resources. The engineers developing the present breed of cars are unquestionably among the world's very best. Imagine that we get to the stage when racing cars must be run on renewable energy alone, with zero emissions. It might be hard to sell certain technologies to contemporary motorists, but it would be straightforward to showcase them within the perfectly structured framework of a grand prix. Hydrogen, for instance, is difficult to retail in the short term but could easily be supplied to a racing circuit for three days – and compatible engines already exist.

What, you wonder, am I getting at? Are you concerned that such a move would no longer truly be representative of F1? Well, do contemporary F1 cars look anything like the Bugattis we see racing at historic events, such as Monterey in August, and do today's laptops look anything like the computers of the 1950s? All we need is a little imagination and courage – that would suffice. Imagination is not lacking in F1, and I cannot envisage for one second that courage could be in short supply either.

CBC2

Y

✚

L

ARM

FLAGS

RADIO

DM DI EL
DX   E
RADIO   EH CBC2

Alice

Bo

-1 0 1+
-2   2+
-3   3+
-4   4+
             TQ

1 2 3 4
            5
1   6   REV
A   7
B
C

DRINK

SF

SC

Scuderia Ferrari Marlboro

The 2007 Formula 1 season consigned Ferrari's name to history books as winner of the Manufacturers' Title – its 15th. The championship was overshadowed by the so-called "spy story" which eventually saw McLaren Mercedes stripped of all the points it had scored. On the track, however, the battle was one of the most thrilling ever. Technical report and drawings by **Paolo d'Alessio**.

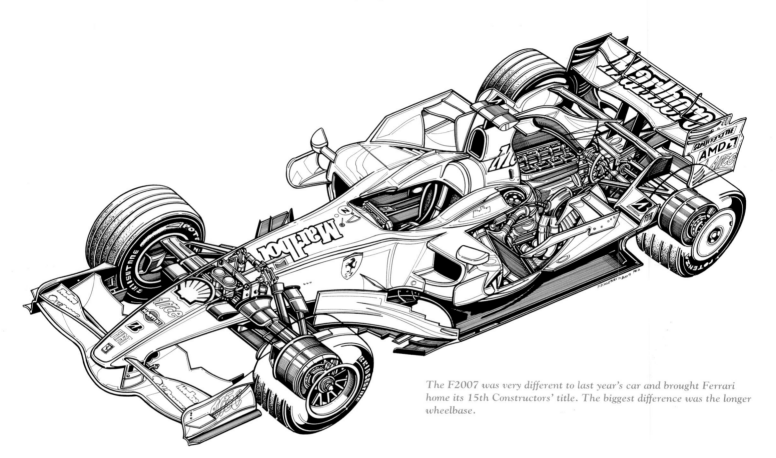

The F2007 was very different to last year's car and brought Ferrari home its 15th Constructors' title. The biggest difference was the longer wheelbase.

When the F2007 was unveiled early in January 2007, the British press was damning in its praise, writing it off as too conventional to be truly competitive. Adrian Newey, one of the most successful and highly paid engineers in F1, was even more critical. According to him, the F2007's longer wheelbase (some 8-10 cm longer than the 248 F1's) was an unforgivable mistake – an unjustifiable choice that may have effectively put Ferrari out of the running for the title before the car even turned a wheel. They could not have been more wrong. Without taking into consideration the tracks that really did not suit the F2007 (such as Monte-Carlo and the Hungaroring), the long wheelbase proved itself more than up to the task.

While the new car maintained the layout of last year's 248 F1, the differences were such that Ferrari's engineers talked of a new direction for the team's single-seaters. There were new aerodynamics (a straighter nose cone, shorter, more profiled side pods, new rear wing profiles), new front suspension (the keel under the chassis was done

away with and the lower wishbones were mounted directly onto the monocoque), new mountings for new radiators and, above all, a different weight distribution to take full advantage of the Bridgestones.

The F2007 was also the single-seater that changed most radically during the season compared to the launch version. Again most of these changes regarded the aero package, with a new engine cover, new bargeboards and flat floor. But from the Hungarian GP the car was also upgraded with new rear suspension featuring a third transverse shock absorber mounted on the gearbox which controlled ride height.

The only real problem faced by the team was the car's lack of reliability. What was once Ferrari's strongest point came sorely to lack and it was Räikkönen and Massa who paid the price. Without the problems that hit Massa in Australia and at Monza, and Räikkönen's retirement in Spain or in Germany the championship would have gone differently. Even without the F.I.A.'s sanctions.

Kimi Räikkönen

Ferrari intervened quite heavily on the F2007's aerodynamics for the Spanish Grand Prix, with a new engine cover and a new vent design.

Felipe Massa

The F2007's upper wishbones play an integral part of the car's aero package, increasing downforce over the front axle.

Jean Todt, general director

Stefano Domenicali, sporting director

A big design change for Ferrari was the adoption of the mounting point for the lower wishbones on the lower side of the monocoque.

Aldo Costa, chassis engineer

Everything that increases downforce helps – these triangular wings half-way up the fuselage made their debut at Silverstone.

The rear discs are now part and parcel of the aerodynamics, using the turning motion of the disc itself and the heat coming out of it to generate downforce.

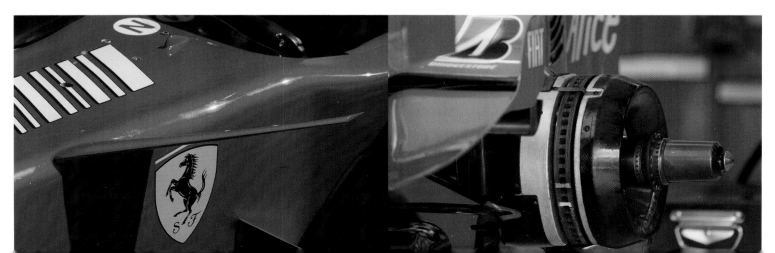

Vodafone McLaren-Mercedes

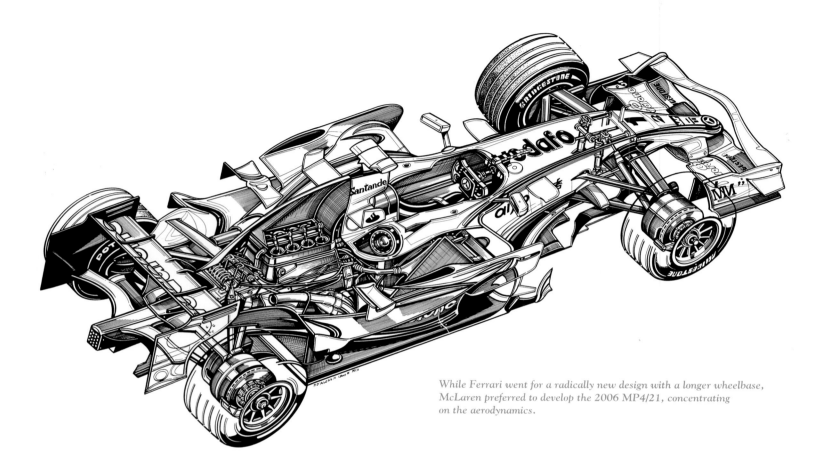

While Ferrari went for a radically new design with a longer wheelbase, McLaren preferred to develop the 2006 MP4/21, concentrating on the aerodynamics.

McLaren-Mercedes paid dearly for their involvement in the Ferrari spy story. But even if it was true that important data was passed to Paragon from Maranello via Nigel Stepney, the McLaren MP4/22 and the Ferrari F2007 were conceptually very different. The origins of the MP4/22 can be traced right back to 2003 when Adrian Newey designed its precursor, the less than competitive MP4/18.

Newey's concept was potentially a winner, let down however by reliability problems and by an aero package that was insufficiently developed to work properly. Over the winter of 2006 his successors – Paddy Lowe, Neil Oatley and that other protagonist of the spy story, Mike Coughlan – set to work with typical British pragmatism to optimise the over 11,000 elements that made up last year's car (the MP4/21) without revolutionising it and, at the same time, avoiding the extreme solutions that had cost the team so much in the recent past (such as in 2005).

The 2007 car thus had a lot in common with the 2006 car, starting with the tiny side pods with almost triangular air intakes and with the lower section heavily cut away.

The front suspension was mounted directly on the monocoque and the rear section was again very narrow and low. McLaren's engineers worked hard on the upper surface of the side pods and on the lateral chimneys in order to speed up and clean up the air flow heading towards the rear wing.

Right from the first GP of the year a series of evolutions were introduced that made the MP4/22 even more competitive, including the highly original "bridge" front wing flap which passed over the nose and was fixed to the end plates. With its chassis and aero package sorted, their next concern was reliability, the team's real enemy last year. And Mercedes pulled it off this time round, helped in part by the F.I.A.'s ruling on a lower, 19,000 rpm rev limit. The V8 (known as the FO108T) proved itself to be on a par with the Ferrari and BMW units, wiping away all fears at the start of the season and, above all, memories of last year's downfall. Which, unlike this year, was not the doing of outside circumstances.

Fernando Alonso

A comparison of the 2006 and 2007 McLarens (left and right respectively). On the 2007 car the front wing support struts are mounted on the central of the three flaps and not on the main front one. This helps increase the air flow under the car.

Lewis Hamilton

On the 2007 MP4/22 the trailing edge of the boomerang flaps on the side pods leads directly to the chimneys.

Ron Dennis, team manager

Norbert Haug, Mercedes motor sport director

McLaren took their upper front wing flap design to an extreme in 2007, developing a bridge solution between the nose cone end plates and thus increasing the total flap surface.

The Mercedes V8 gained considerably in reliability with the mandatory reduction of maximum revs to 19,000 rpm.

A rare photograph in the McLaren pits reveals the entire rear part of the chassis and the rear wing.

BMW Sauber F1 Team

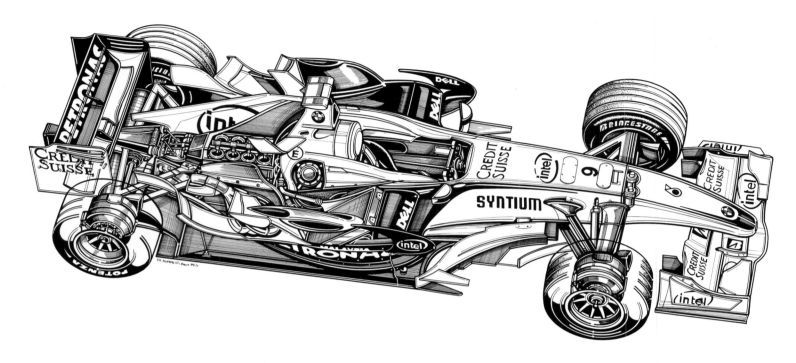

BMW is getting closer to the front runners. After McLaren was disqualified, the team, which is based in Hinwil (Switzerland), came second behind Ferrari in the Constructors' rankings.

Last year's F1.06 was the first ever all-BMW Formula 1 car and was built primarily to gain as much experience and hard data as possible. And secondly to win points. By comparison, the F1.07 was a far more polished and substantial reality, especially in its aero package. The car's surfaces were redefined and huge efforts were made to reduce the performance gap with the top teams (first and foremost Ferrari and Mclaren Mercedes). The single-seaters fielded by Kubica and Heidfeld incorporated a higher, more square-shaped nose cone, new more compact side pods with a tighter "coke-bottle" shape and without any cooling slats, carefully profiled front wing, new bargeboards and an even narrower "waist" at the rear.

Under the skin there were more changes, including to the shape and position of the radiators which were 20 per cent larger than last year's and were used, along with the ballast, to optimise the car's set-up. Combined with improved internal fluid dynamics, they helped improve the BMW V8's performance and durability, the latter an aspect that had left much to be desired last season. The radiators were also mounted very low down – almost horizontally – to help lower the centre of gravity as much as possible.

Powering the F1.07 was the modified V8 (known internally as the BMW P86/7) which had shown so much promise last year (remember rookie Kubica's fine third place at the Italian GP?) and which, this year, also gained in reliability. And the team's second place in the Constructors' championship behind no less than Ferrari and ahead of Renault was proof enough of the unit's competitiveness. The same could not be said for the new "seamless" gearbox which gave Mario Theissen's engineers quite a few sleepless nights early in the season.

On the other hand, unlike several other teams, such as Renault, BMW-Sauber adapted quite painlessly from last year's Michelins to this year's Bridgestones. The BMWs were relatively unaffected by the problems of excessive wear and graining of the soft compound tyres, or by low grip with the harder compound, experienced by rivals. That was no uncertain advantage in what proved to be the definitive transition year for BMW which now has its eyes on the title for the coming seasons.

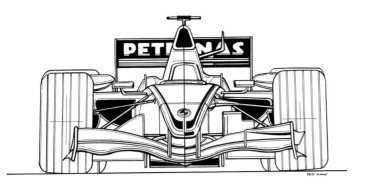

Nick Heidfeld

The BMW Sauber F1 07's new nose cone and front wing, smaller side pods and the McLaren-style horns to the sides of the engine air intake.

Robert Kubica

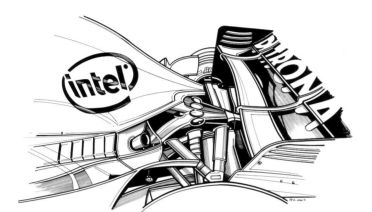

Sebastian Vettel

In the second half of the season, BMW – like other leading teams – introduced new rear bodywork with a reduced section engine cover.

Mario Theissen, team director

The F1 07's upper wishbones act as small wing sections, as do the half-shafts which have their own aerodynamic fairings to increase downforce over the rear axle.

Again to increase downforce over the rear axle BMW developed these mini wings at the end of the transmission.

This photograph illustrates how high the front section of the monocoque is to help channel air below the car.

ING Renault F1 Team

Giancarlo Fisichella

Heikki Kovalainen

Flavio Briatore, team principal

Pat Symmonds, technical director

A lot was expected of Renault after it had won the last two seasons' Constructors' titles, but 2007 turned out to be a complete let down. It could be argued that part of the problem lay with Fernando Alonso's move to McLaren. However, what really put the dampers on Renault's season was the change from the Michelin radials (developed and built around the team's car) to the Bridgestones.

Just like McLaren, the Enstone-based team opted for continuity with the R27. The chief engineer, Pat Symonds intimated that this was a foregone conclusion for two reasons. Firstly because the reigning world champion team could not simply ditch the design of a car that had brought them the title and, secondly, because starting with a known entity would have helped adapting the new car to the Bridgestones. The change to the single supply of tyres also hampered the team from an aerodynamic point of view. The different structure of the Japanese tyre led to a 5 per cent reduction in downforce, forcing the aerodynamicists to modify the shape of the single-seater and its wings.

The Renault was, for example, the first to use the sword-like protuberances (subsequently copied by McLaren and Ferrari) either side of the bodywork ahead of the cockpit to increase pressure in that area. The increase in the number of wings and flaps earned the R27 the nickname "hedgehog". Although vital, the aerodynamics alone could not offset other areas that were lacking, such as the set-up problem caused by the front suspension. Up until last year the Renault solution of a vee-shaped single keel on which the lower wishbone was mounted was optimal. But this year demonstrated that it was better to mount the suspension directly on the monocoque, as pioneered by Ferrari and McLaren, and Renault was forced to re-jig its front suspension on several occasions. The V8 (RS27) also proved less competitive than the units from direct rivals, Ferrari, Mercedes and BMW.

Renault was penalised by the move to the Bridgestone tyres which also affected the car's aerodynamics.

AT&T Williams

Nico Rosberg

Alexander Wurz   Kazuki Nakajima

Frank Williams, team owner

Patrick Head, team manager

While Toyota had a disappointing year, quite the opposite could be said for Williams, effectively a satellite team for the Japanese constructor. After Williams' worst season in three decades in 2006 when it only scored 11 points, Sir Frank and his technical staff proved that, even on a relatively shoe-string budget, their engineering *savoir faire* was unchanged. And their desire to win was in no way dented, as was proved by the way the team's structure was revolutionised to turn the situation around. Sam Michael stayed on as Technical Director, but with more limited powers, and Jon Tomlinson (ex-Renault), Ed Wood and John Russell were taken on alongside him. These experienced engineers came up with a single-seater that, even if it was not revolutionary, was maniacal in its detail.

Some of the aerodynamic solutions adopted on the FW29 – such as the refined nose cone, the compact side-pods or the sinuous radiators that followed the profile of the body panels – were very convincing and inspired other leading teams. As did the seamless gearbox which Williams first introduced in 2006 on the FW28. This technological solution was quickly adopted by all the teams. So by the end of 2007 Williams – thanks to McLaren's disqualification – finished the season fourth in the constructors' rankings, behind Ferrari, BMW and Renault, and well ahead of Toyota itself.

Equipped with Toyota's V8, Williams managed better results than Toyota itself. Bottom right: the McLaren-inspired bridge solution for the front wing used towards the end of the season.

Red Bull Racing

David Coulthard

Mark Webber

Adrian Newey, chief technical officer

Geoff Willis, technical director

Take one of the world's foremost (and highest paid in recent decades) racing car designers, give him a white sheet, a large budget and Renault's V8 that won the 2006 World Championship, and sit back with eyes set on victory. That was the logic, but the first car produced by Adrian Newey brought more delusion than satisfaction to Dietrich Mateschitz's leading team.

The sum of the 2007 season added up to too many retirements, consistent running in the middle of the pack, and a top speed that wasn't going to worry the big teams or get Red Bull up into the F1 hierarchy. That simply was not satisfactory for a team that has ambitions of glory. Yet on paper at least the RB3 seemed to have all the right ingredients to succeed. Adrian Newey had tried to correct the defects of the previous car, making good use of his previous designs. The result was a single-seater that lay somewhere between the 2006 Red Bull and the McLaren MP4/21, a car of his own design. Compared to the McLaren the RB3 had a more rotund and curved nose. Newey's signature could instead be seen in the "zero keel" monocoque design – with the lower front wishbone mounted directly to the chassis – the compact side pods with trapezoidal intakes, and a few engineering details, such as the brake callipers mounted at the bottom of the discs to reduce the centre of gravity. Other touches included the radiators mounted partly inside the lower part of the chassis to reduce the frontal section. But the overall result was light years away from the cars fielded by Alonso and Hamilton and many feel that it will be some time before Red Bull can truly compete at the highest levels.

More was expected of Red Bull who could claim the highest paid designer in F1, as well as the same engine used by Renault in its championship season last year.

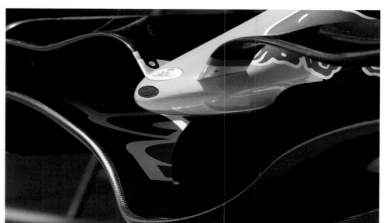

Panasonic Toyota Racing

Jarno Trulli

Ralf Schumacher

Tadashi Yamashina, team principal

Pascal Vasselon, technical director

Unfortunately there is little positive to say about Toyota's F1 performance in 2007, even though at the beginning of the year the team announced that this was going to be a turn-around season for them. Despite the Toyota veterans Hewett and Tomita being replaced by Tadashi Yamashina, there was no change in the results attained. Quite the opposite, in fact, with even worse results than in previous seasons even though they could count on a certain continuity, fielding the same drivers (Trulli and Schumacher) as last year, as well as the same Bridgestone tyres. Those two elements alone were not sufficient, as the TF 107 was out-performed by other more evolved single-seaters.

Many in the business felt that the 2007 Toyota was, in fact, far too conservative to be competitive despite being fitted with the same gearbox as that developed by Williams. Highlight of the car was the aero package, including the original nose cone that debuted successfully in Australia. And even if the overall performance was reasonable, reliability problems side-lined the cars on too many occasions. Then there was the poor launch control function which wiped out Jarno Trulli's best qualifying efforts to get the car high up on the starting grid, only to fall back at the lights.

Toyota can count on virtually unlimited resources, but on the track the results lack, and the long-awaited win has yet to materialize.

Scuderia Toro Rosso

Vitantonio Liuzzi

Scott Speed

Sebastian Vettel

Gerhard Berger,　　　　*Franz Tost,*
team owner　　　　　*technical director*

When the Faenza-based Minardi was sold a couple of seasons ago to Dietrich Mateschitz's group with Gerhard Berger as team manager, the future looked rosy. It looked even more so at the end of the 2006 season with the arrival of a single-seater designed by Adrian Newey (albeit a photocopy of the Red Bull RB3) and the Ferrari V8 (056), the supply of which was guaranteed after Red Bull dropped it in favour of Renault's 2006 championship-winning unit. But it was not sufficient and Toro Rosso was once more an also-ran.

The first signs that all was not as it should be came during winter testing, when Berger started talking of a transition year and a team that would not be able to worry the bigger teams due to too small a budget. So the most that could be expected would be the occasional flash in the pan. But things went even worse than anticipated and the season turned into an odyssey marked by a series of mechanical failures. The main culprit was the new seamless transmission which proved too fragile to complete a full GP. But another aspect of their lack of competitiveness was that while the design was fruit of the synergy with Red Bull Technology, the lack of an adequately dimensioned engineering structure at the team's base in Faenza meant they were unable to implement developments over the season, and were forced to await the modifications carried out by Newey on the Red Bull RB3.

With limited budget and development possibilities, Toro Rosso made the best of its Newey-designed chassis and Ferrari engine, even showing some promise towards the end of the season.

Honda Racing F1 Team

Jenson Button

Rubens Barrichello

Yasuhiro Wada, Honda Racing president

Nick Fry, technical director

After Jenson Button's splendid victory in Hungary and a 2006 season that ended on a high note, great things were expected of Honda this year. Instead 2007 turned into a bit of a disaster. And that despite having invested heavily in the new car – the RA107. The single-seater was designed without compromises and was extremely interesting from both the aerodynamics and chassis points of view.

The fuller forms that characterised the RA106 were dropped in favour of more streamlined ones and a higher nose-cone as per the latest F1 trends, the suspension was mounted directly to the monocoque, and the side-pods were reduced in size while the narrow rear section of the bodywork was the most extreme ever seen in F1, with the body panels literally just coating the mechanical components. Underneath there were new, more rounded radiators which were closely enveloped by the body panels to reduce drag, and a new engine – the RA807E – which on paper looked to be both powerful and reliable.
But from the moment the car took to the track it was evident that there was a fundamental flaw in the design. It was later discovered that the problem lay with the wind tunnel's calibration which undermined all the best efforts made by Honda's engineers. And the situation failed to improve when they eventually fielded the "B" version. It was better at that point to concentrate on 2008's car and relegate the 2007 season to the history books.

If Toyota's performance was a disappointment, Honda's was nigh-on disastrous. The crux of the problem was the car – the RA107. Blame Honda's new wind tunnel settings, which were wrong. The change to Bridgestone tyres didn't help either.

Super Aguri
F1 Team

Takuma Sato

Anthony Davidson

Aguri Suzuki, team principal

Daniel Audetto, managing director

David beat Goliath or, in other words, minnow Super Aguri outclassed the mighty Honda at its own game. It may seem incredible, but that's precisely what happened in 2007, with Aguri Suzuki's single-seaters regularly finishing ahead of the official works cars driven by Jenson Button and Rubens Barrichello. The reason can be traced back to the end of the 2006 season, when Honda decided to recycle that year's car, putting the project in the hands of the satellite team run by Suzuki. The decision was taken partly to assist the struggling Japanese team, putting them in the position to field a well-developed single-seater. Suffice it to recall that with this car, the RA106, Jenson Button clocked up Honda's first ever F1 win in 40 years. So it was a good starting point if it could be developed to work well with the Bridgestone tyres. Which it was, with just a few modifications to the aerodynamics, such as new front wings and new barge boards.

Thus improved the SA07 was regularly battling in the middle of the pack and made the points on a couple of occasions. That was no bad thing for a team that last year was forced to field old 2002-vintage Arrows which had been modified to respect the latest F.I.A. norms. From lapping six or seven seconds slower than the front runners last year to getting Sato into the points this year is a significant achievement in modern F1.

Aguri Suzuki's tiny team managed what many thought to be the impossible – out-run Honda (at least until the penultimate Grand Prix) using the big team's 2006 car with just a few modifications.

Etihad Aldar Spyker F1 Team

Adrian Sutil

Christijan Albers

Sakon Yamamoto   *Markus Winkelhock*

Mike Gascoyne, technical director

In just eight short years, this team has gone from the levels of 1999, when Heinz-Harald Frentzen was even in with a chance of the title, to fighting for its very survival. The team in question is Spyker, née Jordan, née Midland – the one which has changed hands most frequently over recent years, passing from Eddie Jordan to the Russian magnate Alex Shnaider, then to Michiel Mol and Victor Muller who, before the start of the Italian GP, bought a majority holding and changed the name to Spyker. It didn't finished there, because then the team changed hands again, the new courtier being Indian businessman Vijay Mallya who was attracted by the idea of fielding his own car at the upcoming Indian GP. His interest is in part justified, for not only does the F8-VIIB project show promise, but it is also powered by a Ferrari V8 (the 056 version).

Spyker debuted the Mike Gascoyne-designed single-seater at Monza in September 2007 and the car retained effectively little of the model that started the season. The new car differed in the aero package (new nose cone with unusual front wing supports, smaller side pods, new internal fluid dynamics and different radiator lay-out), and featured a different weight distribution and a slightly different wheelbase to adapt better to the new single-supplier tyre. The radical changes made a significant improvement to the car's performance and bode well for the future.

After a terrible start to the year, the debut of the F8-VIIB – the first Spyker to be completely designed by Gascoyne – at Monza saw the team's performance improve greatly, enabling them to make the best use of the Ferrari engine.

Australian Grand Prix

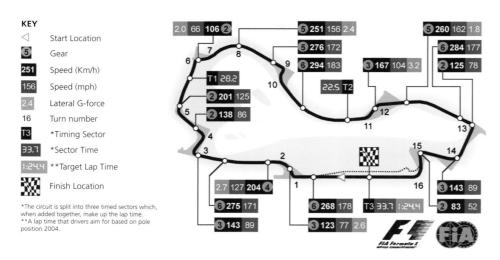

KEY

◁ Start Location
⑤ Gear
251 Speed (Km/h)
156 Speed (mph)
2.4 Lateral G-force
16 Turn number
T3 *Timing Sector
33.7 *Sector Time
1:24.4 **Target Lap Time
🏁 Finish Location

*The circuit is split into three timed sectors which,
when added together, make up the lap time.
**A lap time that drivers aim for based on pole
position 2004.

Albert Park, Melbourne, Australia – 18 March
Lap length: 5.303 km/3.295 miles
No. of laps: 58
Race distance: 307.574 km/191.110 miles
Weather: sunny and warm

QUALIFYING

	Driver	Car	Chassis number	Time
1	K. Räikkönen	Ferrari	F2007-261	1'26.072"
2	F. Alonso	McLaren	MP4/22-03	1'26.493"
3	N. Heidfeld	BMW	F1.07-04	1'26.556"
4	L. Hamilton	McLaren	MP4/22-05	1'26.755"
5	R. Kubica	BMW	F1.07-05	1'27.347"
6	G. Fisichella	Renault	R27-02	1'27.634"
7	M. Webber	Red Bull	RB3-02	1'27.934"
8	J. Trulli	Toyota	TF107-04	1'28.404"
9	R. Schumacher	Toyota	TF107-03	1'28.692"
10	T. Sato	Super Aguri	SA07-04	1'28.871"
11	A. Davidson	Super Aguri	SA07-03	1'26.909"
12	N. Rosberg	Williams	FW29-03	1'26.914"
13	H. Kovalainen	Renault	R27-03	1'26.964"
14	J. Button	Honda	RA107-04	1'27.264"
15	A. Wurz	Williams	FW29-04	1'27.393"
16	F. Massa*	Ferrari	F2007-260	no time
17	R. Barrichello	Honda	RA107-02	1'27.679"
18	S. Speed	Toro Rosso	STR2-01	1'28.305"
19	D. Coulthard	Red Bull	RB3-01	1'28.579"
20	V. Liuzzi	Toro Rosso	STR2-02	1'29.267"
21	A. Sutil	Spyker	F8-VII/03	1'29.339"
22	C. Albers**	Spyker	F8-VII/02	1'31.932"

(*) dropped 10 places after changing engine
(**) started from pit-lane

MELBOURNE

Pole position, victory and fastest lap - Räikkönen didn't waste any time marking his territory at Ferrari. His team-mate, Massa, was let down by his gearbox during qualifying, so was relegated to the back of the pack. Starting with a full tank, Felipe managed to fight his way back to 6th at the chequered flag. Alongside Kimi in second place on the grid was Alonso who was overtaken at the start by both Heidfeld and Hamilton, third and fourth in qualifying. Nick fell back after his first pit-stop (he'd started light on fuel and with soft tyres), but eventually finished fourth after Kubica retired. It wasn't until Fernando's second pit-stop that he managed to pass his team-mate for second place in what was an impressive F1 debut for rookie Lewis, both McLaren drivers making it to the podium. Way back in the running – 13th Saturday and 10th Sunday – Kovalainen would have liked to have had a similar start to his season. Fisichella in the other Renault didn't shine, either – 6th on the grid and 5th in the race – much to Briatore's chagrin. Rosberg finished 7th, the best of the Toyota-powered cars, ahead of the official Toyotas driven by Ralf Schumacher and Jarno Trulli. Wurz in the second Williams was removed from the running by Coulthard's airborne Red Bull, and the Hondas had a very poor showing, qualifying behind the Super Aguris.

RESULT

	Driver	Car	Time	Laps	Stops
1	K. Räikkönen	Ferrari	1hr25'28.770"	58	2
2	F. Alonso	McLaren	+ 7.350"	58	2
3	L. Hamilton	McLaren	+ 18.595"	58	2
4	N. Heidfeld	BMW	+ 38.763"	58	2
5	G. Fisichella	Renault	+ 1'06.469"	58	2
6	F. Massa	Ferrari	+ 1'06.805"	58	1
7	N. Rosberg	Williams	+ 1 lap	57	2
8	R. Schumacher	Toyota	+ 1 lap	57	2
9	J. Trulli	Toyota	+ 1 lap	57	2
10	H. Kovalainen	Renault	+ 1 lap	57	2
11	R. Barrichello	Honda	+ 1 lap	57	2
12	T. Sato	Super Aguri	+ 1 lap	57	2
13	M. Webber	Red Bull	+ 1 lap	57	2
14	V. Liuzzi	Toro Rosso	+ 1 lap	57	2
15	J. Button	Honda	+ 1 lap	57	2*
16	A. Davidson	Super Aguri	+ 2 laps	56	2
17	A. Sutil	Spyker	+ 2 laps	56	2*

(*) one drive-through penalty for Button, two for Sutil
Laps in the lead: Räikkönen 52, Hamilton 4, Alonso 2

RETIREMENTS

A. Wurz	Williams	collision	48	1
D. Coulthard	Red Bull	collision	48	2
R. Kubica	BMW	gearbox	36	1
S. Speed	Toro Rosso	puncture	28	1
C. Albers	Spyker	crash	10	

FASTEST LAP

K. Räikkönen	Ferrari	1'25.235"	41

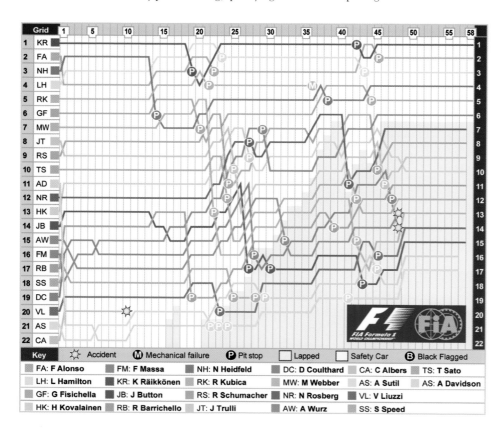

Key		
☆ Accident	Ⓜ Mechanical failure	Ⓟ Pit stop	⬜ Lapped	⬜ Safety Car	Ⓑ Black Flagged

FA: F Alonso	FM: F Massa	NH: N Heidfeld	DC: D Coulthard	CA: C Albers	TS: T Sato
LH: L Hamilton	KR: K Räikkönen	RK: R Kubica	MW: M Webber	AS: A Sutil	AS: A Davidson
GF: G Fisichella	JB: J Button	RS: R Schumacher	NR: N Rosberg	VL: V Liuzzi	
HK: H Kovalainen	RB: R Barrichello	JT: J Trulli	AW: A Wurz	SS: S Speed	

Malaysian Grand Prix

KEY

◁ Start Location
5 Gear
251 Speed (Km/h)
156 Speed (mph)
2.4 Lateral G-force
16 Turn number
T3 *Timing Sector
33.7 *Sector Time
1:24.4 **Target Lap Time
🏁 Finish Location

*The circuit is split into three timed sectors which, when added together, make up the lap time.
**A lap time that drivers aim for based on pole position 2004.

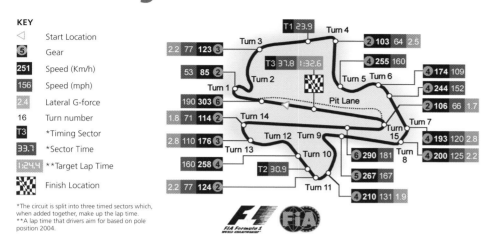

Sepang, Kuala Lumpur, Malaysia – 8 April
Lap length: 5.543 km / 3.444 miles
No. of laps: 56
Race distance: 310.408 km/192.887 miles
Weather: sunny and warm

QUALIFYING

	Driver	Car	Chassis number	Time
1	F. Massa	Ferrari	F2007-260	1'35.043"
2	F. Alonso	McLaren	MP4/22-01	1'35.310"
3	K. Räikkönen	Ferrari	F2007-261	1'35.479"
4	L. Hamilton	McLaren	MP4/22-05	1'36.045"
5	N. Heidfeld	BMW	F1.07-05	1'36.543"
6	N. Rosberg	Williams	FW29-03	1'36.829"
7	R. Kubica	BMW	F1.07-04	1'36.896"
8	J. Trulli	Toyota	TF107-04	1'36.902"
9	R. Schumacher	Toyota	TF107-03	1'37.078"
10	M. Webber	Red Bull	RB3-02	1'37.345"
11	H. Kovalainen	Renault	R27-01	1'35.630"
12	G. Fisichella	Renault	R27-04	1'35.706"
13	D. Coulthard	Red Bull	RB3-01	1'35.766"
14	T. Sato	Super Aguri	SA07-04	1'35.945"
15	J. Button	Honda	RA107-04	1'36.088"
16	V. Liuzzi	Toro Rosso	STR2-02	1'36.145"
17	S. Speed	Toro Rosso	STR2-01	1'36.578"
18	A. Davidson	Super Aguri	SA07-03	1'36.816"
19	R. Barrichello*	Honda	RA107-02	1'36.827"
20	A. Wurz	Williams	FW29-04	1'37.326"
21	C. Albers	Spyker	F8-VII-01	1'38.279"
22	A. Sutil	Spyker	F8-VII-03	1'38.415"

(*) dropped 10 places after changing engine; started from pit-lane

SEPANG

Massa on pole was beaten to the first corner by both McLarens at the start. Lap after lap Hamilton helped Alonso build up a good lead. Slowed by the Brit, Massa attempted a passing manoeuvre that succeeded only in losing him two places after an off. A few laps later and the top five places were cast. Alonso was uncatchable and brought home McLaren's first race win in one and a half seasons. Cherry on the cake was Lewis's second place after fighting off Räikkönen and setting the fastest lap. Fourth again, Heidfeld separated the two disappointing Ferraris, finishing ahead of an unconvincing Massa. Ineffective in qualifying (no higher than the 6th row on the grid), the Renaults took home four championship points with Fisichella 6th and Kovalainen 8th, sandwiching Trulli's Toyota. The reigning World Championship team was helped by an engine breakage in Rosberg's Williams, and by Kubica's tyre and gearbox woes. Once more the Hondas were invisible and the Red Bulls less competitive in the race than in qualifying. After a broken gearbox relegated Wurz to 19th place on the grid, his impressive battle back up the field to 9th at the flag really would have deserved a point.

RESULT

	Driver	Car	Time	Laps	Stops
1	F. Alonso	McLaren	1hr32'14.930"	56	2
2	L. Hamilton	McLaren	+ 17.557"	56	2
3	K. Räikkönen	Ferrari	+ 18.339"	56	2
4	N. Heidfeld	BMW	+ 33.777"	56	2
5	F. Massa	Ferrari	+ 36.705"	56	2
6	G. Fisichella	Renault	+ 1'05.638"	56	2
7	J. Trulli	Toyota	+ 1'10.690"	56	2
8	H. Kovalainen	Renault	+ 1'12.015"	56	2
9	A. Wurz	Williams	+ 1'29.924"	56	2
10	M. Webber	Red Bull	+ 1'33.500"	56	2
11	R. Barrichello	Honda	+ 1 lap	55	2
12	J. Button	Honda	+ 1 lap	55	2
13	T. Sato	Super Aguri	+ 1 lap	55	2
14	S. Speed	Toro Rosso	+ 1 lap	55	2
15	R. Schumacher	Toyota	+ 1 lap	55	2
16	A. Davidson	Super Aguri	+ 1 lap	55	2
17	V. Liuzzi	Toro Rosso	+ 1 lap	55	3
18	R. Kubica	BMW	+ 1 lap	55	2

Laps in the lead: Alonso 52, Hamilton 2, Räikkönen 1, Heidfeld 1

RETIREMENTS

N. Rosberg	Williams	engine	42	2
D. Coulthard	Red Bull	brakes	36	2
C. Albers	Spyker	gearbox	7	
A. Sutil	Spyker	crash	1	

FASTEST LAP

L. Hamilton	McLaren	1'36.701"	22

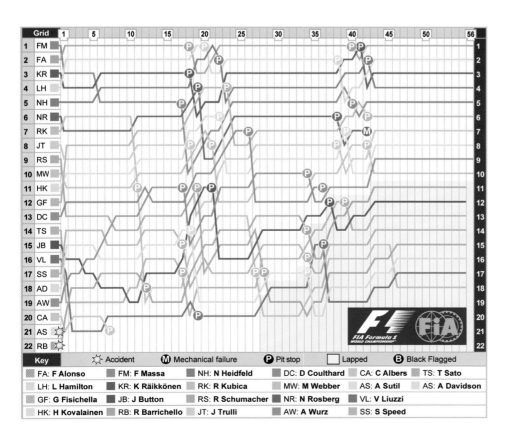

Grid

Grid	1	5	10	15	20	25	30	35	40	45	50	56
1	FM
2	FA
3	KR
4	LH
5	NH
6	NR
7	RK
8	JT
9	RS
10	MW
11	HK
12	GF
13	DC
14	TS
15	JB
16	VL
17	SS
18	AD
19	AW
20	CA
21	AS
22	RB

Key: ☆ Accident | Ⓜ Mechanical failure | Ⓟ Pit stop | ☐ Lapped | Ⓑ Black Flagged

FA: F Alonso	FM: F Massa	NH: N Heidfeld	DC: D Coulthard	CA: C Albers	TS: T Sato
LH: L Hamilton	KR: K Räikkönen	RK: R Kubica	MW: M Webber	AS: A Sutil	AS: A Davidson
GF: G Fisichella	JB: J Button	RS: R Schumacher	NR: N Rosberg	VL: V Liuzzi	
HK: H Kovalainen	RB: R Barrichello	JT: J Trulli	AW: A Wurz	SS: S Speed	

Bahrain Grand Prix

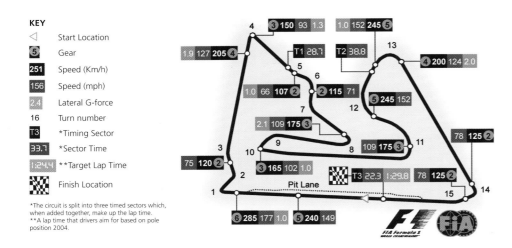

SAKHIR

Author of his second consecutive pole position, Massa wasn't foiled at the start this time, but the McLarens managed to block Räikkönen. A shunt involving Button, Speed and Sutil brought the safety car out, after which Felipe and Lewis pulled away from Fernando, Kimi – weighed down by more fuel – and Heidfeld. Hamilton's second set of tyres were down on performance to the extent that Räikkönen was able to catch him up. But towards the end and with hard tyres it was Lewis's turn to put pressure on Massa, although without really threatening the Ferrari driver. Alonso also found the harder Bridgestones better, but the improvement came too late to improve on his modest 5th place behind Heidfeld, with Räikkönen – who had passed Nick at the first pit-stop – in third. Kubica had a fairly solitary race to bring home his first three championship points. The rest of the group was more tightly knit and saw plenty of action, thanks to the Red Bulls – unfortunately both side-lined by mechanical breakages – and the Williams which finished just outside the points. Trulli had a bad start but recovered two points after passing the Renaults of Fisico and Kovalainen, both slowed by excessive rear tyre wear when running with full tanks after the first pit-stop.

Manama, Bahrain – 15 April
Lap length: 5.412 km/3.363 miles
No. of laps: 57
Race distance: 308.238 km/191.539 miles
Weather: sunny and hot

QUALIFYING

	Driver	Car	Chassis number	Time
1	F. Massa	Ferrari	F2007-260	1'32.652"
2	L. Hamilton	McLaren	MP4/22-05	1'32.935"
3	K. Räikkönen	Ferrari	F2007-261	1'33.131"
4	F. Alonso	McLaren	MP4/22-01	1'33.192"
5	N. Heidfeld	BMW	F1.07-05	1'33.404"
6	R. Kubica	BMW	F1.07-03	1'33.710"
7	G. Fisichella	Renault	R27-04	1'34.056"
8	M. Webber	Red Bull	RB3-02	1'34.106"
9	J. Trulli	Toyota	TF107-04	1'34.154"
10	N. Rosberg	Williams	FW29-03	1'34.399"
11	A. Wurz	Williams	FW29-04	1'32.915"
12	H. Kovalainen	Renault	R27-01	1'32.935"
13	A. Davidson	Super Aguri	SA07-03	1'33.082"
14	R. Schumacher	Toyota	TF107-03	1'33.294"
15	R. Barrichello	Honda	RA107-03	1'33.624"
16	J. Button	Honda	RA107-05	1'33.731"
17	T. Sato	Super Aguri	SA07-04	1'33.984"
18	V. Liuzzi	Toro Rosso	STR2-02	1'34.024"
19	S. Speed	Toro Rosso	STR2-01	1'34.333"
20	A. Sutil	Spyker	F8-VII-03	1'35.280"
21	D. Coulthard	Red Bull	RB3-01	1'35.341"
22	C. Albers	Spyker	F8-VII-01	1'35.533"

RESULT

	Driver	Car	Time	Laps	Stops
1	F. Massa	Ferrari	1hr33'27.515"	57	2
2	L. Hamilton	McLaren	+ 2.360"	57	2
3	K. Raikkonen	Ferrari	+ 10.839"	57	2
4	N. Heidfeld	BMW	+ 13.831"	57	2
5	F. Alonso	McLaren	+ 14.426"	57	2
6	R. Kubica	BMW	+ 45.925"	57	2
7	J. Trulli	Toyota	+ 1'21.371"	57	2
8	G. Fisichella	Renault	+ 1'21.701"	57	2
9	H. Kovalainen	Renault	+ 1'29.411"	57	2
10	N. Rosberg	Williams	+ 1'29.916"	57	2
11	A. Wurz	Williams	+ 1 lap	56	2
12	R. Schumacher	Toyota	+ 1 lap	56	2
13	R. Barrichello	Honda	+ 1 lap	56	2
14	C. Albers	Spyker	+ 2 laps	55	2
15	A. Sutil	Spyker	+ 4 laps	53	3
16	A. Davidson	Super Aguri	+ 6 laps (engine)	51	1

Laps in the lead: Massa 51, Hamilton 4, Raikkonen 2

RETIREMENTS

M. Webber	Red Bull	gearbox	41	2
D. Coulthard	Red Bull	transmission	36	1
T. Sato	Super Aguri	engine	34	1
V. Liuzzi	Toro Rosso	hydraulics	26	2*
J. Button	Honda	collision	1	
S. Speed	Toro Rosso	collision	1	

(*) drive-through penalty for having overtaken under yellow flags

FASTEST LAP

F. Massa	Ferrari	1'34.067"	42

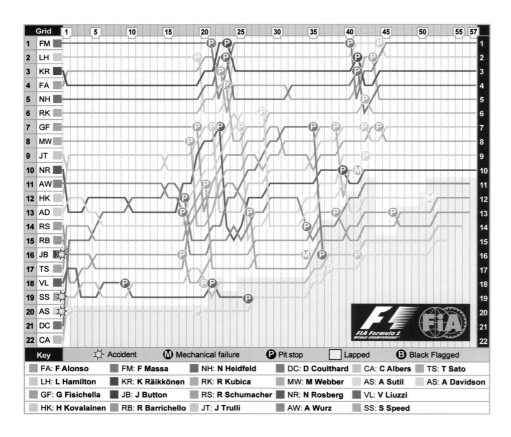

Key		
☆ Accident	Ⓜ Mechanical failure	Ⓟ Pit stop
▢ Lapped	Ⓑ Black Flagged	

FA: F Alonso	FM: F Massa	NH: N Heidfeld	DC: D Coulthard
CA: C Albers	TS: T Sato		
LH: L Hamilton	KR: K Räikkönen	RK: R Kubica	MW: M Webber
AS: A Sutil	AS: A Davidson		
GF: G Fisichella	JB: J Button	RS: R Schumacher	NR: N Rosberg
VL: V Liuzzi			
HK: H Kovalainen	RB: R Barrichello	JT: J Trulli	AW: A Wurz
SS: S Speed			

Spanish Grand Prix

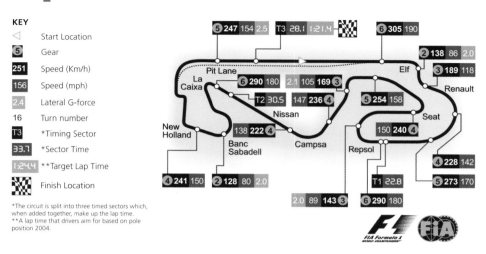

KEY

◁   Start Location

5   Gear

251   Speed (Km/h)

156   Speed (mph)

2.4   Lateral G-force

16   Turn number

T3   *Timing Sector

33.7   *Sector Time

1:24.4   **Target Lap Time

🏁   Finish Location

*The circuit is split into three timed sectors which, when added together, make up the lap time.
**A lap time that drivers aim for based on pole position 2004.

BARCELONA

Alonso went wheel to wheel with Massa into the first corner to try to take the lead, but just when it seemed he would succeed, the cars touched forcing Ferdinand off. The McLaren driver lost two places and Felipe headed off into the distance, his solitary race troubled only by flames from spilt fuel during refuelling. Hamilton had passed Räikkönen at the start and managed to gain on the Ferrari driver even though both were carrying similar amounts of fuel, more than their team-mates. Kimi was soon in Alonso's sights, but the duel wasn't to last long – Räikkönen was sidelined by electrical problems after 10 laps. The BMWs challenged Alonso for a podium finish until Heidfeld was eliminated from the running when he left a pit-stop with a wheel loose. Kubica went on to take a good fourth place well ahead of Coulthard who was slowed towards the end by gearbox problems. Even having lost a few gears he still managed to pick up Red Bull's first points of the season (5th), keeping Rosberg and Kovalainen at bay. Both Renaults were slowed by a defective refuelling rig. This cost Fisichella the 8th place as he was beaten to the line by Sato who thus took home Super Aguri's first point this year. Hamilton found himself leading the Drivers' rankings and McLaren pulled away in the Constructors' standings.

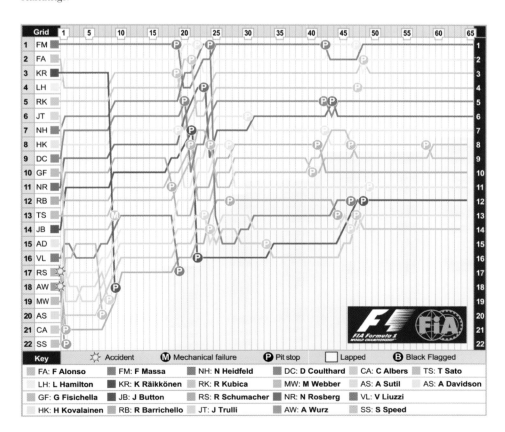

Barcelona, Spain – 13 May
Lap length: 4.655 km/2.892 miles
No. of laps: 65
Race distance: 302.449 km/187.942 miles
Weather: sunny and warm

QUALIFYING

	Driver	Car	Chassis number	Time
1	F. Massa	Ferrari	F2007-260	1'21.421"
2	F. Alonso	McLaren	MP4/22-06	1'21.451"
3	K. Räikkönen	Ferrari	F2007-262	1'21.723"
4	L. Hamilton	McLaren	MP4/22-05	1'21.785"
5	R. Kubica	BMW	F1.07-07	1'22.253"
6	J. Trulli*	Toyota	TF107-04	1'22.324"
7	N. Heidfeld	BMW	F1.07-05	1'22.389"
8	H. Kovalainen	Renault	R27-03	1'22.568"
9	D. Coulthard	Red Bull	RB3-03	1'22.749"
10	G. Fisichella	Renault	R27-04	1'22.881"
11	N. Rosberg	Williams	FW29-05	1'21.968"
12	R. Barrichello	Honda	RA107-02	1'22.097"
13	T. Sato	Super Aguri	SA07-04	1'22.115"
14	J. Button	Honda	RA107-04	1'22.120"
15	A. Davidson	Super Aguri	SA07-02	1'22.295"
16	V. Liuzzi	Toro Rosso	STR2-03	no time
17	R. Schumacher	Toyota	TF107-05	1'22.666"
18	A. Wurz	Williams	FW29-04	1'22.769"
19	M. Webber	Red Bull	RB3-02	1'23.398"
20	A. Sutil	Spyker	F8-VII-03	1'23.811"
21	C. Albers	Spyker	F8-VII-04	1'23.990"
22	S. Speed	Toro Rosso	STR2-04	no time

(*) started from pit-lane

RESULT

	Driver	Car	Time	Laps	Stops
1	F. Massa	Ferrari	1hr31'36.230"	65	2
2	L. Hamilton	McLaren	+ 6.790"	65	2
3	F. Alonso	McLaren	+ 17.456"	65	2
4	R. Kubica	BMW	+ 31.615"	65	2
5	D. Coulthard	Red Bull	+ 58.331"	65	2
6	N. Rosberg	Williams	+ 59.538"	65	2
7	H. Kovalainen	Renault	+ 1'02.128"	65	3
8	T. Sato	Super Aguri	+ 1 lap	64	2
9	G. Fisichella	Renault	+ 1 lap	64	3
10	R. Barrichello	Honda	+ 1 lap	64	2
11	A. Davidson	Super Aguri	+ 1 lap	64	2
12	J. Button	Honda	+ 1 lap	64	2*
13	A. Sutil	Spyker	+ 2 laps	63	2
14	C. Albers	Spyker	+ 2 laps	63	2*

(*) drive-through penalty
Laps in the lead: Massa 55, Hamilton 8, Heidfeld 2

RETIREMENTS

Nick Heidfeld	BMW	gearbox	47	2
Ralf Schumacher	Toyota	roadholding	45	2
Vitantonio Liuzzi	Toro Rosso	hydraulics	20	
Scott Speed	Toro Rosso	puncture	10	
Kimi Räikkönen	Ferrari	electrics	10	
Jarno Trulli	Toyota	fuel pressure	9	
Mark Webber	Red Bull	hydraulics	8	
Alexander Wurz	Williams	collision	1	

FASTEST LAP

F. Massa	Ferrari	1'22.680"	14

Monaco Grand Prix

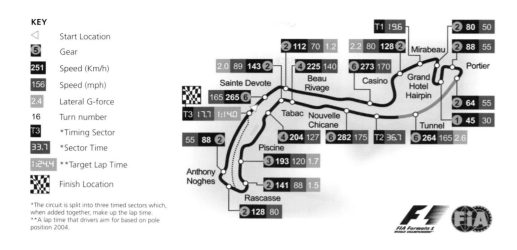

KEY

◁ Start Location
5 Gear
251 Speed (Km/h)
156 Speed (mph)
2.4 Lateral G-force
16 Turn number
T3 *Timing Sector
33.7 *Sector Time
1:24.4 **Target Lap Time
🏁 Finish Location

*The circuit is split into three timed sectors which, when added together, make up the lap time.
**A lap time that drivers aim for based on pole position 2004.

MONACO

For the first time this season, Ferrari did not dominate qualifying. Räikkönen broke his suspension after clipping a barrier and was classified 16th, while Massa – never really at ease on the tight road circuit – recorded the 3rd fastest time, some way behind the impressive McLarens. Hamilton – who on Thursday had made his first error of the season at the Sainte-Dévote – held on to the pole position right up until the last minute, when it was snatched from under his nose by Alonso. Fisichella made encouraging progress (4th) as did the Hondas (9th and 10th), while the Toyotas dropped back and Coulthard (13th) was penalised for obstructing Kovalainen (15th). The race turned into something of a procession. Hamilton stuck so close to Alonso's tailpipes that Ron Dennis even went to the lengths of pulling his young protégé in early for his first pit-stop to ensure they would bring home the 1-2. Massa finished third at over a minute from the McLarens. Fisichella confirmed Renault's return to form, easily keeping the BMWs (5th and 6th) at bay. Rosberg provided plenty of action during qualifying and the first few laps, and Wurz (7th) pulled off a fine drive to resist pressure from Räikkönen who, stuck in traffic, was the day's big loser. Scott Speed's performance also warrants a mention, finishing as he did 9th despite starting from 18th on the grid and edging out the Hondas. 18 cars took the chequered flag.

Monte-Carlo, Monaco – 27 May
Lap length: 3.340 km/2.075 miles
No. of laps: 78
Race distance: 260.520 km/161.887 miles
Weather: sunny and warm

QUALIFYING

	Driver	Car	Chassis number	Time
1	F. Alonso	McLaren	MP4/22-06	1'15.726"
2	L. Hamilton	McLaren	MP4/22-05	1'15.905"
3	F. Massa	Ferrari	F2007-260	1'15.967"
4	G. Fisichella	Renault	R27-04	1'16.285"
5	N. Rosberg	Williams	FW29-05	1'16.439"
6	M. Webber	Red Bull	RB3-02	1'16.784"
7	N. Heidfeld	BMW	F1.07-05	1'16.832"
8	R. Kubica	BMW	F1.07-07	1'19.955"
9	R. Barrichello	Honda	RA107-02	1'17.498"
10	J. Button	Honda	RA107-04	1'17.939"
11	D. Coulthard*	Red Bull	RB3-03	1'16.319"
12	A. Wurz	Williams	FW29-04	1'16.662"
13	V. Liuzzi	Toro Rosso	STR2-03	1'16.703"
14	J. Trulli	Toyota	TF107-04	1'16.988"
15	H. Kovalainen	Renault	R27-03	1'17.125"
16	K. Räikkönen	Ferrari	F2007-262	no time
17	A. Davidson	Super Aguri	SA07-03	1'18.250"
18	S. Speed	Toro Rosso	STR2-04	1'18.390"
19	A. Sutil	Spyker	F8-VII-03	1'18.418"
20	R. Schumacher	Toyota	TF107-05	1'18.539"
21	T. Sato	Super Aguri	SA07-04	1'18.554"
22	C. Albers	Spyker	F8-VII-02	no time

(*) penalised for having disturbed Kovalainen

RESULT

	Driver	Car	Time	Laps	Stops
1	F. Alonso	McLaren	1hr40'29.329"	78	2
2	L. Hamilton	McLaren	+ 4.095"	78	2
3	F. Massa	Ferrari	+ 1'09.114"	78	2
4	G. Fisichella	Renault	+ 1 lap	77	2
5	R. Kubica	BMW	+ 1 lap	77	1
6	N. Heidfeld	BMW	+ 1 lap	77	1
7	A. Wurz	Williams	+ 1 lap	77	1
8	K. Räikkönen	Ferrari	+ 1 lap	77	1
9	S. Speed	Toro Rosso	+ 1 lap	77	1
10	R. Barrichello	Honda	+ 1 lap	77	2
11	J. Button	Honda	+ 1 lap	77	2
12	N. Rosberg	Williams	+ 1 lap	77	2
13	H. Kovalainen	Renault	+ 1 lap	77	1
14	D. Coulthard	Red Bull	+ 2 laps	76	1
15	J. Trulli	Toyota	+ 2 laps	76	1
16	R. Schumacher	Toyota	+ 2 laps	76	1
17	T. Sato	Super Aguri	+ 2 laps	76	2
18	A. Davidson	Super Aguri	+ 2 laps	76	2*

(*) drive-through penalty
Laps in the lead: Alonso 73, Hamilton 5

RETIREMENTS

C. Albers	Spyker-Ferrari	transmission	70	2
A. Sutil	Spyker-Ferrari	crash	53	1
M. Webber	Red Bull	gearbox	17	
V. Liuzzi	Toro Rosso	crash	1	

FASTEST LAP

F. Alonso	McLaren	1'15.284"	44

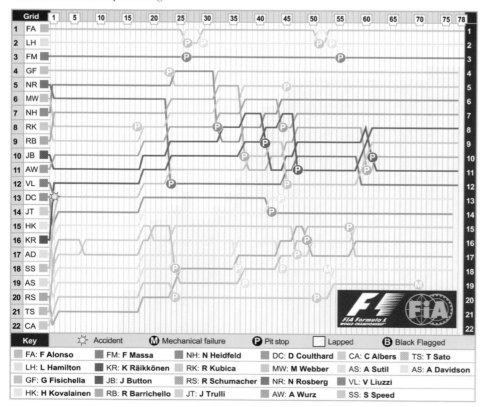

Key		
☼ Accident	Ⓜ Mechanical failure	Ⓟ Pit stop	▢ Lapped	Ⓑ Black Flagged

FA: F Alonso	FM: F Massa	NH: N Heidfeld	DC: D Coulthard	CA: C Albers	TS: T Sato
LH: L Hamilton	KR: K Räikkönen	RK: R Kubica	MW: M Webber	AS: A Sutil	AS: A Davidson
GF: G Fisichella	JB: J Button	RS: R Schumacher	NR: N Rosberg	VL: V Liuzzi	
HK: H Kovalainen	RB: R Barrichello	JT: J Trulli	AW: A Wurz	SS: S Speed	

Canadian Grand Prix

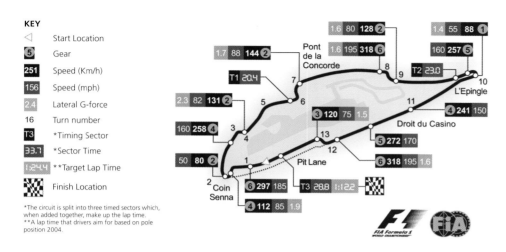

KEY

◁   Start Location

5   Gear

251   Speed (Km/h)

156   Speed (mph)

2.4   Lateral G-force

16   Turn number

T3   *Timing Sector

33.7   *Sector Time

1:24.4   **Target Lap Time

🏁   Finish Location

*The circuit is split into three timed sectors which, when added together, make up the lap time.
**A lap time that drivers aim for based on pole position 2004.

Circuit Gilles Villeneuve, Montreal, Canada – 10 June

Lap length: 4.361 km/2.709 miles
No. of laps: 70
Race distance: 305.270 km/189.694 miles
Weather: sunny and warm

QUALIFYING

	Driver	Car	Chassis number	Time
1	L. Hamilton	McLaren	MP4/22-01	1'15.707"
2	F. Alonso	McLaren	MP4/22-08	1'16.163"
3	N. Heidfeld	BMW	F1.07-05	1'16.266"
4	K. Räikkönen	Ferrari	F2007-262	1'16.411"
5	F. Massa	Ferrari	F2007-260	1'16.570"
6	M. Webber	Red Bull	RB3-02	1'16.913"
7	N. Rosberg	Williams	FW29-05	1'16.919"
8	R. Kubica	BMW	F1.07-07	1'16.993"
9	G. Fisichella	Renault	R27-05	1'17.229"
10	J. Trulli	Toyota	TF107-04	1'17.747"
11	T. Sato	Super Aguri	SA07-04	1'16.743"
12	V. Liuzzi	Toro Rosso	STR2-03	1'16.760"
13	R. Barrichello	Honda	RA107-02	1'17.116"
14	D. Coulthard	Red Bull	RB3-03	1'17.304"
15	J. Button	Honda	RA107-04	1'17.541"
16	S. Speed	Toro Rosso	STR2-04	1'17.571"
17	A. Davidson	Super Aguri	SA07-03	1'17.542"
18	R. Schumacher	Toyota	TF107-05	1'17.634"
19	H. Kovalainen*	Renault	R27-03	1'17.806"
20	A. Wurz	Williams	FW29-04	1'18.089"
21	A. Sutil	Spyker	F8-VII-03	1'18.536"
22	C. Albers**	Spyker	F8-VII-02	1'19.196"

(*) dropped 10 places after changing engine
(**) started from pit-lane

MONTREAL

After taking the first pole position of his career, Hamilton fended off an attack from his team-mate at the first corner forcing Alonso into the first of several excursions onto the grass and letting Heidfeld into second place, a position he would hold until the end. Behind them no less than four safety car stints mixed up the running. Alonso and Rosberg received a stop-and-go penalty for having stopped to refuel when the pit-lane was still closed. Massa and Fisichella were black-flagged for having left the pit-lane under the red light. There was a fright on lap 26 when Kubica had a huge off just before the hairpin. The BMW flew into the air, smashing frontally into a cement wall, before cartwheeling across the track. The impact was such that everyone feared for his life, but the final diagnosis was just a sprained ankle. Webber and Barrichello were both robbed of a possible podium finish by late pit-stops. Both Liuzzi and Trulli missed out on points that were theirs for the taking after making mistakes late in the race. Wurz, who started from 19th place on the grid, crossed the line 3rd for Williams ahead of Kovalainen, who had started last. Räikkönen came a pale 5th, ahead of Sato and a struggling Alonso, while the last point went to Schumacher. Only 12 cars finished this most chaotic of races which saw Hamilton finally take his first victory and write his name in the history books.

RESULT

	Driver	Car	Time	Laps	Stops
1	L. Hamilton	McLaren	1hr44'11.292"	70	2
2	N. Heidfeld	BMW	+ 4.343"	70	2
3	A. Wurz	Williams	+ 5.325"	70	1
4	H. Kovalainen	Renault	+ 6.729"	70	1
5	K. Räikkönen	Ferrari	+ 13.007"	70	2
6	T. Sato	Super Aguri	+ 16.698"	70	3
7	F. Alonso	McLaren	+ 21.936"	70	2*
8	R. Schumacher	Toyota	+ 22.888"	70	2
9	M. Webber	Red Bull	+ 22.960"	70	2
10	N. Rosberg	Williams	+ 23.984"	70	2*
11	A. Davidson	Super Aguri	+ 24.318"	70	3
12	R. Barrichello	Honda	+ 30.439"	70	2

(*) stop-and-go penalty
Laps in the lead: Hamilton 67, Massa 3

RETIREMENTS

J. Trulli	Toyota	crash	58	4
V. Liuzzi	Toro Rosso	crash	54	2
F. Massa	Ferrari	black flag*	51	1
G. Fisichella	Renault	black flag*	51	1
C. Albers	Spyker	crash	47	1
D. Coulthard	Red Bull	gearbox	36	3
R. Kubica	BMW	crash	26	1
A. Sutil	Spyker	crash	21	
S. Speed	Toro Rosso	collision	8	
J. Button	Honda	gearbox	0	

(*) disqualified for failing to respect the red light on pit exit

FASTEST LAP

F. Alonso	McLaren	1'16.367"	46

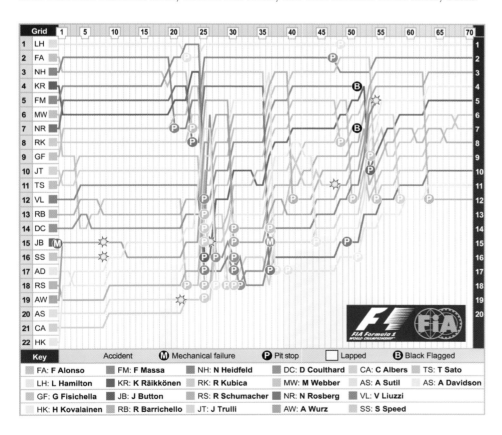

Key				
Accident	**M** Mechanical failure	**P** Pit stop	☐ Lapped	**B** Black Flagged

FA: F Alonso	FM: F Massa	NH: N Heidfeld	DC: D Coulthard	CA: C Albers	TS: T Sato
LH: L Hamilton	KR: K Räikkönen	RK: R Kubica	MW: M Webber	AS: A Sutil	AS: A Davidson
GF: G Fisichella	JB: J Button	RS: R Schumacher	NR: N Rosberg	VL: V Liuzzi
HK: H Kovalainen	RB: R Barrichello	JT: J Trulli	AW: A Wurz	SS: S Speed

United States Grand Prix

KEY

◁ Start Location

5 Gear

251 Speed (Km/h)

156 Speed (mph)

2.4 Lateral G-force

16 Turn number

T3 *Timing Sector

33.7 *Sector Time

1:24.4 **Target Lap Time

🏁 Finish Location

*The circuit is split into three timed sectors which,
when added together, make up the lap time.
**A lap time that drivers aim for based on pole
position 2004

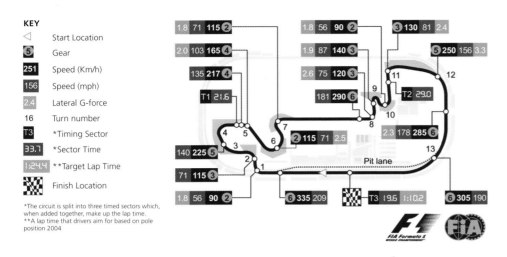

Indianapolis, USA – 17 June
Lap length: 4.192 km/2.605 miles
No. of laps: 73
Race distance: 306.016 km/190.139 miles
Weather: sunny and warm

QUALIFYING

	Driver	Car	Chassis number	Time
1	L. Hamilton	McLaren	MP4/22-01	1'12.331"
2	F. Alonso	McLaren	MP4/22-06	1'12.500"
3	F. Massa	Ferrari	F2007-260	1'12.703"
4	K. Räikkönen	Ferrari	F2007-262	1'12.839"
5	N. Heidfeld	BMW	F1.07-05	1'12.847"
6	H. Kovalainen	Renault	R27-03	1'13.308"
7	S. Vettel	BMW	F1.07-03	1'13.513"
8	J. Trulli	Toyota	TF107-06	1'13.789"
9	M. Webber	Red Bull	RB3-04	1'13.871"
10	G. Fisichella	Renault	R27-03	1'13.953"
11	D. Coulthard	Red Bull	RB3-03	1'12.873"
12	R. Schumacher	Toyota	TF107-05	1'12.920"
13	J. Button	Honda	RA107-04	1'12.998"
14	N. Rosberg	Williams	FW29-05	1'13.060"
15	R. Barrichello	Honda	RA107-02	1'13.201"
16	A. Davidson	Super Aguri	SA07-03	1'13.259"
17	A. Wurz	Williams	FW29-04	1'13.441"
18	T. Sato	Super Aguri	SA07-04	1'13.477"
19	V. Liuzzi	Toro Rosso	STR2-03	1'13.484"
20	S. Speed	Toro Rosso	STR2-04	1'13.712"
21	A. Sutil	Spyker	F8-VII-03	1'14.122"
22	C. Albers	Spyker	F8-VII-02	1'14.597"

INDIANAPOLIS

After having dominated the practice sessions, Alonso was pipped to the pole by 17 hundredths of a second by Hamilton. The Ferraris occupied the second row of the grid, half a second down. Hamilton held on to the lead at the first corner, while Räikkönen dropped two places. Further back the group Vettel cut a corner and Ralf took out Coulthard and Barrichello. Lewis gradually increased his lead over Fernando, but it was never more than three seconds. During his second stint Alonso tried a passing manoeuvre at the end of the straight, but it didn't come off and Hamilton stayed ahead. The same thing happened with Massa and Räikkönen, with Kimi unable to overtake for third place even though he was faster. Lying fourth for a while, Heidfeld first missed a braking point then his gearbox broke. This was to Kovalainen's advantage and he finished a good 5th. On his way to taking three points thanks to a good strategy, Rosberg lost his engine five laps from the end. A final spurt saw Trulli, Webber and Vettel battle for the last points in that order, with Sebastian taking one point on his debut. After a mistake in the opening laps, Fisichella made a fighting comeback but finished out of the points. 10 points now separated the McLaren drivers, with Lewis in the lead and with Ferrari continuing to lose ground.

RESULT

	Driver	Car	Time	Laps	Stops
1	L. Hamilton	McLaren	1hr31'09.965"	73	2
2	F. Alonso	McLaren	+ 1.518"	73	2
3	F. Massa	Ferrari	+ 12.842"	73	2
4	K. Räikkönen	Ferrari	+ 15.422"	73	2
5	H. Kovalainen	Renault	+ 41.402"	73	2
6	J. Trulli	Toyota	+ 1'06.703"	73	2
7	M. Webber	Red Bull	+ 1'07.331"	73	2
8	S. Vettel	BMW	+ 1'07.783"	73	2
9	G. Fisichella	Renault	+ 1 lap	72	1
10	A. Wurz	Williams	+ 1 lap	72	1
11	A. Davidson	Super Aguri	+ 1 lap	72	2
12	J. Button	Honda	+ 1 lap	72	1
13	S. Speed	Toro Rosso	+ 2 laps	71	1
14	A. Sutil	Spyker	+ 2 laps	71	2
15	C. Albers	Spyker	+ 3 laps	70	1
16	N. Rosberg	Williams	+ 5 laps (engine)	68	1
17	V. Liuzzi	Toro Rosso	+ 5 laps (engine)	68	1

Laps in the lead: Hamilton 66, Kovalainen 5, Alonso 1, Massa 1

RETIREMENTS

N. Heidfeld	BMW	gearbox	55	2
T. Sato	Super Aguri	crash	13	
R. Barrichello	Honda	collision	1	
D. Coulthard	Red Bull	collision	1	
R. Schumacher	Toyota	collision	0	

FASTEST LAP

K. Räikkönen	Ferrari	1'13.117"	49

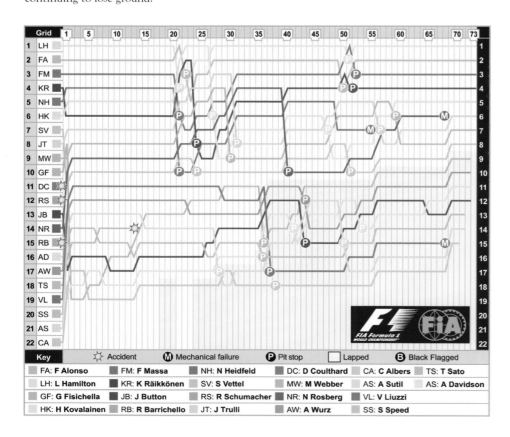

Key		
☆ Accident	Ⓜ Mechanical failure	Ⓟ Pit stop	☐ Lapped	Ⓑ Black Flagged

FA: F Alonso	FM: F Massa	NH: N Heidfeld	DC: D Coulthard	CA: C Albers	TS: T Sato
LH: L Hamilton	KR: K Räikkönen	SV: S Vettel	MW: M Webber	AS: A Sutil	AS: A Davidson
GF: G Fisichella	JB: J Button	RS: R Schumacher	NR: N Rosberg	VL: V Liuzzi	
HK: H Kovalainen	RB: R Barrichello	JT: J Trulli	AW: A Wurz	SS: S Speed	

French Grand Prix

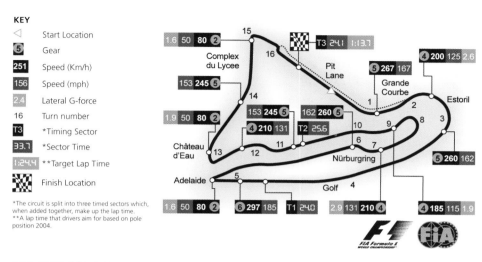

MAGNY-COURS

Ferrari were back in contention in France, just missing out on occupying the front row of the
grid when Hamilton managed to squeeze between Massa and Räikkönen, while Alonso was
relegated to 10th place by gearbox woes. Kimi got the better of Lewis at the start, while the first
lap saw collisions between Trulli and Kovalainen, and between Davidson and Liuzzi.
The F2007s gradually built up a lead over Hamilton, despite the McLaren being lighter on
fuel (Lewis would actually pit three times). The die was cast after the Ferraris' second pit-stop.
Massa was delayed by traffic and Räikkönen rejoined ahead, holding onto the lead until the
end. Pressured for a while by Kubica, Lewis held onto third place to finish in front of the Pole.
Alonso pulled out all the stops to recover lost ground, overtaking both Fisichella and Heidfeld
on the track, but then found himself stuck behind them again after the pit-stops. Heidfeld
preceded Fisichella across the line to take 5th, followed by Alonso and Button who took
Honda's first point of the season. Albers didn't improve his standing in the eyes of his team by
accelerating away from his pit-stop before they'd finished refuelling, with the rig still attached
to his car. Hamilton rose to a 14-point lead over his team-mate in the Drivers' classification
while Ferrari, after their first 1-2 of the season, reduced McLaren's lead to 25 points.

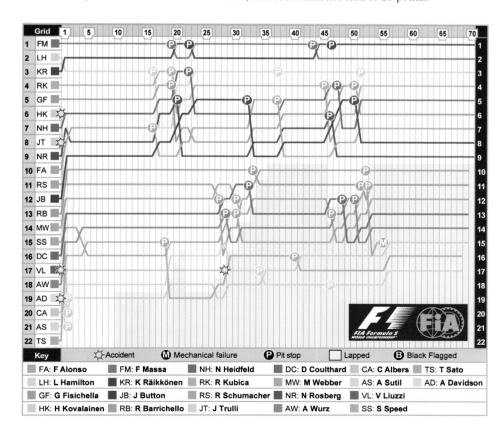

Circuit de Nevers Magny-Cours, France – 1 July

Lap length: 4.411 km/2.741 miles
No. of laps: 70
Race distance: 308.586 km/191.755 miles
Weather: sunny and warm

QUALIFYING

	Driver	Car	Chassis number	Time
1	F. Massa	Ferrari	F2007-260	1'15.034"
2	L. Hamilton	McLaren	MP4/22-04	1'15.104"
3	K. Räikkönen	Ferrari	F2007-262	1'15.257"
4	R. Kubica	BMW	F1.07-03	1'15.493"
5	G. Fisichella	Renault	R27-05	1'15.674"
6	H. Kovalainen	Renault	R27-03	1'15.826"
7	N. Heidfeld	BMW	F1.07-05	1'15.900"
8	J. Trulli	Toyota	TF107-06	1'15.935"
9	N. Rosberg	Williams	FW29-05	1'16.328"
10	F. Alonso	McLaren	MP4/22-06	no time
11	R. Schumacher	Toyota	TF107-05	1'15.534"
12	J. Button	Honda	RA107-04	1'15.584"
13	R. Barrichello	Honda	RA107-02	1'15.761"
14	M. Webber	Red Bull	RB3-04	1'15.806"
15	S. Speed	Toro Rosso	STR2-04	1'16.049"
16	D. Coulthard	Red Bull	RB3-03	no time
17	V. Liuzzi	Toro Rosso	STR2-03	1'16.142"
18	A. Wurz	Williams	FW29-03	1'16.241"
19	T. Sato*	Super Aguri	SA07-04	1'16.244"
20	A. Davidson	Super Aguri	SA07-03	1'16.366"
21	C. Albers	Spyker	F8-VII-02	1'17.826"
22	A. Sutil**	Spyker	F8-VII-03	1'17.915"

(*) dropped 10 places for failing to respect yellow flags at Indianapolis
(**) started from pit-lane with T-car

RESULT

	Driver	Car	Time	Laps	Stops
1	K. Räikkönen	Ferrari	1h30'54.200"	70	2
2	F. Massa	Ferrari	+ 2.414"	70	2
3	L. Hamilton	McLaren	+ 32.153"	70	3
4	R. Kubica	BMW	+ 41.727"	70	2
5	N. Heidfeld	BMW	+ 48.801"	70	2
6	G. Fisichella	Renault	+ 52.210"	70	2
7	F. Alonso	McLaren	+ 56.516"	70	2
8	J. Button	Honda	+ 58.885"	70	2
9	N. Rosberg	Williams	+ 1'08.505"	70	2
10	R. Schumacher	Toyota	+ 1 lap	69	2
11	R. Barrichello	Honda	+ 1 lap	69	2
12	M. Webber	Red Bull	+ 1 lap	69	2
13	D. Coulthard	Red Bull	+ 1 lap	69	2
14	A. Wurz	Williams	+ 1 lap	69	2
15	H. Kovalainen	Renault	+ 1 lap	69	2
16	T. Sato	Super Aguri	+ 2 laps	68	2
17	A. Sutil	Spyker	+ 2 laps	68	2

Laps in the lead: Massa 40, Räikkönen 30

RETIREMENTS

S. Speed	Toro Rosso	gearbox	56	2
C. Albers	Spyker	fuel	29	
J. Trulli	Toyota	collision	1	
A. Davidson	Super Aguri	collision	1	
V. Liuzzi	Toro Rosso	collision	1	

FASTEST LAP

F. Massa	Ferrari	1'16.099"	42

British Grand Prix

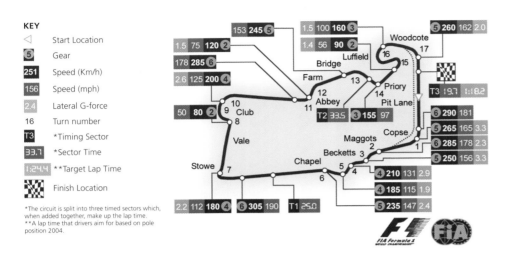

Silverstone, Great Britain – 8 July

Lap length: 5.141 km/3.194 miles
No. of laps: 59
Race distance: 303.214 km/188.446 miles
Weather: sunny and warm

QUALIFYING

	Driver	Car	Chassis number	Time
1	L. Hamilton	McLaren	MP4/22-04	1'19.997"
2	K. Räikkönen	Ferrari	F2007-262	1'20.099"
3	F. Alonso	McLaren	MP4/22-06	1'20.147"
4	F. Massa*	Ferrari	F2007-260	1'20.265"
5	R. Kubica	BMW	F1.07-03	1'20.401"
6	R. Schumacher	Toyota	TF107-05	1'20.516"
7	H. Kovalainen	Renault	R27-03	1'20.721"
8	G. Fisichella	Renault	R27-05	1'20.775"
9	N. Heidfeld	BMW	F1.07-05	1'20.894"
10	J. Trulli	Toyota	TF107-06	1'21.240"
11	M. Webber	Red Bull	RB3-04	1'20.235"
12	D. Coulthard	Red Bull	RB3-03	1'20.329"
13	A. Wurz	Williams	FW29-03	1'20.350"
14	R. Barrichello	Honda	RA107-04	1'20.364"
15	S. Speed	Toro Rosso	STR2-04	1'20.515"
16	V. Liuzzi	Toro Rosso	STR2-03	1'20.823"
17	N. Rosberg	Williams	FW29-05	1'21.219"
18	J. Button	Honda	RA107-05	1'21.335"
19	A. Davidson	Super Aguri	SA07-02	1'21.448"
20	A. Sutil	Spyker	F8-VII-03	1'22.019"
21	T. Sato*	Super Aguri	SA07-04	1'22.045"
22	C. Albers	Spyker	F8-VII-04	1'22.589"

(*) started from pit-lane

SILVERSTONE

In front of an enthusiastic home crowd Hamilton pipped Räikkönen to the pole by a tenth of second, thanks to a lighter fuel load and an error by his rival on his hot lap. Alonso and Massa were 3rd and 4th respectively on the grid, but Felipe's engine stalled at the end of the warm up lap and he was forced to start from the pits. Lewis had a perfect start, but so did Kimi. Hamilton's lead was in doubt the moment he pitted on the 15th lap. And in fact the Ferrari took the advantage and pulled ahead of Lewis, although Kimi was still second as Alonso in the meantime had slipped into first place. This time it was Fernando who took on less fuel to try and maintain his advantage. But to no avail – after his second pit-stop Räikkönen regained the lead and went on to take his third victory of the year. Hamilton finished a distant 3rd, while Massa's impressive charge back up through the field ended with a 5th place, sandwiched between the two BMWs, with Kubica 4th and Heidfeld 6th. The two Renaults took the last points, with Kovalainen 7th and Fisichella 8th, ahead of the two Hondas which were helped by a single pit-stop strategy. Kimi's win was enough to put him back in the running for the title, but he was still 18 points behind Hamilton and six behind Alonso.

RESULT

	Driver	Car	Time	Laps	Stops
1	K. Räikkönen	Ferrari	1hr21'43.077"	59	2
2	F. Alonso	McLaren	+ 2.459"	59	2
3	L. Hamilton	McLaren	+ 39.373"	59	2
4	R. Kubica	BMW	+ 53.319"	59	2
5	F. Massa	Ferrari	+ 54.063"	59	2
6	N. Heidfeld	BMW	+ 56.336"	59	2
7	H. Kovalainen	Renault	+ 1 lap	58	2
8	G. Fisichella	Renault	+ 1 lap	58	2
9	R. Barrichello	Honda	+ 1 lap	58	1
10	J. Button	Honda	+ 1 lap	58	1
11	D. Coulthard	Red Bull	+ 1 lap	58	2
12	N. Rosberg	Williams	+ 1 lap	58	2
13	A. Wurz	Williams	+ 1 lap	58	2
14	T. Sato	Super Aguri	+ 2 laps	57	2
15	C. Albers	Spyker	+ 2 laps	57	2
16	V. Liuzzi	Toro Rosso	+ 6 laps (gearbox)	53	2

Laps in the lead: Räikkönen 24, Alonso 20, Hamilton 15

RETIREMENTS

J. Trulli	Toyota	roadholding	43	2
A. Davidson	Super Aguri	mechanical		

FASTEST LAP

K. Räikkönen	Ferrari	1'20.638"	17

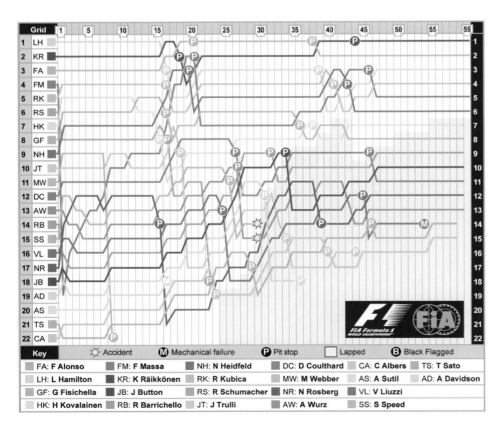

European Grand Prix

KEY

◁ Start Location
5 Gear
251 Speed (Km/h)
156 Speed (mph)
2.4 Lateral G-force
16 Turn number
T3 *Timing Sector
33.7 *Sector Time
1:24.4 **Target Lap Time
Finish Location

*The circuit is split into three timed sectors which,
when added together, make up the lap time.
**A lap time that drivers aim for based on pole
position 2004.

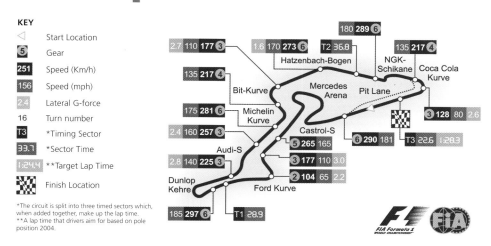

Nürburgring, Germany – 22 July

Lap length: 5.148 km/3.199 miles
No. of laps: 60
Race distance: 308.863 km/191.938 miles
Weather: rainy and cold

QUALIFYING

	Driver	Car	Chassis number	Time
1	K. Räikkönen	Ferrari	F2007-262	1'31.450"
2	F. Alonso	McLaren	MP4/22-06	1'31.741"
3	F. Massa	Ferrari	F2007-260	1'31.778"
4	N. Heidfeld	BMW	F1.07-05	1'31.840"
5	R. Kubica	BMW	F1.07-03	1'32.123"
6	M. Webber	Red Bull	RB3-04	1'32.476"
7	H. Kovalainen	Renault	R27-03	1'32.478"
8	J. Trulli	Toyota	TF107-04	1'32.501"
9	R. Schumacher	Toyota	TF107-05	1'32.570"
10	L. Hamilton	McLaren	MP4/22-01*	1'33.833"
11	N. Rosberg	Williams	FW29-05	1'31.978"
12	A. Wurz	Williams	FW29-03	1'31.996"
13	G. Fisichella	Renault	R27-05	1'32.010"
14	R. Barrichello	Honda	RA107-05	1'32.221"
15	A. Davidson	Super Aguri	SA07-03	1'32.451"
16	T. Sato	Super Aguri	SA07-04	1'32.838"
17	J. Button	Honda	RA107-04	1'32.983"
18	S. Speed	Toro Rosso	STR2-04	1'33.038"
19	V. Liuzzi	Toro Rosso	STR2-03	1'33.148"
20	D. Coulthard	Red Bull	RB3-03	1'33.151"
21	A. Sutil	Spyker	F8-VII-03	1'34.500"
22	M. Winkelhock	Spyker	F8-VII-04	1'35.940"

(*) chassis used in the race after qualifying crash

NÜRBURGRING

Hamilton crashed heavily in qualifying when a wheel came adrift, leaving him 10th on the grid while Räikkönen took pole with Alonso second and Massa third. There was a deluge right after the start and car after car aquaplaned off the first corner, including that of Hamilton who, however, rejoined the race after being hoisted back onto the track by a tractor. Kimi, then first, missed the pit-lane entrance and was forced to do another lap whilst the rest of the pack pitted to change tyres. The rainstorm was so heavy that the race was red-flagged as Winkelhock's Spyker – the only one to start on full wets – was in the lead in his first ever F1 race. At the restart it was Massa, Alonso and Räikkönen who set the pace until Kimi was forced to retire with hydraulic problems. Felipe was heading for victory when, 15 minutes from the end of the race, another cloudburst flooded the track. Alonso caught up with him and, after some wheel-to-wheel dicing, got past, much to Felipe's chagrin. Webber finished third for Red Bull ahead of Wurz and Coulthard. After several frights the BMWs of Heidfled and Kubica took 6th and 7th place respectively, ahead of the Renault of Kovalainen. After coming home 9th and outside the points, Hamilton held onto the leadership for the title, but Alonso was now close on his heels.

RESULT

	Driver	Car	Time	Laps	Stops
1	F. Alonso	McLaren	2hr06'26.358"	60	4
2	F. Massa	Ferrari	+ 8.155"	60	4
3	M. Webber	Red Bull	+ 1'05.674"	60	4
4	A. Wurz	Williams	+ 1'05.937"	60	4
5	D. Coulthard	Red Bull	+ 1'13.656"	60	4
6	N. Heidfeld	BMW	+ 1'20.298"	60	6
7	R. Kubica	BMW	+ 1'22.415"	60	4
8	H. Kovalainen	Renault	+ 1 lap	59	4
9	L. Hamilton	McLaren	+ 1 lap	59	4
10	G. Fisichella	Renault	+ 1 lap	59	4
11	R. Barrichello	Honda	+ 1 lap	59	5
12	A. Davidson	Super Aguri	+ 1 lap	59	6
13	J. Trulli	Toyota	+ 1 lap	59	6

Laps in the lead: Massa 45, Winkelhock 6, Alonso 5, Räikkönen 1, Coulthard 1

RETIREMENTS

K. Räikkönen	Ferrari	hydraulics	34	2
T. Sato	Super Aguri	hydraulics	19	3
R. Schumacher	Toyota	collision	18	3
M. Winkelhock	Spyker	hydraulics	13	2
J. Button	Honda	crash	2	1
N. Rosberg	Williams	crash	2	1
V. Liuzzi	Toro Rosso	crash	2	2
S. Speed	Toro Rosso	crash	2	1
A. Sutil	Spyker	crash	2	1

FASTEST LAP

F. Massa	Ferrari	1'32.853"	34

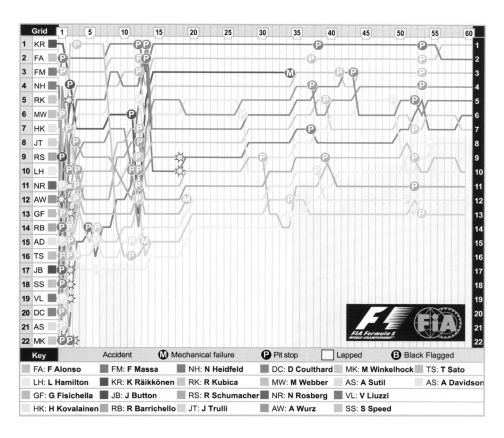

Key					
	Accident	Ⓜ Mechanical failure	Ⓟ Pit stop	☐ Lapped	Ⓑ Black Flagged

FA: F Alonso	**FM: F Massa**	**NH: N Heidfeld**	**DC: D Coulthard**	**MK: M Winkelhock**	**TS: T Sato**
LH: L Hamilton	**KR: K Räikkönen**	**RK: R Kubica**	**MW: M Webber**	**AS: A Sutil**	**AS: A Davidson**
GF: G Fisichella	**JB: J Button**	**RS: R Schumacher**	**NR: N Rosberg**	**VL: V Liuzzi**	
HK: H Kovalainen	**RB: R Barrichello**	**JT: J Trulli**	**AW: A Wurz**	**SS: S Speed**	

Hungarian Grand Prix

KEY

◁   Start Location

5   Gear

251   Speed (Km/h)

156   Speed (mph)

2.4   Lateral G-force

16   Turn number

T3   *Timing Sector

33.7   *Sector Time

1:24.4   **Target Lap Time

🏁   Finish Location

*The circuit is split into three timed sectors which,
when added together, make up the lap time.
**A lap time that drivers aim for based on pole
position 2004.

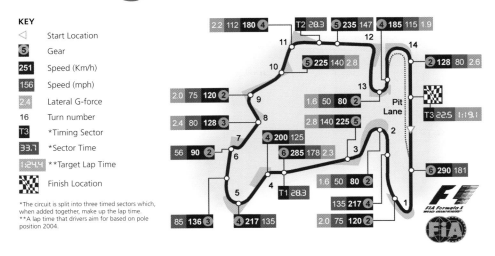

HUNGARORING

A bolt of lightning struck at the end of qualifying. Pole-sitter Alonso was relegated to 6th place on the grid for having deliberately obstructed his own team-mate, Hamilton. Despite being far from the innocent party in events, which provoked a heated exchange with an upset Ron Dennis, Hamilton inherited the pole position ahead of Heidfeld and Räikkönen. Lewis flew away from the lights and Kimi passed Nick, slowed by starting on the dirty side of the track. Alonso was lying 8th at the end of the first lap, but then started to climb back up the pack – the only one to actually do any overtaking. After the first pit-stop Räikkönen closed in on the leading McLaren, reducing the gap by half-way through the race. But he never had the chance to really challenge Hamilton's lead. On a three-stop strategy, Heidfeld soon had Alonso breathing down his neck, but the Spaniard was unable to pass him. Behind Kubica, 5th, Ralf Schumacher returned to form with a good 6th place finish ahead of Rosberg and Kovalainen, while the second Renault only managed 12th, Fisichella having also been penalised after qualifying. The Italian crossed the line ahead of Massa who'd been stuck in traffic after only making it to 14th on the grid. Taking home his third win of the season, Hamilton increased his lead in the standings over Alonso by seven points, but it was now open war between the two McLaren drivers.

Hungaroring, Budapest, Hungary – 6 August
Lap length: 4.381 km/2.722 miles
No. of laps: 70
Race distance: 306.663 km/190.560 miles
Weather: sunny and warm

QUALIFYING

	Driver	Car	Chassis number	Time
1	F. Alonso*	McLaren	MP4/22-06	1'19.674"
2	L. Hamilton	McLaren	MP4/22-05	1'19.781"
3	N. Heidfeld	BMW	F1.07-05	1'20.259"
4	K. Räikkönen	Ferrari	F2007-262	1'20.410"
5	N. Rosberg	Williams	FW29-05	1'20.632"
6	R. Schumacher	Toyota	TF107-05	1'20.714"
7	R. Kubica	BMW	F1.07-03	1'20.876"
8	G. Fisichella*	Renault	R27-05	1'21.079"
9	J. Trulli	Toyota	TF107-06	1'21.206"
10	M. Webber	Red Bull	RB3-04	1'21.256"
11	D. Coulthard	Red Bull	RB3-03	1'20.718"
12	H. Kovalainen	Renault	R27-03	1'20.779"
13	A. Wurz	Williams	FW29-03	1'20.865"
14	F. Massa	Ferrari	F2007-260	1'21.021"
15	A. Davidson	Super Aguri	SA07-02	1'21.127"
16	V. Liuzzi	Toro Rosso	STR2-01	1'21.993"
17	J. Button	Honda	RA107-04	1'21.737"
18	R. Barrichello	Honda	RA107-05	1'21.877"
19	T. Sato	Super Aguri	SA07-04	1'22.143"
20	S. Vettel	Toro Rosso	STR2-04	1'22.177"
21	A. Sutil	Spyker	F8-VII-03	1'22.737"
22	S. Yamamoto	Spyker	F8-VII-04	1'23.774"

(*) dropped five places for having blocked another driver

RESULT

	Driver	Car	Time	Laps	Stops
1	L. Hamilton	McLaren	1hr35'52.991"	70	2
2	K. Räikkönen	Ferrari	+ 0.715"	70	2
3	N. Heidfeld	BMW	+ 43.129"	70	3
4	F. Alonso	McLaren	+ 44.858"	70	2
5	R. Kubica	BMW	+ 47.616"	70	3
6	R. Schumacher	Toyota	+ 50.669"	70	2
7	N. Rosberg	Williams	+ 59.139"	70	3
8	H. Kovalainen	Renault	+ 1'08.104"	70	2
9	M. Webber	Red Bull	+ 1'16.331"	70	3
10	J. Trulli	Toyota	+ 1 lap	69	2
11	D. Coulthard	Red Bull	+ 1 lap	69	2
12	G. Fisichella	Renault	+ 1 lap	69	2
13	F. Massa	Ferrari	+ 1 lap	69	2
14	A. Wurz	Williams	+ 1 lap	69	2
15	T. Sato	Super Aguri	+ 1 lap	69	2
16	S. Vettel	Toro Rosso	+ 1 lap	69	2
17	A. Sutil	Spyker	+ 2 laps	68	2
18	R. Barrichello	Honda	+ 2 laps	68	2

Laps in the lead: Hamilton 70

RETIREMENTS

V. Liuzzi	Toro Rosso	electrics	43	1
A. Davidson	Super Aguri	collision	42	1
J. Button	Honda	engine	36	1
S. Yamamoto	Spyker	crash	5	

FASTEST LAP

K. Räikkönen	Ferrari	1'20.047"	70

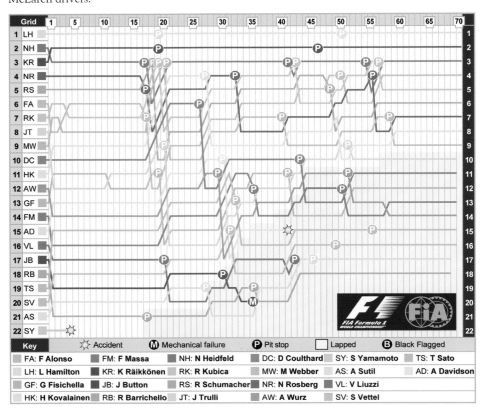

Key				
FA: F Alonso	FM: F Massa	NH: N Heidfeld	DC: D Coulthard	SY: S Yamamoto	TS: T Sato
LH: L Hamilton	KR: K Räikkönen	RK: R Kubica	MW: M Webber	AS: A Sutil	AD: A Davidson
GF: G Fisichella	JB: J Button	RS: R Schumacher	NR: N Rosberg	VL: V Liuzzi	
HK: H Kovalainen	RB: R Barrichello	JT: J Trulli	AW: A Wurz	SV: S Vettel	

☆ Accident   Ⓜ Mechanical failure   Ⓟ Pit stop   ☐ Lapped   Ⓑ Black Flagged

Turkish Grand Prix

KEY

◁ Start Location
5 Gear
251 Speed (Km/h)
156 Speed (mph)
2.4 Lateral G-force
16 Turn number
T3 *Timing Sector
33.7 *Sector Time
1:24.4 **Target Lap Time
🏁 Finish Location

*The circuit is split into three timed sectors which, when added together, make up the lap time.
**A lap time that drivers aim for based on pole position 2004.

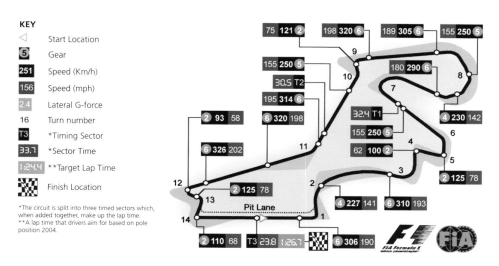

Istanbul, Turkey – 26 August
Lap length: 5.338 km/3.317 miles
No. of laps: 58
Race distance: 309.356 km/192.258 miles
Weather: sunny and hot

QUALIFYING

	Driver	Car	Chassis number	Time
1	F. Massa	Ferrari	F2007-263	1'27.329"
2	L. Hamilton	McLaren	MP4/22-01	1'27.373"
3	K. Räikkönen	Ferrari	F2007-262	1'27.546"
4	F. Alonso	McLaren	MP4/22-06	1'27.574"
5	R. Kubica	BMW	F1.07-03	1'27.722"
6	N. Heidfeld	BMW	F1.07-08	1'28.037"
7	H. Kovalainen	Renault	R27-03	1'28.491"
8	N. Rosberg	Williams	FW29-05	1'28.501"
9	J. Trulli	Toyota	TF107-06	1'28.740"
10	G. Fisichella	Renault	R27-05	1'29.322"
11	A. Davidson	Super Aguri	SA07-03	1'28.002"
12	M. Webber	Red Bull	RB3-04	1'28.013"
13	D. Coulthard	Red Bull	RB3-05	1'28.100"
14	R. Barrichello*	Honda	RA107-05	1'28.188"
15	J. Button*	Honda	RA107-04	1'28.220"
16	A. Wurz	Williams	FW29-03	1'28.390"
17	V. Liuzzi	Toro Rosso	STR2-03	1'28.798"
18	R. Schumacher	Toyota	TF107-05	1'28.809"
19	T. Sato	Super Aguri	SA07-02	1'28.953"
20	S. Vettel	Toro Rosso	STR2-05	1'29.408"
21	A. Sutil	Spyker	F8-VII-01	1'29.891"
22	S. Yamamoto	Spyker	F8-VII-02	1'31.479"

(*) dropped 10 places after changing engine

ISTANBUL

Second in qualifying behind Massa and ahead of Räikkönen, Hamilton struggled to get a clean start away from the dirty part of the track and was out-accelerated by the Finn. Alonso did even worse, with both BMW-Saubers slipping past. Further back the pack Trulli was knocked into a spin by Fisichella at the first corner. The two Ferraris gained slightly on Hamilton, while Alonso would have to wait until the first round of pit-stops to finally get ahead of the Kubica-Heidfeld duo. But by then he had already lost too much time to be in the running for the podium. And yet fate would hand him a chance, thanks to Hamilton. Whilst Lewis was doing his best to keep up with the Ferraris before his second pit-stop, he blew his front right tyre. By the time he made it back to the pits, both Fernando and Heidfeld had passed him. Hamilton would have to make do with a 5th place, challenged by a competitive Kovalainen. Rosberg and Kubica, just ahead of Fisichella, battled it out for 7th place, the final standing seeing them finish in that order in a race that saw only one retirement (Webber). At one point seemingly ready to attack Massa, Räikkönen backed off and settled for second place, with Massa repeating his 2006 success and overtaking Kimi in the drivers' standings by one point. Lewis clung on to a 5-point lead in the Championship.

RESULT

	Driver	Car	Time	Laps	Stops
1	F. Massa	Ferrari	1hr26'42.161"	58	2
2	K. Räikkönen	Ferrari	+ 2.275"	58	2
3	F. Alonso	McLaren	+ 26.181"	58	2
4	N. Heidfeld	BMW	+ 39.674"	58	2
5	L. Hamilton	McLaren	+ 45.085"	58	2
6	H. Kovalainen	Renault	+ 46.169"	58	2
7	N. Rosberg	Williams	+ 55.778"	58	2
8	R. Kubica	BMW	+ 56.707"	58	2
9	G. Fisichella	Renault	+ 59.491"	58	2
10	D. Coulthard	Red Bull	+ 1'11.009"	58	2
11	A. Wurz	Williams	+ 1'19.628"	58	2
12	R. Schumacher	Toyota	+ 1 lap	57	1
13	J. Button	Honda	+ 1 lap	57	2
14	A. Davidson	Super Aguri	+ 1 lap	57	2
15	V. Liuzzi	Toro Rosso	+ 1 lap	57	2
16	J. Trulli	Toyota	+ 1 lap	57	2
17	R. Barrichello	Honda	+ 1 lap	57	2
18	T. Sato	Super Aguri	+ 1 lap	57	1
19	S. Vettel	Toro Rosso	+ 1 lap	57	2
20	S. Yamamoto	Spyker	+ 2 laps	56	2
21	A. Sutil	Spyker	+ 5 laps	53	2

Laps in the lead: Massa 55, Hamilton 1, Alonso 1, Kovalainen 1

RETIREMENT

M. Webber	Red Bull	hydraulics	9

FASTEST LAP

K. Räikkönen	Ferrari	1'27.295"	57

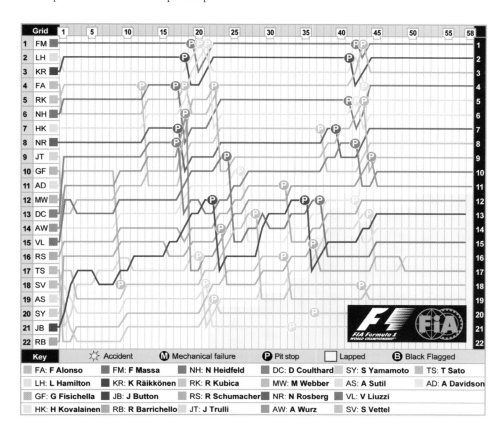

Italian Grand Prix

KEY

◁ Start Location

5 Gear

251 Speed (Km/h)

156 Speed (mph)

2.4 Lateral G-force

16 Turn number

T3 *Timing Sector

33.7 *Sector Time

1:24.4 **Target Lap Time

🏁 Finish Location

*The circuit is split into three timed sectors which, when added together, make up the lap time.
**A lap time that drivers aim for based on pole position 2004.

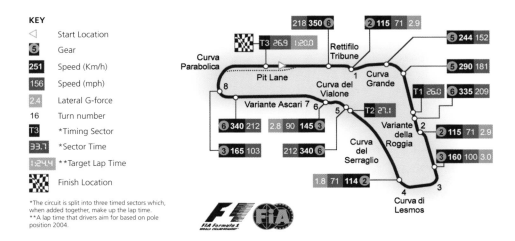

Monza, Italy – 9 September
Lap length: 5.793 km/3.600 miles
No. of laps: 53
Race distance: 306.720 km/190.596 miles
Weather: sunny and warm

QUALIFYING

	Driver	Car	Chassis number	Time
1	F. Alonso	McLaren	MP4/22-06	1'21.997"
2	L. Hamilton	McLaren	MP4/22-01	1'22.034"
3	F. Massa	Ferrari	F2007-263	1'22.549"
4	N. Heidfeld	BMW	F1.07-08	1'23.174"
5	K. Räikkönen	Ferrari	F2007-262	1'23.183"
6	R. Kubica	BMW	F1.07-03	1'23.446"
7	H. Kovalainen	Renault	R27-03	1'24.102"
8	N. Rosberg	Williams	FW29-05	1'24.382"
9	J. Trulli	Toyota	TF107-06	1'24.555"
10	J. Button	Honda	RA107-04	1'25.165"
11	M. Webber	Red Bull	RB3-04	1'23.166"
12	R. Barrichello	Honda	RA107-03	1'23.176"
13	A. Wurz	Williams	FW29-03	1'23.209"
14	A. Davidson	Super Aguri	SA07-03	1'23.274"
15	G. Fisichella	Renault	R27-02	1'23.325"
16	S. Vettel	Toro Rosso	STR2-04	1'23.351"
17	T. Sato	Super Aguri	SA07-02	1'23.749"
18	R. Schumacher	Toyota	TF107-05	1'23.787"
19	V. Liuzzi	Toro Rosso	STR2-03	1'23.886"
20	D. Coulthard	Red Bull	RB3-05	1'24.019"
21	A. Sutil	Spyker	F8-VII-03	1'24.669"
22	S. Yamamoto	Spyker	F8-VII-04	1'25.084"

MONZA

McLaren proved unbeatable on their rivals' home turf. Alonso took the pole position ahead of Hamilton. Massa was in third place over half a second down, while the second Ferrari was seriously damaged in a crash Saturday morning, and Räikkönen was happy to take fifth fastest time behind Heidfeld with a gap that hinted Kimi was qualifying on a full tank. There was a big scare on lap two when Coulthard had a massive off after hitting Fisichella, bringing the safety car out. While the McLarens pulled out a lead, Massa pitted on lap 9. A lap later and he was back in – to retire. The roadholding of his car pointed to a mechanical failure waiting to happen. This left Kimi alone to defend the local colours. His one-stop strategy would almost work. After the leading McLarens pitted for the second time, he was lying between them, behind Fernando and ahead of Lewis. The Italian hopes lasted two laps before Hamilton passed the Ferrari in a risky but beautifully-executed overtaking manoeuvre braking into the first chicane. The same move enabled Kubica to regain fifth place behind Heidfeld after a messy first pit-stop had compromised his race. Behind the BMWs were the valiant Rosberg, a competitive Kovalainen and Button who managed to bring home Honda's second point of the season. Monza was Alonso's fourth victory of the season, bringing him up to three points behind his team-mate.

RESULT

	Driver	Car	Time	Laps	Stops
1	F. Alonso	McLaren	1hr18'37.806"	53	2
2	L. Hamilton	McLaren	+ 6.062"	53	2
3	K. Räikkönen	Ferrari	+ 27.325"	53	1
4	N. Heidfeld	BMW	+ 56.562"	53	2
5	R. Kubica	BMW	+ 1'00.558"	53	2
6	N. Rosberg	Williams	+ 1'05.810"	53	1
7	H. Kovalainen	Renault	+ 1'06.751"	53	2
8	J. Button	Honda	+ 1'12.368"	53	1
9	M. Webber	Red Bull	+ 1'15.879"	53	1
10	R. Barrichello	Honda	+ 1'16.958"	53	1
11	J. Trulli	Toyota	+ 1'17.736"	53	1
12	G. Fisichella	Renault	+ 1 lap	52	1
13	A. Wurz	Williams	+ 1 lap	52	1
14	A. Davidson	Super Aguri	+ 1 lap	52	1
15	R. Schumacher	Toyota	+ 1 lap	52	1
16	T. Sato	Super Aguri	+ 1 lap	52	1
17	V. Liuzzi	Toro Rosso	+ 1 lap	52	1
18	S. Vettel	Toro Rosso	+ 1 lap	52	1
19	A. Sutil	Spyker	+ 1 lap	52	2
20	S. Yamamoto	Spyker	+ 1 lap	52	2

Laps in the lead: Alonso 48, Hamilton 5

RETIREMENTS

F. Massa	Ferrari	suspension	10	1
D. Coulthard	Red Bull	crash	1	

FASTEST LAP

1	F. Alonso	McLaren	1'22.871"	15

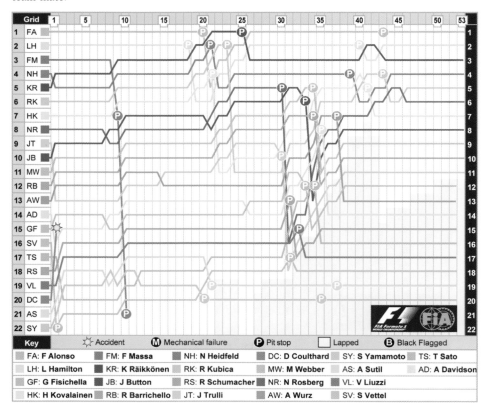

Grid											
1	FA
2	LH
3	FM
4	NH
5	KR
6	RK
7	HK
8	NR
9	JT
10	JB
11	MW
12	RB
13	AW
14	AD
15	GF
16	SV
17	TS
18	RS
19	VL
20	DC
21	AS
22	SY

Key ☆ Accident Ⓜ Mechanical failure Ⓟ Pit stop ▢ Lapped Ⓑ Black Flagged

FA: F Alonso	**FM: F Massa**	**NH: N Heidfeld**	**DC: D Coulthard**	**SY: S Yamamoto** · **TS: T Sato**
LH: L Hamilton	**KR: K Räikkönen**	**RK: R Kubica**	**MW: M Webber**	**AS: A Sutil** · **AD: A Davidson**
GF: G Fisichella	**JB: J Button**	**RS: R Schumacher**	**NR: N Rosberg**	**VL: V Liuzzi**
HK: H Kovalainen	**RB: R Barrichello**	**JT: J Trulli**	**AW: A Wurz**	**SV: S Vettel**

Belgian Grand Prix

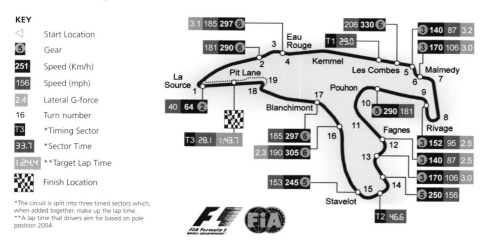

SPA-FRANCORCHAMPS

A thunderbolt hit even before the cars turned a wheel – accused of industrial espionage against Ferrari, McLaren were fined $100 million and were excluded from the Constructors' championship title race. The drivers vindicated the British team on Friday, but on Saturday it was Ferrari's turn to show a clean pair of heels. Räikkönen took pole ahead of Massa and Alonso, with less than a tenth of a second separating the three cars. Hamilton was fourth, four tenths down, followed by Kubica and Fisichella who was relegated to 11th place after having to change his engine. The start was a closely fought thing, with the two McLarens side by side through la Source and Raidillon. Alonso managed to get the upper hand, but was still behind the Ferraris. Räikkönen led from start to finish and neither his team-mate nor the McLarens could get near enough to worry him. The top four drivers finished in the same order as the qualifying, followed by Heidfeld who had been delayed on the first lap. There was a lot of action behind the leaders with Kovalainen racing with a very full tank and yet managing to keep most of the field behind him at length. Rosberg (6th) and Webber (7th) managed to get past, but Kubica, who had managed to work his way back up the field, wasn't so lucky, finding himself stuck behind the Renault again after his second pit stop. Sutil deserves a mention, finishing heroically 14th with the struggling Spyker. Hamilton came away from Belgium with his lead over Alonso reduced to two points, and 13 over Kimi.

Spa-Francorchamps, Belgium – 16 September
Lap length: 7.004 km/4.352 miles
No. of laps: 44
Race distance: 308.176 km/191.500 miles
Weather: sunny

QUALIFYING

	Driver	Car	Chassis number	Time
1	K. Räikkönen	Ferrari	F2007-262	1'45.994"
2	F. Massa	Ferrari	F2007-263	1'46.011"
3	F. Alonso	McLaren	MP4/22-06	1'46.091"
4	L. Hamilton	McLaren	MP4/22-01	1'46.406"
5	R. Kubica*	BMW	F1.07-03	1'46.996"
6	N. Rosberg	Williams	FW29-05	1'47.334"
7	N. Heidfeld	BMW	F1.07-08	1'47.409"
8	M. Webber	Red Bull	RB3-04	1'47.524"
9	J. Trulli	Toyota	TF107-04	1'47.798"
10	H. Kovalainen	Renault	R27-03	1'48.505"
11	G. Fisichella**	Renault	R27-02	1'46.603"
12	R. Schumacher	Toyota	TF107-05	1'46.618"
13	D. Coulthard	Red Bull	RB3-03	1'46.800"
14	J. Button	Honda	RA107-04	1'46.955"
15	V. Liuzzi	Toro Rosso	STR2-03	1'47.115"
16	A. Wurz	Williams	FW29-03	1'47.394"
17	S. Vettel	Toro Rosso	STR2-04	1'47.581"
18	R. Barrichello	Honda	RA107-05	1'47.954"
19	T. Sato	Super Aguri	SA07-02	1'47.980"
20	A. Sutil	Spyker	F8-VII-03	1'48.044"
21	A. Davidson**	Super Aguri	SA07-03	1'48.199"
22	S. Yamamoto	Spyker	F8-VII-04	1'49.577"

(*) dropped 10 places after changing engine
(**) started from pit-lane

RESULT

	Driver	Car	Time	Laps	Stops
1	K. Räikkönen	Ferrari	1hr20'39.066"	44	2
2	F. Massa	Ferrari	+ 4.695"	44	2
3	F. Alonso	McLaren	+ 14.343"	44	2
4	L. Hamilton	McLaren	+ 23.615"	44	2
5	N. Heidfeld	BMW	+ 51.879"	44	2
6	N. Rosberg	Williams	+ 1'16.876"	44	2
7	M. Webber	Red Bull	+ 1'20.639"	44	2
8	H. Kovalainen	Renault	+ 1'25.106"	44	1
9	R. Kubica	BMW	+ 1'25.661"	44	2
10	R. Schumacher	Toyota	+ 1'28.574"	44	1
11	J. Trulli	Toyota	+ 1'43.653"	44	2
12	V. Liuzzi	Toro Rosso	+ 1 lap	43	1
13	R. Barrichello	Honda	+ 1 lap	43	1
14	A. Sutil	Spyker	+ 1 lap	43	2
15	T. Sato	Super Aguri	+ 1 lap	43	2
16	A. Davidson	Super Aguri	+ 1 lap	43	1
17	S. Yamamoto	Spyker	+ 1 lap	43	2

Laps in the lead: Räikkönen 42, Massa 2

RETIREMENTS

J. Button	Honda	hydraulics	36	2
A. Wurz	Williams	fuel	34	3
D. Coulthard	Red Bull	hydraulics	29	1
S. Vettel	Toro Rosso	steering	8	1
G. Fisichella	Renault	suspension	1	

FASTEST LAP

F. Massa	Ferrari	1'48.036"	34

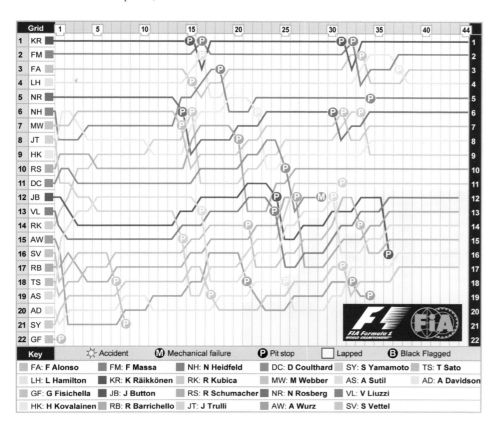

Key	☆ Accident	Ⓜ Mechanical failure	Ⓟ Pit stop	☐ Lapped	Ⓑ Black Flagged
FA: F Alonso	**FM: F Massa**	**NH: N Heidfeld**	**DC: D Coulthard**	**SY: S Yamamoto**	**TS: T Sato**
LH: L Hamilton	**KR: K Räikkönen**	**RK: R Kubica**	**MW: M Webber**	**AS: A Sutil**	**AD: A Davidson**
GF: G Fisichella	**JB: J Button**	**RS: R Schumacher**	**NR: N Rosberg**	**VL: V Liuzzi**	
HK: H Kovalainen	**RB: R Barrichello**	**JT: J Trulli**	**AW: A Wurz**	**SV: S Vettel**	

Japanese Grand Prix

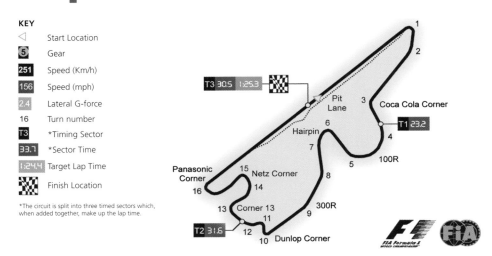

Fuji, Japan – 30 September
Lap length: 4.563 km/2.835 miles
No. of laps: 67
Race distance: 305.721 km/189.975 miles
Weather: heavy rain and mist

QUALIFYING

	Driver	Car	Chassis number	Time
1	L. Hamilton	McLaren	MP4/22-05	1'25.368"
2	F. Alonso	McLaren	MP4/22-06	1'25.438"
3	K. Räikkönen	Ferrari	F2007-262	1'25.516"
4	F. Massa	Ferrari	F2007-263	1'25.765"
5	N. Heidfeld	BMW	F1.07-08	1'26.505"
6	N. Rosberg*	Williams	FW29-05	1'26.728"
7	J. Button	Honda	RA107-04	1'26.913"
8	M. Webber	Red Bull	RB3-04	1'26.914"
9	S. Vettel	Toro Rosso	STR2-04	1'26.973"
10	R. Kubica	BMW	F1.07-03	1'27.225"
11	G. Fisichella	Renault	R27-02	1'26.033"
12	H. Kovalainen	Renault	R27-03	1'26.232"
13	D. Coulthard	Red Bull	RB3-03	1'26.247"
14	J. Trulli	Toyota	TF107-04	1'26.253"
15	V. Liuzzi**	Toro Rosso	STR2-03	1'26.948"
16	R. Schumacher	Toyota	TF107-05	no time
17	R. Barrichello	Honda	RA107-05	1'27.323"
18	A. Wurz	Williams	FW29-03	1'27.454"
19	A. Davidson	Super Aguri	SA07-03	1'27.564"
20	A. Sutil	Spyker	F8-VII-03	1'28.628"
21	T. Sato	Super Aguri	SA07-02	1'28.792"
22	S. Yamamoto	Spyker	F8-VII-04	1'29.668"

(*) dropped 10 places after changing engine
(**) started from pit-lane

FUJI

The deluge that hit the foot of Mount Fuji was such that the start and the first part of the race was held behind the safety car which, however, did not prevent a couple of spins. The Ferraris started on the wrong tyre compound, the only team to do so because, according to Jean Todt, they had not received the official communication prior to the start making the extreme wets mandatory, and were forced to pit to change over. After the restart the McLarens that monopolised the front of the grid sped away and Wurz lost it big time and hit Massa. While the F2007s made up lost ground, Alonso gave his all to try and close the gap with his team-mate. He tried too hard and on lap 41 crashed badly. This was his first DNF, and one which weighed heavily on his title bid. The race was again interrupted by the safety car, and that's when Vettel harpooned Webber when they were lying a fantastic 3rd and 2nd respectively. As a result – and with Hamilton safely in the lead – there was a sprint between the two Finnish drivers for the podium. Kovalainen managed to hold off Räikkönen until the end. Coulthard and Fisichella finished 4th and 5th, while Heidfeld was left on foot by a mechanical problem at the start of the last lap. A huge battle between Massa and Kubica saw Felipe get the upper hand and squeeze the BMW out for three points. Liuzzi passed Sutil to take a point for Toro Rosso, only to see it taken away because he'd overtaken the Spyker under yellow flags. With his lead up to 12 points over Fernando and 17 over Kimi, Hamilton was a step closer to the title.

RESULT

	Driver	Car	Time	Laps	Stops
1	L. Hamilton	McLaren	2hr00'34.579"	67	1
2	H. Kovalainen	Renault	+ 8.377"	67	1
3	K. Räikkönen	Ferrari	+ 9.478"	67	3
4	D. Coulthard	Red Bull	+ 20.297"	67	1
5	G. Fisichella	Renault	+ 38.864"	67	1
6	F. Massa	Ferrari	+ 49.042"	67	4
7	R. Kubica	BMW	+ 49.285"	67	2
8	A. Sutil	Spyker	+ 1'00.129"	67	1
9	V. Liuzzi*	Toro Rosso	+ 1'20.622"	67	2
10	R. Barrichello	Honda	+ 1'28.342"	67	2
11	J. Button	Honda	+ 1 lap (gearbox)	66	1
12	S. Yamamoto	Spyker	+ 1 lap	66	2
13	J. Trulli	Toyota	+ 1 lap	66	2
14	N. Heidfeld	BMW	+ 2 laps (electrics)	65	1
15	T. Sato	Super Aguri	+ 2 laps	65	4

Laps in the lead: Hamilton 55, Webber 5, Vettel 3, Kovalainen 3, Fisichella 1
(*) 25" penalty for having overtaken under yellow flags

RETIREMENTS

R. Schumacher	Toyota	puncture	55	4
A. Davidson	Super Aguri	accelerator	54	1
N. Rosberg	Williams	electronics	49	2
S. Vettel	Toro Rosso	collision	46	2
M. Webber	Red Bull	collision	45	1
F. Alonso	McLaren	crash	41	1
A. Wurz	Williams	crash	19	1

FASTEST LAP

L. Hamilton	McLaren	1'28.193"	27

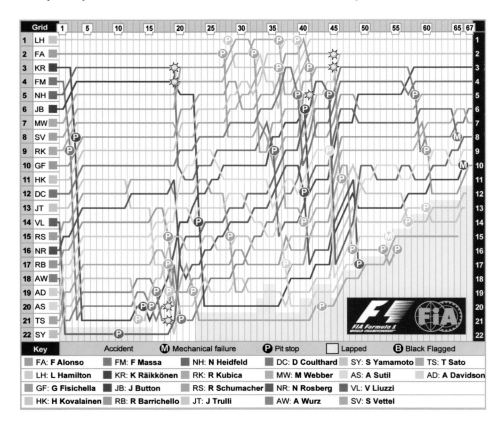

Chinese Grand Prix

◁ Start Location

5 Gear

251 Speed (Km/h)

156 Speed (mph)

2.4 Lateral G-force

16 Turn number

T3 *Timing Sector

33.7 *Sector Time

1:24.4 **Target Lap Time

🏁 Finish Location

*The circuit is split into three timed sectors which, when added together, make up the lap time.
**A lap time that drivers aim for based on pole position 2004

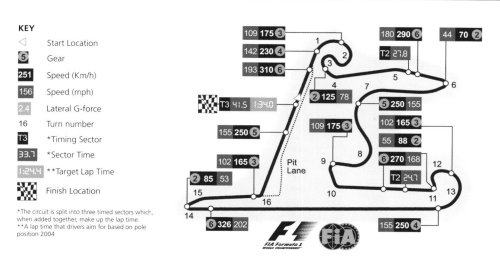

ZHUHAI

The Chinese GP turned out to be the second wet race in a week. Fastest in qualifying thanks to running light on fuel, Hamilton made a quick getaway and behind him the Ferraris kept close to edge out Alonso (4th on the grid) who, for a moment, had succeeded in splitting them. Coming out of the first round of pit-stops, Räikkönen rejoined the race on Hamilton's tail. Fernando managed to pass Massa who was having tyre problems, and as the track dried the Ferrari driver was not alone. Hamilton was in evident difficulty with worn wets, but he had no intention of letting Kimi pass, even though the Ferrari was clearly a lot faster. It took Räikkönen two laps to get past the McLaren, leaving Lewis to defend his third place from Alonso. At this point Lewis's rear right tyre had worn through to the carcass, forcing him to pit on lap 31, but he arrived too fast at the entrance to the pit lane and ended up in the gravel. An inglorious end to his race. Räikkönen and Alonso thus both picked up valuable points in the drivers' table, allowing them to stay in the running for the title going into the last race. Massa came third and it was a day of rejoicing for Toro Rosso, with Vettel an excellent 4th and Liuzzi 6th. Button split the two Toro Rossos to come home 5th – Honda's best result of the season, on the contrary to BMW. Kubica had just inherited the lead when he was eliminated by a hydraulics failure, and Heidfeld couldn't do any better than 7th. The last point of the day was fought over by four Renault-powered cars, with Coulthard coming out best ahead of Kovalainen, Webber and Fisichella. Hamilton 107 points, Alonso 103, Räikkönen 100: Interlagos was going to be hot!

Shanghai Circuit, Zhuhai, China – 7 October
Lap length: 5.451 km/3.387 miles
No. of laps: 56
Race distance: 305.066 km/189.568 miles
Weather: rainy and cold

QUALIFYING

	Driver	Car	Chassis number	Time
1	L. Hamilton	McLaren	MP4/22-01	1'35.908"
2	K. Räikkönen	Ferrari	F2007-262	1'36.044"
3	F. Massa	Ferrari	F2007-263	1'36.221"
4	F. Alonso	McLaren	MP4/22-06	1'36.576"
5	D. Coulthard	Red Bull	RB3-03	1'37.619"
6	R. Schumacher	Toyota	TF107-05	1'38.013"
7	M. Webber	Red Bull	RB3-04	1'38.153"
8	N. Heidfeld	BMW	F1.07-08	1'38.455"
9	R. Kubica	BMW	F1.07-03	1'38.472"
10	J. Button	Honda	RA107-04	1'39.285"
11	V. Liuzzi	Toro Rosso	STR2-03	1'36.862"
12	S. Vettel*	Toro Rosso	STR2-04	1'36.891"
13	J. Trulli	Toyota	TF107-04	1'36.959"
14	H. Kovalainen	Renault	R27-03	1'36.991"
15	A. Davidson	Super Aguri	SA07-03	1'37.247"
16	N. Rosberg	Williams	FW29-05	1'37.483"
17	R. Barrichello	Honda	RA107-05	1'37.251"
18	G. Fisichella	Renault	R27-02	1'37.290"
19	A. Wurz	Williams	FW29-03	1'37.456"
20	T. Sato	Super Aguri	SA07-02	1'38.218"
21	A. Sutil	Spyker	F8-VII-03	1'38.668"
22	S. Yamamoto	Spyker	F8-VII-04	1'39.336"

(*) dropped five places for having blocked another driver

RESULT

	Driver	Car	Time	Laps	Stops
1	K. Räikkönen	Ferrari	1hr37'58.395"	56	2
2	F. Alonso	McLaren	+9.806"	56	2
3	F. Massa	Ferrari	+12.891"	56	2
4	S. Vettel	Toro Rosso	+53.509"	56	1
5	J. Button	Honda	+1'06.666"	56	2
6	V. Liuzzi	Toro Rosso	+1'13.673"	56	2
7	N. Heidfeld	BMW	+1'14.224"	56	2
8	D. Coulthard	Red Bull	+1'20.750"	56	2
9	H. Kovalainen	Renault	+1'21.186"	56	1
10	M. Webber	Red Bull	+1'24.685"	56	2
11	G. Fisichella	Renault	+1'26.683"	56	2
12	A. Wurz	Williams	+1 lap	55	2
13	J. Trulli	Toyota	+1 lap	55	1
14	T. Sato	Super Aguri	+1 lap	55	2
15	R. Barrichello	Honda	+1 lap	55	3
16	N. Rosberg	Williams	+2 laps	54	3
17	S. Yamamoto	Spyker	+3 laps	53	4

Laps in the lead: Räikkönen 21, Hamilton 24, Kubica 1

RETIREMENTS

R. Kubica	BMW	hydraulics	33	1
L. Hamilton	McLaren	crash	30	1
R. Schumacher	Toyota	crash	25	1
A. Sutil	Spyker	crash	24	1
A. Davidson	Super Aguri	brakes	11	

FASTEST LAP

F. Massa	Ferrari	1'37.454"	56

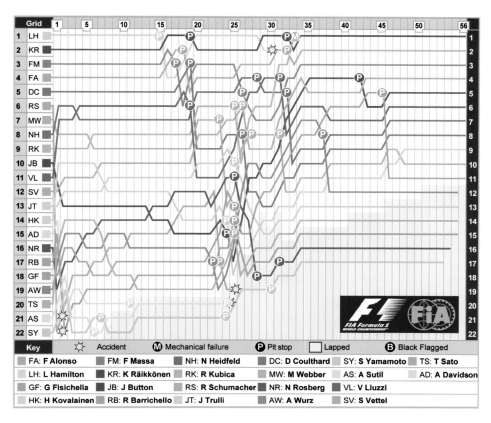

Grid	
1	LH
2	KR
3	FM
4	FA
5	DC
6	RS
7	MW
8	NH
9	RK
10	JB
11	VL
12	SV
13	JT
14	HK
15	AD
16	NR
17	RB
18	GF
19	AW
20	TS
21	AS
22	SY

Key
☼ Accident Ⓜ Mechanical failure Ⓟ Pit stop ☐ Lapped Ⓑ Black Flagged

FA: **F Alonso**	FM: **F Massa**	NH: **N Heidfeld**	DC: **D Coulthard**	SY: **S Yamamoto**	TS: **T Sato**
LH: **L Hamilton**	KR: **K Räikkönen**	RK: **R Kubica**	MW: **M Webber**	AS: **A Sutil**	AD: **A Davidson**
GF: **G Fisichella**	JB: **J Button**	RS: **R Schumacher**	NR: **N Rosberg**	VL: **V Liuzzi**	
HK: **H Kovalainen**	RB: **R Barrichello**	JT: **J Trulli**	AW: **A Wurz**	SV: **S Vettel**	

Brazilian Grand Prix

KEY

◁   Start Location

5   Gear

251   Speed (Km/h)

156   Speed (mph)

2.4   Lateral G-force

16   Turn number

T3   *Timing Sector

33.7   *Sector Time

1:24.4   **Target Lap Time

🏁   Finish Location

*The circuit is split into three timed sectors which, when added together, make up the lap time.
**A lap time that drivers aim for based on pole position 2004.

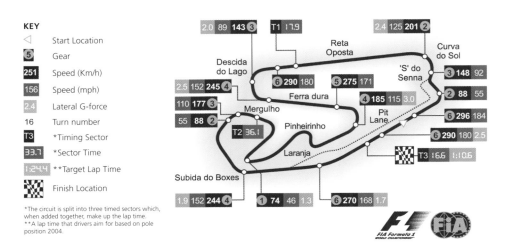

INTERLAGOS

What a cliff-hanger! With Massa on pole in front of his home crowd, Hamilton had the best grid position of all the drivers still in with a chance of the title – 2nd ahead of Räikkönen and Alonso. But at the start Lewis was passed by both opponents and, as he tried to repass Fernando at the end of the first straight, he braked late, went wide and rejoined in 9th place. That was just the start of Hamilton's problems as, a few laps later, he rolled almost to a standstill with no gears until he managed to reset the McLaren's electronics. That left him in 18th place! At the front of the pack the Ferraris built up a strong lead and Alonso gradually lost contact until he literally became a target for Kubica who was lying in 4th place but on a three-stop strategy. Nothing really changed after the first round of pit-stops, but Kimi clocked up two fast laps after Massa pitted, and that was sufficient to see him rejoin in the lead by a whisker after his own pit-stop. This was a vital moment as the potential 10 points would ensure that Kimi would take the title as long as Alonso didn't finish higher than 3rd and Hamilton 5th. But Lewis was way back and could only manage two points despite a curious strategy that saw him pit three times in all. Räikkönen went on to win, with Massa 2nd and Alonso a minute behind in 3rd place. Fernando finished ahead of a battling trio made up of Rosberg, Kubica and Heidfeld. Hamilton in 7th place was followed over the line by Trulli who thus picked up the last point of the season.

Interlagos Circuit, Sao Paulo, Brazil – 21 October
Lap length: 4.309 km/2.677 miles
No. of laps: 71
Race distance: 305.909 km/190.067 miles
Weather: sunny and warm

QUALIFYING

	Driver	Car	Chassis number	Time
1	F. Massa	Ferrari	F2007-263	1'11.931"
2	L. Hamilton	McLaren	MP4/22-05	1'12.082"
3	K. Räikkönen	Ferrari	F2007-262	1'12.322"
4	F. Alonso	McLaren	MP4/22-03	1'12.356"
5	M. Webber	Red Bull	RB3-04	1'12.928"
6	N. Heidfeld	BMW	F1.07-08	1'13.081"
7	R. Kubica	BMW	F1.07-03	1'13.129"
8	J. Trulli	Toyota	TF107-03	1'13.195"
9	D. Coulthard	Red Bull	RB3-05	1'13.272"
10	N. Rosberg	Williams	FW29-05	1'13.477"
11	R. Barrichello	Honda	RA107-02	1'12.932"
12	G. Fisichella	Renault	R27-02	1'12.968"
13	S. Vettel	Toro Rosso	STR2-01	1'13.058"
14	V. Liuzzi	Toro Rosso	STR2-03	1'13.251"
15	R. Schumacher	Toyota	TF107-05	1'13.351"
16	J. Button	Honda	RA107-04	1'13.469"
17	H. Kovalainen	Renault	R27-03	1'14.078"
18	T. Sato	Super Aguri	SA07-02	1'14.098"
19	K. Nakajima	Williams	FW29-03	1'14.417"
20	A. Davidson	Super Aguri	SA07-03	1'14.596"
21	A. Sutil	Spyker	F8-VII-03	1'15.217"
22	S. Yamamoto	Spyker	F8-VII-04	1'15.487"

RESULT

	Driver	Car	Time	Laps	Stops
1	K. Räikkönen	Ferrari	1hr28'15.270"	71	2
2	F. Massa	Ferrari	+ 1.493"	71	2
3	F. Alonso	McLaren	+ 57.019"	71	2
4	N. Rosberg	Williams	+ 1'02.848"	71	2
5	R. Kubica	BMW	+ 1'10.957"	71	2
6	N. Heidfeld	BMW	+ 1'11.317"	71	2
7	L. Hamilton	McLaren	+ 1 lap	70	3
8	J. Trulli	Toyota	+ 1 lap	70	3
9	D. Coulthard	Red Bull	+ 1 lap	70	3
10	K. Nakajima	Williams	+ 1 lap	70	2
11	R. Schumacher	Toyota	+ 1 lap	70	2
12	T. Sato	Super Aguri	+ 2 laps	69	2
13	V. Liuzzi	Toro Rosso	+ 2 laps	69	3
14	A. Davidson	Super Aguri	+ 3 laps	68	3

Laps in the lead: Massa 46, Räikkönen 24, Alonso 1

RETIREMENTS

Adrian Sutil	Spyker	brakes	43	6
Rubens Barrichello	Honda	engine	40	3
Heikki Kovalainen	Renault	crash	35	1
Sebastian Vettel	Toro Rosso	hydraulics	34	2
Jenson Button	Honda	engine	20	
Mark Webber	Red Bull	gearbox	14	
Sakon Yamamoto	Spyker	collision	2	1
Giancarlo Fisichella	Renault	collision	2	1

FASTEST LAP

K. Räikkönen	Ferrari	1'12.445"	66

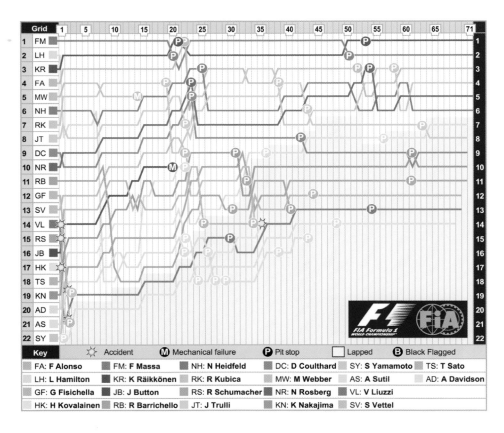

Key	☆ Accident	Ⓜ Mechanical failure	Ⓟ Pit stop	☐ Lapped	Ⓑ Black Flagged
FA: F Alonso	**FM: F Massa**	**NH: N Heidfeld**	**DC: D Coulthard**	**SY: S Yamamoto**	**TS: T Sato**
LH: L Hamilton	**KR: K Räikkönen**	**RK: R Kubica**	**MW: M Webber**	**AS: A Sutil**	**AD: A Davidson**
GF: G Fisichella	**JB: J Button**	**RS: R Schumacher**	**NR: N Rosberg**	**VL: V Liuzzi**	
HK: H Kovalainen	**RB: R Barrichello**	**JT: J Trulli**	**KN: K Nakajima**	**SV: S Vettel**	

DRIVERS' CHAMPIONSHIP

Pos.	Driver	Australia	Malaysia	Bahrain	Spain	San Marino	Canada	USA	France	Great Britain	Europe	Hungary	Turkey	Italy	Belgium	Japan	China	Brazil	Points
1	Kimi Räikkönen (FIN)	10	6	6	-	1	4	5	10	10	-	8	8	6	10	6	10	10	110
2	Lewis Hamilton (GB)	6	8	8	8	8	10	10	6	6	0	10	4	8	5	10	-	2	109
3	Fernando Alonso (E)	8	10	4	6	10	2	8	2	8	10	5	6	10	6	-	8	6	109
4	Felipe Massa (BR)	3	4	10	10	6	-	6	8	4	8	0	10	-	8	3	6	8	94
5	Nick Heidfeld (D)	5	5	5	-	3	8	-	4	3	3	6	5	5	4	0	2	3	61
6	Robert Kubica (POL)	-	0	3	5	4	-	-	5	5	2	4	1	4	0	2	-	4	39
7	Heikki Kovalainen (FIN)	0	1	0	2	0	5	4	-	2	1	1	3	2	1	8	0	-	30
8	Giancarlo Fisichella (I)	4	3	1	0	5	-	0	3	1	0	0	0	0	-	4	0	-	21
9	Nico Rosberg (D)	2	-	0	3	0	0	0	0	0	-	2	2	3	3	-	0	5	20
10	David Coulthard (GB)	-	-	-	4	0	-	-	0	0	4	0	0	-	-	5	1	0	14
11	Alex Wurz (A)	-	0	0	-	2	6	0	0	0	5	0	0	0	-	-	0	-	13
12	Mark Webber (AUS)	0	0	-	-	0	0	2	0	-	6	0	-	0	2	-	0	-	10
13	Jarno Trulli (I)	0	2	2	-	0	-	3	-	-	0	0	0	0	0	0	0	1	8
14	Sebastian Vettel (D)							1				0	0	0	-	-	5	-	6
15	Jenson Button (GB)	0	0	-	0	0	-	0	1	0	-	0	1	-	0	-	4	-	6
16	Ralf Schumacher (D)	1	0	0	-	0	1	-	0	-	-	3	0	0	-	-	0	-	5
17	Takuma Sato (J)	0	0	-	1	0	3	-	0	-	-	0	0	0	0	0	0	0	4
18	Vitantonio Liuzzi (I)	0	0	-	-	-	-	0	-	0	-	-	0	0	0	0	3	0	3
19	Adrian Sutil (D)	0	-	0	0	-	-	0	0	-	-	0	0	0	0	1	-	-	1
20	Rubens Barrichello (BR)	0	0	0	0	0	0	-	0	0	0	0	0	0	0	0	0	-	0
21	Scott Speed (US)	-	0	-	-	0	-	0	-	-									0
22	Kazuki Nakajima (JPN)																0		0
23	Anthony Davidson (GB)	0	0	0	0	0	0	0	-			-	0	0	0	-	-	0	0
24	Sakon Yamamoto (JPN)											0	0	0	0	0	0	-	0
25	Christijan Albers (NL)	-	-	0	0	0	-	0	-	0									0
-	Markus Winkelhock (D)										-								0

CONSTRUCTORS' CHAMPIONSHIP

Pos.	Team	Australia	Malaysia	Bahrain	Spain	San Marino	Canada	USA	France	Great Britain	Europe	Hungary	Turkey	Italy	Belgium	Japan	China	Brazil	Points
1	Scuderia Ferrari Marlboro	13	10	16	10	7	4	11	18	14	8	8	18	6	18	9	16	18	204
2	BMW Sauber F1 Team	5	5	8	5	7	8	1	9	8	5	10	6	9	4	2	2	7	101
3	ING Renault F1 Team	4	4	1	2	5	5	4	3	3	1	1	3	2	1	12	0	0	51
4	AT&T Williams	2	0	0	3	2	6	0	0	0	5	2	2	3	3	0	0	5	33
5	Red Bull Racing	0	0	0	4	0	0	2	0	0	10	0	0	0	2	5	1	0	24
6	Panasonic Toyota Racing	1	2	2	0	0	1	3	0	0	0	3	0	0	0	0	0	1	13
7	Scuderia Toro Rosso	0	0	0	0	0	0	0	0	0	0	0	0	0	0	8	0	0	8
8	Honda Racing F1 Team	0	0	0	0	0	0	0	1	0	0	0	1	0	0	4	0	0	6
9	Super Aguri F1 Team	0	0	0	1	0	3	0	0	0	0	0	0	0	0	0	0	0	4
10	Etihad Aldar Spyker F1 Team	0	0	0	0	0	0	0	0	0	0	0	0	0	0	1	0	0	1
-	Vodafone McLaren Mercedes*	-	-	-	-	-	-	-	-	-	-	-	-	-	-	-	-	-	0

* McLaren's drivers totalled 218 points between them, but the F.I.A. removed the team's points in the Constructors' Championship in the aftermath of the spy story. Standings were provisional at the time of going to print pending an appeal presented by McLaren after the last race.

GP2 – RESULTS

Pos.	Drivers	Team	Bahrain	Spain	Monaco	France	Great Britain	Germany	Hungary	Turkey	Italy	Belgium	Spain	Points
1	Timo Glock (D)	iSport	14	17	6	2	-	14	2	11	12	1	9	88
2	Lucas Di Grassi (BR)	Art Grand Prix	4	10	4	11	8	9	8	10	3	10	-	77
3	Giorgio Pantano (I)	Campos	-	1	8	14	-	5	-	8	13	-	10	59
4	Luca Filippi (I)	Super Nova	16	-	5	10	4	-	-	2	13	8	1	59
5	Kazuki Nakajima (J)	DAMS	2	1	-	1	11	10	8	3	-	-	8	44
6	Javier Villa (E)	Racing Engineering	-	6	-	8	-	7	7	-	3	5	6	42
7	Adam Carroll (GB)	Petrol Ofisi FMS Int.	-	-	-	-	9	-	15	10	1	1	-	36
8	Bruno Senna (BR)	Arden	5	13	-	6	-	-	-	1	9	-	-	34
9	Andreas Zuber (UAE)	iSport	6	-	-	-	14	-	7	1	2	-	-	30
10	Borja Garcia (E)	Durango	4	4	-	-	-	-	6	7	-	-	7	28

Team standings: 1. iSport International, 118 points; 2. ART Grand Prix, 87; 3. Campos Grand Prix, 80; 4. Super Nova International, 78; 5. DAMS, 67; 6. Racing Engineering, 51; 7. Arden International, 44; 8. Durango, 44; 9. FMS International, 37; 10. Trident Racing, 35; 11. Minardi Piquet Sports, 22; 12. DPR, 15; 13. BCN Competicion, 4

Timo Glock, 2007 GP2 Champion.

United nations

A1GP – the self-styled World Cup of Motorsport – was initially greeted with cynicism, as an ambitious gimmick with slim prospects of long-term success. But that was in 2004. Today, the concept's driving forces believe they are absolutely on the right track. **Simon Arron** introduces us to the series and to the people at its helm.

An action-packed start for the 22-car A1 line-up at Taupo (New Zealand). Nico Hülkenberg (Germany) leads Loïc Duval (France) into the first corner.

Tony Teixeira

Pete da Silva

Unveiled on March 30, 2004, A1GP represented a fresh concept in international motorsport. Although the notion of a one-make single-seater category was nothing new – A1GP features Lola-built chassis, Zytek 3.4-litre V8 engines and Cooper control tyres – the focus most certainly was: the champion would not be a driver, but a nation. Established racing teams – with a proven pedigree in GP2, F3000, F3, Formula Renault and elsewhere – would run cars in the colours of competing countries. Each was free to swap and change drivers throughout the campaign, which would begin during the European autumn – as other mainstream series were drawing to a close – and conclude the following spring.

The format of each weekend would, like the cars, be identical, with a qualifying session to determine the grid for a sprint race the following morning – and the result of that would settle the line-up for a main event, complete with mandatory pit stop, later in the day. Points are award on a 10-9-8-7-6-5-4-3-2-1 basis to the top 10 finishers in the main event and 6-5-4-3-2-1 to the first six nations in the sprint. There is also one bonus point available for the weekend's fastest race lap. The first races took place at Brands Hatch, England, on September 25, 2005. Nelson Piquet Jr. scored a double race victory for Brazil, but France went on to win the inaugural title. Germany emerged triumphant during

the second season and the third began at Zandvoort, Holland, on September 30, 2007. The campaign was still in progress as *Automobile Year* closed for press.

As motor sport series go, few have had a potentially quirkier provenance. A1GP's original front man was Sheikh Maktoum Hasher Maktoum Al Maktoum, a member of Dubai's ruling dynasty. His family had strong sporting connections – in the world of horse racing – but his homeland had a threadbare motor sport culture. Yet here he was, outlining a bold new initiative that would tap into fresh markets and provide motor racing teams with a revenue stream during the European winter, their traditional off-season. Few believed him, not least because similar concepts – Premier 1 Grand Prix and Formula Supertec, to name but two – had failed to get off the ground, despite a barrage of hyperbole. A1GP turned out to be different, though. The first race took place, as promised, in late 2005 and, despite some teething problems, the series reached its conclusion. In the intervening period, Maktoum has stepped down (RAB Capital from London taking up an 80% stake in the operation) to leave the reins to A1GP co-founder and chairman Tony Teixeira and chief executive officer Pete da Silva. *Automobile Year* spoke to the South African duo about their fight to gain acceptance and their hopes for the future.

"Grid Girls" carrying the participating nations' flags add colour and spectacle to the start.

Since the interview took place, A1GP announced a partnership with Ferrari (to start with the 2008/09 season) regarding the development of both engines and chassis. Another demonstration of the series' success.

AUTOMOBILE YEAR: How do you assess A1GP's position after its first two seasons?
TONY TEIXEIRA: Everything we set out to achieve has been done. Obviously there has been a lot of criticism and we have had a few hurdles to cross, but our concept has remained the same since the start – nation versus nation. We're tapping into the passion of each country, taking racing to places F1 doesn't go. I wouldn't say, though, that we are deliberately targeting areas F1 avoids. I see A1GP as a complement to F1 – it's a case of going to places where we fit. We learned a lot in season one. At the Lausitzring in Germany, for instance, we attracted about 7,000 people to a venue with 150,000 seats. It was just too big for us. In season two I don't think we've had an event that attracted fewer than 50,000-60,000 people over the weekend. I think we're beginning to find our niche markets.

AY: You take great care to avoid comparisons with Formula One, but the outside world is forever drawing parallels…
PETE DA SILVA: I always say, "Hey, we're only 20 months old". We keep getting compared to F1, but that's an honour at this stage in our development. The F1 world championship has been going for almost

60 years. Do we have 60 years to get established? Absolutely not, but I would like three or four. Since I came on board in January 2007, I have been putting building blocks in place.
TT: F1 will always be there, for the next 300 years or whatever, and anything else would look out of place at venues such as Monaco. We're trying to establish 12 or 15 races that suit our market. There are more than 200 countries in the world, so there has to be enough room for everybody.

AY: Even so, the market is very crowded just south of F1. We've got GP2, A1GP, the World Series by Renault, the new Superleague Formula… Isn't there a risk of saturation?
TT: It's good for fans. If there are more series out there, they can decide what they want to watch. We've always said we're into *motortainment*: we're not into technology. We want to entertain people. We want people to come along, have a good time and start shouting for their countries. On the other hand, it's bad for the sport when guys come along and announce something that doesn't subsequently happen. In those circumstances people start to take the sport as a whole less seriously. You get sponsors asking questions: the guys who announce stuff but do nothing end up hurting everyone. If you announce it, you have to go through with it.

AY: What were the main criteria when it came to deciding where to race?
PDS: People have said we were lucky in choosing certain

On the narrow street circuit of Mexico City things are particularly tight: Here ex-Formula 1 Minardi driver Alex Yoong from Malaysia battles with Britain's Oliver Jarvis and Germany's Christian Vietoris.

countries for our events, but there's no such thing as luck. It was strategic. We chose nations that love motor sport but didn't have top-level racing of this calibre. We also targeted up-and-coming nations. We believe Pakistan, Indonesia, South Africa and so on must have significant talent pools. Not all motor racing heroes have to come from Brazil, Britain, France, Germany or Italy.

AY: How are things stacking up financially?
TT: Year one was all about investment – I've seen stories saying we lost $200 million, but when you start a new business, build a new house or whatever you first have to invest. We invested $200 million to set up A1GP and in year two we anticipated a small loss, as in $20 million to $30 million. Given what we're doing, that's small. I think we are on target to break even or make a small profit in year three. In a business like this you can't simply go out and start making money from day one. It's impossible. We haven't yet started to capitalise on all the potential revenue streams – I'm talking about merchandising, betting… all the basic things such as which drinks companies or food suppliers are allowed at events. Once you're established companies will want to talk about such deals, but that's all to come. We are exactly where we thought we would be.
PDS: In the business world, people would be suspicious if you made a profit in year one. They expect a loss, and the same – but on a smaller scale – in year two.

By year three you should be breaking even and then you get into the black – that's the mindset I'm in.
AY: What expansion plans do you have?
TT: I don't see us going over 14 races per season in the short term. Expansion will come via the countries that take part in A1, when they set up their own feeder series. We're going to call that A2. A rule will come that says unless you win your national A2 championship you can't race in A1. Countries competing today have a time limit in which to set up a national series – this is A1, the national championship will be A2 and there'll also be A3, a development formula. The A2 series winners will become the national representatives in A1 and that's where we're going to grow.

AY: Which hurdles still have to be overcome?
TT: We need more terrestrial TV coverage, but the fact remains that we're going out in about 140 countries. Most of our broadcasts are live and I'm beginning to concur with F1 that our races in the Far East should perhaps run later in the day, so that they're at the right time for European TV. We have to work on getting better coverage in the next few years.
PDS: I've learned that one marketing plan doesn't suit all. When we went to Taupo in New Zealand, it was amazing. I didn't even have to show my passport. When they saw A1 on my shirt they said, "Fine, come on through". In Sydney, though, it was more like, "A1GP? Who are you?" The two events were physically very

Switzerland clinched a surprising pole position on the Sepang (Malaysia) Grand Prix circuit. 23-year-old Neel Jani defends his lead from Nicolas Lapierre going into the first corner, but the Swiss driver had dropped back to fourth place by the end of the race.

close, but the markets are significantly different. We had the same template for those two markets but we won't do that again. If we have 11 races we'll have 11 separate templates. We'll treat each one very differently.

AY: Do you foresee any significant technical changes?
TT: Not really. We wanted to keep things simple. The car is the right size – it's very reliable and just right for the drivers' level of experience.

AY: GP2 is presently recognised as F1's official ante-chamber. Would you like people to look at A1GP in a similar light?
PDS: I think recognition will come in due course. The timing of our season gives us access to drivers who want to build a profile ahead of the European campaign. At one race in season two we had an average podium age of 18 years 6 months – and that's magic, a barometer of real young talent. Would Nico Hülkenberg have made such a name for himself without A1GP? I don't think so.

AY: Where do you see A1GP 10 years from now?
TT: I see a series embraced by 25 nations – but then we might have 60 countries fighting for a place on the main A1 grid. It could almost be like a World Cup situation, where you have a knock-out – that's the sort of growth we might get. We have set a goal of 28 A1 teams at the max and we want to represent the world.

PDS: I want to see passion, like you get at football matches. We want to grow, but I tell people, "How do you eat an elephant? Piece by piece, because otherwise you choke". That's the approach we have to take.

AY: Any message for the cynics?
PDS: I relish the fact people doubt us: it heightens the challenge.

After France had won the inaugural A1GP season in 2005/2006,
it was Germany's turn to dominate the series in 2006/2007
with the promising young driver Nico Hülkenberg (centre).

A1GP SEASON 2006/07 FINAL STANDINGS

Pos	A1 Team	Points	Starts	Wins	Podiums	Top 10s	Poles*	F.Laps
1	Germany	128	22	9	14	19	3	5
2	New Zealand	93	22	3	11	18	2	4
3	Great Britain	92	22	3	10	19	2	2
4	France	67	22	-	8	15	-	-
5	Netherlands	57	22	1	1	17	1	-
6	Malaysia	55	22	3	3	13	1	2
7	Italy	52	22	1	4	12	-	1
8	Switzerland	50	22	1	1	18	1	1
9	USA	42	22	-	2	15	-	2
10	Mexico	35	22	-	4	7	-	2
11	Canada	33	22	-	1	12	-	1
12	Czech Republic	27	22	-	1	8	-	-
13	Australia	25	22	-	3	6	-	-
14	South Africa	24	22	1	2	8	1	2
15	China	22	22	-	1	10	-	-
16	India	13	22	-	-	6	-	-
17	Portugal	10	8	-	-	3	-	-
18	Brazil	9	22	-	-	4	-	-
19	Ireland	8	22	-	-	5	-	-
20	Singapore	3	14	-	-	1	-	-
21	Indonesia	1	22	-	-	3	-	-
22	Pakistan	1	22	-	-	1	-	-
23	Lebanon	0	22	-	-	-	-	-
24	Greece	0	4	-	-	-	-	-

* only one qualifying session per race week-end, determining grid positions for the sprint race.

Scotsman Franchitti emulates Jim Clark

Dario Franchitti had a crazy season in 2007, capturing his first IndyCar Series championship literally with ups and downs. Franchitti emerged from the 17-race schedule with several memorable moments, led by his Indianapolis 500 victory. He also flipped his car twice, drove into the side of team-mate Marco Andretti, ran into a championship rival and was handed the series title when Scott Dixon ran out of fuel on the final lap of the season. "I thought winning the Indy 500 was a great feeling, but this feels different," he said of the title. "I guess because it's a whole year rolled into one." Andretti also flipped twice, the first coming at the end of the 500. Dan Wheldon found himself nose to nose with an angry Danica Patrick after their contact at Milwaukee, there was a pit road fight at Watkins Glen, N.Y., and Tony Kanaan got criticized for protecting Franchitti and his wounded car in Sonoma, California. Dixon spun on the tight Detroit street circuit only to be accused of intentionally letting his car roll into Franchitti's path. It was a wild year. Season highlights by **Curt Cavin**.

Tony Kanaan didn't win this June night race in Richmond, Virginia, but he got plenty hot in the second half of the season, winning three times in a four-race stretch (Michigan, Kentucky and Detroit) to put him in the championship chase right up to the end of the season.

Dario Franchitti won his first Indianapolis 500 in unusual fashion, splashing down the front straightaway after rain fell on the 166th lap (of 200). The scene was reminiscent of Buddy Rice's rain-shortened victory in 2004, and it started a run of three wins in five races for the driver who would go on to win the IndyCar Series championship.

This was actually the second of two flips of Marco Andretti's car in 2007. The first came at the end of the Indianapolis 500 when he turned into Dan Wheldon's path. Here, contact with Tony Kanaan launched him off course at Mid-Ohio. He escaped both without injury.

Scott Dixon (left) might have led the next-to-last lap of the Indy-car season at Chicagoland, but his engine sputtered without fuel in the third turn of the final circuit, allowing Dario Franchitti to sweep wide and take the race victory and series championship. Dixon finished second in each.

Leaving on a high note

Once again, writes **Curt Cavin**, teams in the Champ Car World Series thought they could keep Sébastien Bourdais at bay. Once again, they couldn't. The Frenchman bound for Formula 1 delivered yet another exemplary title-worthy performance, pulling away from his competitors in the second half of the season. Bourdais, already the champion for the past three years, delivered a pair of strong stretches to lead with his Newman/Haas/Lanigan Racing car. He won three consecutive races (Long Beach, Houston and Portland) before struggling briefly. But that was followed by a string of three wins in four races to build an advantage over Justin Wilson and rookie Robert Doornbos, among others. The race in Portland, Ore., not only was Champ Car's first caution-free race since 2000, it became the 100th victory in the series for team owners Carl Haas and actor Paul Newman. Despite having taken 26 of those wins, Bourdais played his role down. "I don't think I made history," he said. "I participated in it." The season also saw the debut of Graham Rahal, the son of 1986 Indianapolis 500 winner Bobby Rahal, a three-time CART champion.

This sums up how the first race of Sébastien Bourdais' title defence went in 2007. During the Las Vegas weekend he had a mechanical failure in practice, three tyre punctures, contact with two drivers in the race and a wall slap in the tunnel. "The worst weekend I can remember," he said. Will Power won the race.

Sébastien Bourdais (left) took the lead of the Edmonton race at the start from Will Power, whose car slipped on the paint markings in his grid slot, and the championship advantage from Robert Doornbos, who fell a lap behind on lap 69 after contact with Alex Tagliani. That turned a three-horse race into a 20-point lead for the three-time series champion.

Will Power won his second career Champ Car race in rainy conditions in Toronto, but the real action was behind him. Simon Pagenaud and Alex Tagliani made contact in the fourth turn of the opening lap to ignite a chain reaction that collected six additional cars.

Robert Doornbos ended up in a mess with Jan Heylen on the opening lap of the race in San Jose, California, but Doornbos and his Minardi Team USA crew recovered with smart pit strategy to score their second victory of the season. Doornbos made only two fuel stops to take command.

Dario Franchitti didn't understand what it meant to win Indy and its prestigious BorgWarner Trophy when he arrived for his first 500 in 2002. Now, his accomplishment matches that of his hero, the late Jim Clark, a Scotsman who won Indy in 1965.

Sébastien Bourdais gave Champ Car's most successful team, Newman/Haas/Lanigan Racing, its 100th victory in open-wheel racing with this 13.5-second win over Justin Wilson in Portland, Oregon. Mario Andretti scored the team's first win at Elkhart Lake, Wisconsin, in 1983.

While Dario Franchitti couldn't rely on the same Honda advantage that propelled Tony Kanaan (2004) and Dan Wheldon (2005) to IndyCar Series championships, he still gave Andretti Green Racing its third title in four years. The team won nine of the 17 races this past season.

INDY 500 – RESULTS

Pos.	Driver	Team	Car	S	QS	Laps	LL	Earnings	Points
1	Dario Franchitti	Canadian Club	DH	3	225.191	166	34	$1,645,233	50
2	Scott Dixon	Target Chip Ganassi Racing	DH	4	225.122	166	11	$719,067	40
3	Helio Castroneves	Team Penske	DH	1	225.817	166	19	$646,303	35
4	Sam Hornish Jr.	Team Penske	DH	5	225.109	166	2	$360,389	32
5	Ryan Briscoe	Symantec Luczo Dragon Racing	DH	7	224.410	166	0	$302,305	30
6	Scott Sharp	Patron Sharp Rahal Letterman	DH	12	223.875	166	0	$368,305	28
7	Tomas Scheckter	Vision Racing	DH	10	222.877	166	0	$304,105	26
8	Danica Patrick	Motorola	DH	8	224.076	166	0	$298,005	24
9	Davey Hamilton	HP Vision Racing	DH	20	222.327	166	0	$268,905	22
10	Vitor Meira	Delphi Panther	DH	19	222.333	166	0	$280,305	20

Key: S= Starting position; QS= Qualifying speed (mph); LL= Laps in the lead; Pts= Points scored; DH= Dallara Honda; PH= Panoz Honda

IRL – FINAL STANDINGS

Pos.	Driver	Starts	Poles	Wins	Top 5	Top 10	Winnings	Points
1	Dario Franchitti	17	4	4	13	16	$4,017,583	637
2	Scott Dixon	17	2	4	13	16	$2,152,417	624
3	Tony Kanaan	17	2	5	12	13	$1,754,269	576
4	Dan Wheldon	17	1	2	6	11	$1,336,855	466
5	Sam Hornish Jr.	17	0	1	8	12	$1,323,789	465
6	Helio Castroneves	17	7	1	6	11	$1,659,603	446
7	Danica Patrick	17	0	0	4	11	$1,182,055	424
8	Scott Sharp	17	1	0	3	10	$1,212,505	421
9	Buddy Rice	17	0	0	3	11	$1,010,205	360
10	Tomas Scheckter	17	0	0	2	9	$1,064,905	357

CHAMP CAR – DRIVER STANDINGS

Pos.	Driver	Points	Wins	Poles	Winnings
1	Sébastien Bourdais	332	7	6	$686,000
2	Justin Wilson	270	1	2	$471,500
3	Robert Doornbos	262	2	0	$489,500
4	Will Power	234	2	4	$439,000
5	Graham Rahal	220	0	0	$361,500
6	Neel Jani	218	0	0	$360,500
7	Bruno Junqueira	216	0	0	$357,500
8	Simon Pagenaud	213	0	0	$336,000
9	Oriol Servia	212	0	0	$337,500
10	Alex Tagliani	197	0	0	$313,500

Standings after 13 out of 14 races; Bourdais has clinched the championship.

Audi makes it seven

Ńobody, from company executive vice-president Frédéric Saint-Geours downwards, expected Peugeot to win the 24-Hours of Le Mans in 2007, reports **Michael Cotton**. If one of the two diesel-powered 908 HDi FAP coupés were to finish the race, in any position, it would be regarded as a success, a springboard for a victory bid in 2008. Well, Audi's R10 diesel did achieve its second victory at the Sarthe but the Germans had a nail-biting day on Sunday after the second of three cars crashed out of the reckoning with eight hours to go, and with two healthy Peugeots breathing on the necks of Frank Biela, Emanuele Pirro and Marco Werner.

One of the V12-powered Peugeots retired unexpectedly with an oil pressure failure two hours from the end and the other, driven by Sébastien Bourdais, Pedro Lamy and Stéphane Sarrazin, was none too healthy entering the final lap, in heavy rain, but Bourdais was able to take the flag in second place and perform a victory dance in front of the packed grandstands. "It was an awesome way to finish a crazy race," said Bourdais.

Le Mans hero Henri Pescarolo, veteran of 40 Le Mans enduros as a driver and entrant, saw his Judd-powered Pescarolo finish in third position, 11 laps behind the winning Audi R10 diesel and by no means disgraced. There was another Pescarolo-Judd, privately entered by the British Rollcentre Racing team, in fourth position.

All four cars belong to the LMP1 class. The 24-Hours are run is four classes, two for Prototype sports cars (LMP) and two for Grand Touring cars (LM-GT). The more powerful cars are in the upper categories, LMP1 and GT1, supported by manufacturers, while private "customer" teams feature in the less powerful, and less expensive LMP2 and GT2 groups.

Aston Martin Racing threw off their jinx to win the GT1 category with the DBR9, fifth overall and just a lap ahead of the Corvette Racing C6.R. In GT2 the Porsche marque, which had been struggling in early-season races with the new 997 model 911 RSR, achieved a fine victory thanks to the French IMSA Performance Matmut team. It finished 15th overall. One had to go down to the 18th position to find the winner of the LMP2 class, the Binnie Motorsports Lola Zytek.

Audi Sport achieved their seventh victory at Le Mans in eight years, and it was the second at the Sarthe for the diesel-powered R10 TDI. The Big Wheel, an historic feature of the Esses fairground, has been moved to the infield near the Ford chicane, affording spectators an unique view of the Porsche Curves, treacherous as heavy rain lashed the track in the last hour. Challenging the Audi in shot, though many laps behind, is the GT1 class-winning Aston Martin DBR9.

James Bond drove an Aston Martin, though not at Le Mans, and the "works" team was allowed to race with the numbers 007 and 009. The concession by the ACO brought them luck, reversing three defeats by the American Corvette Racing team at the Sarthe. Six DBR9s started the 24-Hours and all finished, although the "Bond" 007 lost the class lead at the 16-hour mark with a damaged splitter, leaving 009 to win in the hands of David Brabham, Rickard Rydell and Darren Turner.

Rookie Mike Rockenfeller completed only two laps of the big circuit before losing control of his Audi R10 at Tertre Rouge, pressing-on on a damp surface. "The driver is trying to find a gear to bring the car back" announced team director Dr Wolfgang Ullrich, not realising that the back of the car was wrecked.

Conditions at Le Mans were sometimes fine, sometimes foul, but Pescarolo Sport drivers Emmanuel Collard, Jean-Christophe Boullion and Romain Dumas drove a perfect race to third place overall in their Judd V10-powered Pescarolo, "winners of the petrol engine class," said the team boss.

Zytek has sprung to prominence in the LMP2 category with engines and chassis, but Binnie Motorsports ran a Lola chassis powered by the Zytek V8 engine to win the second-tier prototype category at Le Mans. Scottish-born American Bill Binnie teamed up with Allen Timpany and Chris Buncombe to achieve the victory, after finishing second in class last year.

Audi R10 TDI

With Formula 1, Le Mans represents the most challenging competition in which manufacturers can measure up and demonstrate their technical know-how. This year Peugeot joined Audi in the battle for diesel-powered supremacy in the LMP1 class with the 908 HDi FAP. **Michael Cotton** reports on these and on the other top contenders from each class.

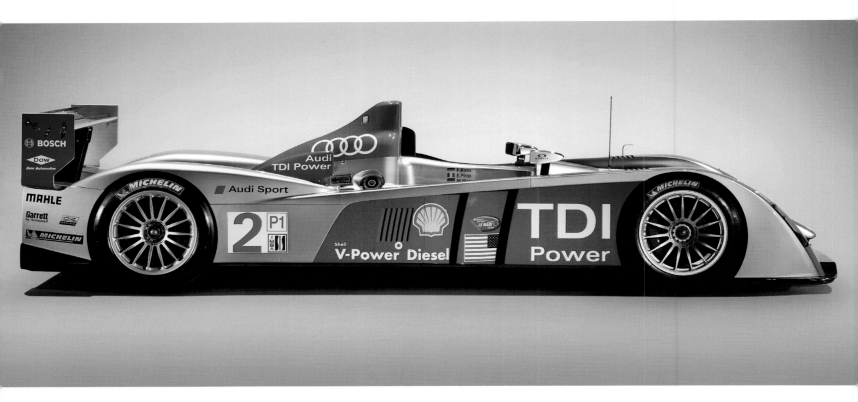

LMP1

Diesel engines dominated the 24-Hours of Le Mans in June 2007, and Audi achieved their seventh victory at the Sarthe in no more than nine years. Yet, with rain sweeping the 13.629 kilometre circuit at regular intervals, and with fierce competition from Peugeot on their debut appearance, the result was not as predictable as in recent years.

Audi's R10 TDI, powered by a bespoke 5.5-litre aluminium V12 diesel engine, swept all before it in 2006 and was favourite for a second successive Le Mans victory. During the winter, engine designer Ulrich Baretzky concentrated on making the engine more efficient, finding improvements in consumption, durability and drivability. The engine management system was optimised by Audi and Bosch, some engine parts were lightened and internal friction reduced. Also, the two diesel

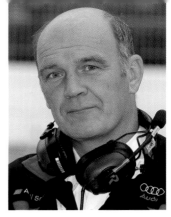

Wolfgang Ullrich, team principal

particulate filters were made smaller and lighter so Audi, like Peugeot, could claim to be pioneering environmentally friendly technology on the race track.

Power was still quoted at 650 bhp, "a minimum of 650 bhp!" says Baretzky, but the power curve was noticeably improved, the torque peaking at 1,100 Nm. So too was the traction control system, which worked overtime in sometimes very wet track conditions. Like any production diesel engine, the Audi R10 TDI's power unit could not be taken usefully beyond 5,000 rpm, and in contrast to high-revving gasoline engines the diesels sounded muffled and muted.

The ACO reduced the fuel tank capacity by 10 per cent, from 90 litres to 81 litres, in order to reduce the clear advantage of diesel engines over gasoline engines. And yet, with all the improvements, including some minor but significant aerodynamic modifications carried out by

chassis and body designer Wolfgang Appel, the Audis were still able to complete 12 or 13 laps on each tank of fuel, instead of 13 or 14 laps the previous year.

Michelin contributed to the success of the Audi and Peugeot teams with continued progress in tyre technology, paying special attention to the enormous amounts of traction required by the diesel engines. Just making those 16-inch wide (405 mm) tyres to grip with full torque applied in dry conditions was no mean feat.

Audi's rookie driver Mike Rockenfeller lost control of his R10 at Tertre Rouge in the second hour and crashed heavily into the guardrail, caught out by slick white paint in mixed conditions. Tom Kristensen was denied his eighth victory, which looked almost certain on Sunday morning, when a rear wheel became detached at the fast Indianapolis curve, rendering Dindo Capello a helpless passenger.

Peugeot 908 HDi FAP

LMP1

Even in the days before the 24-Hours of Le Mans, Peugeot's management would have settled for a good finish with not too many problems. The 908 HDi FAP twin-turbo diesel had only begun its test programme in January and despite two victories in the Le Mans Series, had not run a full 24-hour test without failures. To finish in second position overall, behind the Audi R10 TDI, was beyond the most optimistic expectations of the Peugeot team, and this result builds their confidence in aiming at outright victory in 2008.

Peugeot made the decision to design the 908 FAP with closed, coupé-style bodywork in anticipation of new rules which will be introduced by the ACO in 2010. A closed cockpit has less drag than an open car, a key factor on the Le Mans circuit with a fastest lap average speed of 237 km/h, but there are negative factors too, such as greater frontal

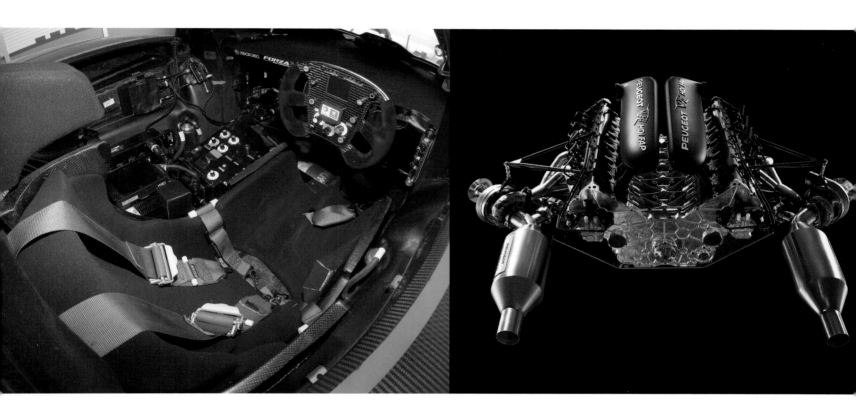

area, higher centre of gravity, less downforce on the rear wing, and poor cockpit access for the drivers. The design team was led by Bruno Famin, and Paolo Catone was named as the head of the 908 project. Under him, Guillaume Cattelani led the aerodynamics team which had the difficult task of sending enough cooling air to the 5.5-litre V12 diesel engine while keeping drag at a minimum. Claude Guillois' engine team designed the wide angle (100-degree) V12 from a clean sheet of paper and achieved some impressive figures: 700 horsepower and 1,200 Nm of torque. Like Audi, Peugeot ran the Dow Automotive diesel particulate filters.

Bosch supplied the MS17 engine management system which has much in common with Audi's MS14, and Peugeot worked with Ricardo to hone the longitudinal six-speed gearbox, which has an electro-pneumatic control. Like its predecessor, the 905 coupé (pictured left) which won at Le Mans in 1992 and 1993, the 908

had electrically controlled power steering. Le Mans born Sébastien Bourdais set the fastest time for Peugeot at the official test day, June 3 which guaranteed a record crowd, numbered at 250,920 over the race weekend. His team-mate Stéphane Sarrazin set the fastest qualifying lap, too, so Peugeot's new 908 clearly had the speed to match Audi in single-lap qualifying.

The race, though, soon told a different story as the three Audis were able to control the race from the front, lapping not far off their qualifying times, while the two Peugeots raced at a steadier pace, the Bourdais car a lap down after three hours. Then his car, the faster of the two, was delayed by a seized rear wheel bearing and went four laps down, but was still able to claim second place overall, though in the late stages was handicapped by the same falling oil pressure that retired the sister car in the penultimate hour.

Pescarolo-Judd

Henri Pescarolo, team owner

LMP1

Pescarolo Sport was founded in 2000 by Henri Pescarolo, the four-times Le Mans winning driver, competing in the first four years with sports-prototypes made by his neighbour at Le Mans, Yves Courage. He then developed his own bodywork on the Courage chassis, renaming the cars 'Pescarolo', and relying on Judd V10 engines. In the past three years, Pescarolo Sport had claimed a fourth place overall at Le Mans, then two second positions. It would be much harder to reach the podium in 2007, Pescarolo expected, with Audi running three R10s and Peugeot two 908s, their diesel engines having a proven superiority in lap times.

The 2007 model Pescarolo was based on the Courage LC70 carbon monocoque chassis, with unique bodywork designed by Claude Galopin, the team's technical director. Judd supplied the engine, as usual, the latest 5.5-litre GV5.5 V10 rated at 650 bhp at 7,000 rpm, and 660 Nm of torque at 6,000 rpm. Prepared to the same minimum weight as the diesels, 925 kg, the Pescarolo had far less torque and had less punch out of the chicanes and slow corners.

In race condition the Pescarolo-Judd was not far off the pace of the Peugeots, and the team's lead car was able to finish in third position overall, ahead of the "customer car" of Rollcentre Racing.

Lola Zytek B05/40

William Binnie, team director

LMP2

The combination of Lola's B05/40 chassis and Zytek's
3.4-litre V8 engine came together to win the LMP2
class at Le Mans. Bill Binnie, the Glasgow-born,
Boston resident driver formed his own team in 2005 and
this was his fourth appearance at the Sarthe, with co-drivers
Allen Timpany and Chris Buncombe. Binnie Motorsports
won the category handsomely, despite spending much
of the last hour in the pits with waterlogged ignition.

Lola's Julian Sole designed the carbon monocoque chassis,
based on the company's original LMP1 chassis which debuted
in 2005, and was assisted by Dan Cox on body design.
It was weighed at 795 kg at Le Mans scrutineering, some 45 kg
above the minimum for the category, and the car was powered
by Zytek's 90-degree V8 engine which develops 520 bhp
at 9,500 rpm with a single 42.9 mm inlet air restrictor in place.
Maximum torque was 530 Nm at 7,500 rpm, driving through
a Lola designed transverse 6-speed sequential gearbox.

Aston Martin DBR9

David Richards, team owner

LMGT1

Six Aston Martin DBR9s started the 24-Hours of Le Mans and all finished, one of them winning the GT1 category in fifth position overall and ending Chevrolet's winning run.

AMR's technical director and race team manager George Howard-Chappell was responsible for the design and development of the DBR9 racing car, which is built at the Prodrive facility. Like the production model, the DB9, the GT1 car has a very stiff extruded aluminium chassis which is glued and bolted together in sections. In the event of an accident, the entire front end including the engine can be unbolted at the bulkhead, or the rear subframe can be detached along with the gearbox and differential.

The roll cage is a separate structure and the chassis is built around it, a process that takes no more than four hours. All the bodywork is made by Prodrive in carbon-fibre. The DBR9 was on the minimum weight of 1,250 kg.

The 6-litre V12 "modular" engine was made by Ford in Cologne, then completely rebuilt and modified by AMR, with dry sump lubrication and Magnetti Marelli Pectel T10S engine management. The engine develops 575 bhp at 7,000 rpm and 700 Nm of torque at 5,250 rpm, with two 30.7 mm inlet air restrictors in place. An Xtrac longitudinal transmission is placed at the rear, a six-speed sequential unit with manual shifting.

Porsche 997 GT3 RSR

Raymond Narac, team director

LMGT2

Porsche's engineers in Weissach were faced with a risk in developing the 911 GT3 RSR race car, but it was a risk that had to be taken. The outgoing 996 model 911 had won the GT2 category at Le Mans seven times in succession, but the modern 997 model was 100mm wider, and heavier.

The capacity of the flat-six engine increased from 3.6 to 3.8 litres, and Porsche decided to go into a higher band in GT2, with a minimum weight of 1,225 kg, an increase of 100 kg. The benefit was to be allowed larger diameter inlet air restrictors, of 30.3 mm instead of 29.0 mm, raising the power to 485 bhp at 8,500 rpm and the torque to 435 Nm at 7,250 rpm. Offsetting the higher weight, the 997 model has a 10 per cent stiffer bodyshell, with the roll cage installed, and races with 14-inch wide rear wheels, instead of 12-inch wide.

Would the updates be sufficient to improve lap times, especially over a full driver stint? The answer was affirmative, but the proven Ferrari 430 GT model remained a formidable rival, and two different Ferrari teams led the category

at Le Mans before running into difficulties. At the finish, Porsche teams were placed first and third in GT2 led by the IMSA Performance Matmut 997 GT3 RSR driven by Raymond Narac, Patrick Long and Richard Lietz.

Circuit des 24 Heures, Le Mans, France · 16-17 June
Circuit length: 13.629 km
Distance covered by the winning team: 5,029 km
Weather conditions: partly sunny with scattered showers

			1h	2h	3h	4h	5h	6h	7h	8h	9h	10h	11h	12h	13h	14h	15h	16h	17h	18h	19h	20h	21h	22h	23h	24h		
1	Peugeot 908 Hdi FAP	8																									1	1
2	Audi R10 TDi	2																	2								8	2
3	Peugeot 908 Hdi FAP	7																					7				16	3
4	Audi R10 TDi	1																									18	4
5	Audi R10 TDi	3																									009	5
6	Pescarolo Judd	16																									63	6
7	Courage LC7 AER	13																									008	7
8	Pescarolo Judd	18																									15	8
9	Dome S101.5 Judd	14																									007	9
10	Creation Judd CA07	9																									54	10
11	Lola B07/17 Judd	15																									100	11
12	Courage LC70 AER	12																									72	12
13	Pescarolo Judd	17																									17	13
14	Lola Audi B07/10	5																									67	14
15	Zytek 07S/2	33																									76	15
16	Lola B06/10 AER	19																									55	16
17	Lola B05/40 AER	40																									59	17
18	Lola B05/40 Zytek	31																									31	18
19	Radical SR9 AER	21																									99	19
20	Zytek 07S/2	32																									19	20
21	MG Lola EX264 AER	25																									93	21
22	Courage LC75 AER	35																25									78	22
23	Aston Martin DBR9	008																									82	23
24	Saleen S7-R	55																									73	24
25	Pilbeam MP93 Judd	20																									14	25
26	Corvette C6R	64																									12	26
27	Aston Martin DBR9	009																									33	27
28	Pescarolo Judd	44																									70	28
29	Corvette C6-R	63																				83					006	29
30	Aston Martin DBR9	59																	87									30
31	Saleen S7-R	54																										31
32	Aston Martin DBR9	100																										32
33	Corvette C6-R	72																										33
34	Aston Martin DBR9	007																	97									34
35	Corvette C6-R	70									80																	35
36	Courage LC75 AER	24												13				35										36
37	Corvette C5-R	73																										37
38	Aston Martin DBR9	006															24											38
39	Ferrari F430 GT	87												20														39
40	Porsche 997 GT3 RSR	76										80																40
41	Ferrari F430 GT	97									40																	41
42	Porsche 997 GT3 RSR	80																										42
43	Lamborghini Murcielago	53																										43
44	Porsche 997 GT3 RSR	93								44																		44
45	Ferrari F430 GT	99							86	5																		45
46	Ferrari 550 Maranello	67							71																			46
47	Spyker C8 Spyder GT2R	85						81	9																			47
48	Panoz Esperante GTLM	81						29																				48
49	Spyker C8 Spyder GT2R	86				3																						49
50	Panoz Esperante GTLM	82				64																						50
51	Ferrari F430 GT	83																										51
52	Porsche 997 GT3 RSR	71		21																								52
53	Ferrari F430 GT	78		32																								53
54	Dome Mader S101-5	29		53																								54

KEY
LMP 1
LMP 2
LMGT 1
LMGT 2

FINAL STANDINGS

Pos	N.	Cat.	Car	Team	Drivers	Laps	Km/h	Best lap
1	1	LMP1	Audi R10 TDI	Audi Sport North America	Biela F./Pirro E./Werner M.	369	209.152	3:27.739
2	8	LMP1	Peugeot 908 Hdi FAP	Team Peugeot Total	Lamy P./Sarrazin S./Bourdais S.	359	203.473	3:27.633
3	16	LMP1	Pescarolo Judd	Pescarolo Sport	Collard E./Boullion J-C./Dumas R.	358	201.920	3:33.886
4	18	LMP1	Pescarolo Judd	Rollcentre Racing	Barbosa J./Hall S./Short M.	347	196.314	3:37.633
5	009	LMGT1	Aston Martin DBR9	Aston Martin Racing	Brabham D./Rydell R./Turner D.	343	193.741	3:49.641
6	63	LMGT1	Corvette C6.R	Corvette Racing	O'Connell J./Magnussen J./Fellows R.	342	193.491	3:50.929
7	008	LMGT1	Aston Martin DBR9	AMR Larbre Comp.	Bouchut C./Gollin F./Elgaard C.	341	192.757	3:49.504
8	15	LMP1	Lola B07/17 Judd	Charouz Racing	Charouz J./Mucke S./Yoong A.	338	190.898	3:32.945
9	007	LMGT1	Aston Martin DBR9	Aston Martin Racing	Enge T./Herbert J./Kox P.	337	191.011	3:48.969
10	54	LMGT1	Saleen S7R	Team Oreca	Groppi L./Prost N./Belloc J-P.	337	190.247	3:51.852
11	100	LMGT1	Aston Martin DBR9	AMR BMS	Babini F./Davies J./Malucelli M.	336	190.447	3:52.281
12	72	LMGT1	Corvette C6.R	Alphand Aventures	Policand J./Goueslard P./Alphand L.	327	184.535	3:55.445
13	17	LMP1	Pescarolo Judd	Pescarolo Sport	Primat H./Tinseau C./Treluyer B.	325	183.583	3:35.406
14	67	LMGT1	Ferrari 550 Maranello	Convers Menx Team	Vasiliev A./Kostka T./Pergl R.	322	182.119	4:01.593
15	76	LMGT2	Porsche 997 GT3 RSR	IMSA Performance	Narac R./Lietz R./Long P.	320	180.918	4:05.109
16	55	LMGT1	Saleen S7-R	Team Oreca	Ortelli S./Ayari S./Lapierre N.	318	180.244	3:51.148
17	59	LMGT1	Aston Martin DBR9	Team Modena	Garcia A./Menten J./Fittipaldi C.	318	180.096	3:53.449
18	31	LMP2	Lola B05/40 Zytek	Binnie Motorsports	Binnie B./Timpany A./Buncombe C.	318	179.613	3:48.312
19	99	LMGT2	Ferrari F430 GT	Risi Competizione	Krohn T./Jonsson N./Braun C.	314	177.161	4:08.187
20	19	LMP1	Lola B06/10 AER	Chamberlain Synergy	Evans G./Berridge B./Owen P.	310	175.131	3:42.471
21	93	LMGT2	Porsche 997 GT3 RSR	Autorlando Sport	Simonsen A./Nielsen L.E./Ehret P.	309	175.060	4:07.575
22	78	LMGT2	Ferrari F430 GT	AF Corse	Macari J./Aucott B./Newey A.	308	173.978	4:12.281
23	82	LMGT2	Panoz Esperante	Team LNT	Tomlinson L./Dean R./Bell R.	308	173.819	4:11.082
24	73	LMGT1	Corvette C5-R	Alphand Aventures	Blanchemain J-L./Vosse V./Andre D.	306	172.919	3:57.250
25	14	LMP1	Dome S101.5 Judd	Racing For Holland	Lammers J./Hart D./Bleekemolen J.	305	172.554	3:33.836
26	12	LMP1	Courage LC70 AER	Courage Competition	Frei A./Cochet J./Besson B.	305	172.105	3:34.469
27	33	LMP2	Zytek 07S/2	Barazi Epsilon	Fernandez A./Kurozawa H./Kerr R.	301	170.599	3:39.309
28	70	LMGT1	Corvette C6.R	PSI Experience	Smet D./Gosselin Cy./Peter Ph.	289	163.086	3:54.398
29	006	LMGT1	Aston Martin DBR9	AMR Larbre Comp.	Bornhauser P./Berville R./Fisken G.	272	153.444	4:01.000

Retirements

	N.	Cat.	Car	Team	Drivers	Laps	Km/h	Best lap
	7	LMP1	Peugeot 908 Hdi FAP	Team Peugeot Total	Gene M./Minassian N./Villeneuve J.	338	205.074	3:27.968
	2	LMP1	Audi R10 TDI	Audi Sport North America	Capello R./Kristensen T./McNish A.	262	215.963	3:27.176
	32	LMP2	Zytek 07S/2	Barazi Epsilon	Barazi J./Vergers M./Ojjeh K.	252	180.519	3:40.946
	83	LMGT2	Ferrari F430 GT	GPC Sport	Villaroel J./Rosenblad C./Marsh M.	252	165.874	4:09.371
	25	LMP2	MG Lola EX264 AER	RML	Erdos T./Newton M./Wallace A.	251	180.415	3:45.773
	87	LMGT2	Ferrari F430 GT	Scuderia Ecosse	Niarchos C./Kirkaldy A./Mullen T.	241	185.018	4:05.300
	35	LMP2	Courage LC75 AER	Saulnier Racing	Nicolet J./Filhol A./Jouanny B.	224	164.665	3:50.336
	97	LMGT2	Ferrari F430 GT	Risi Competizione	Salo M./Melo J./Mowlem J.	223	171.803	4:05.222
	24	LMP2	Courage LC75 AER	Noel Del Bello	Petrov V./Halliday L./Ianetta R.	198	153.811	3:47.280
	13	LMP1	Courage LC70 AER	Courage Competition	Gounon J-M./Moreau G./Johansson S.	175	171.943	3:37.576
	85	LMGT2	Spyker C8 Spyder GT2R	Spyker Squadron	Belicchi A./Caffi A./Chiesa A.	145	173.468	4:15.965
	40	LMP2	Lola B05/40 AER	Quifel ASM Team	Amaral M./De Castro M./Hughes W.	137	166.801	3:41.891
	20	LMP2	Pilbeam MP93 Judd	Pierre Bruneau	Rostan M./Pickering G./MacAllister C.	126	134.544	3:57.218
	80	LMGT2	Porsche 997 GT3 RSR	Flying Lizard Motorsport	Van Overbeek J./Bergmeister J./Neiman S.	124	177.686	4:03.821
	44	LMP2	Pescarolo Judd	Kruse Motorsport	Burgess T./De Pourtales J./Siedler N.	98	143.185	3:51.168
	86	LMGT2	Spyker C8 Spyder GT2R	Spyker Squadron	Janis J./Hezemans M./Kane J.	70	175.113	4:10.050
	71	LMGT2	Porsche 997 GT3 RSR	Seikel Motorsport	Collin P./Felbermayr H./Felbermayr H. Jr.	68	169.949	4:15.445
	5	LMP1	Lola Audi B07/10	Swiss Spirit	Deletraz J-D./Fassler M./Alexander I.	62	95.451	3:37.493
	81	LMGT2	Panoz Esperante	Team LNT	Kimber-Smith T./Watts D./Milner T.	60	151.369	4:10.417
	29	LMP2	Dome Mader S101-5	T2M Motorsport	Longechal R./Yamagishi Y./Terada Y.	56	141.430	4:01.305
	9	LMP1	Creation Judd CA07	Creation Autosportif Ltd	Campbell-Walter J./Ortiz F./Nakano S.	55	105.850	3:38.478
	3	LMP1	Audi R10 TDI	Audi Sport Team Joest	Luhr L./Premat A./Rockenfeller M.	23	205.799	3:33.229
	64	LMGT1	Corvette C6.R	Corvette Racing	Beretta O./Gavin O./Papis M.	22	188.186	3:55.136
	21	LMP2	Radical SR9 AER	Bruichladdich Radical	Greaves T./Moseley S./Liddell R.	16	195.340	3:48.884
	53	LMGT1	Lamborghini Murciélago	J-LOC	Isao N./Yogo A./Yamanishi K.	1		

The podium at Le Mans was logically made up of LMP1 entries, but the third place obtained by Pescarolo against the much faster diesel-powered cars fielded by Audi and Peugeot was a surprise.

Peugeot gets the lion's share

A truly impressive Le Mans Series line-up included for the first time Peugeot's diesel-powered
908 HDi FAP, but it was only a small step in the right direction, comments **Andrew Cotton**.
Series organisers had been hoping for a world class battle between Peugeot and Audi, but Audi
opted for the American market and the ALMS, leaving Peugeot to compete with Pescarolo,
Zytek, Creation and Lola. The French manufacturer won each of the first five races. Yet the
scoring system, coupled with officious pit lane marshals at Silverstone that hindered the series
leaders Pedro Lamy and Stéphane Sarrazin, meant that Pescarolo once again stood a chance
of winning his third successive title, at the final race, the Mil Milhas Brasil in November.
There were so many entries that organisers were forced to select a grid for the small
and inadequate Valencia circuit, though the remaining races boasted impressive
numbers, more than 40 cars at each event, and each class was well represented.

The LMP2 class did not have the complication of manufacturer involvement from Porsche and Acura, and was the richer for it. The season was closely contested between Lola, Zytek, Courage, Dome and Pescarolo, the title falling to the RML Lola of Tommy Erdos and Mike Newton, here at the Nürburgring, the only double-winner of the European season.

Peugeot's diesel-powered 908 HDi FAPs started each of the European races from pole position, like here in Monza, sometimes as much as three seconds faster than anyone else, and won each race too. There were problems with wheel bearings, a clutch at Valencia and bodywork damage at Silverstone, but Pedro Lamy and Stéphane Sarrazin led the standings prior to the inaugural Brazilian race in November.

Saleen's S7R was always considered to be the most competitive GT1 package, with a seven-litre V8 engine mid-mounted. Run by the multiple FIA GT, ALMS and Le Mans champions ORECA on Michelin tyres, the car dominated, winning four of the five European races on its way to the title. The car of leaders Stéphane Ortelli and Soheil Ayari is seen here at the Nürburgring.

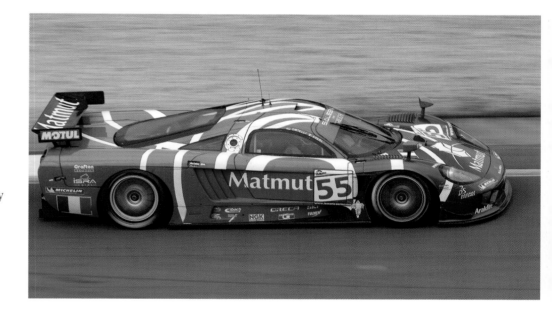

The GT2 battle went to Ferrari, completing a clean sweep for the Italian manufacturer in the ALMS, FIA GT Championship, and Le Mans Series. Robert Bell, here teamed up for the win with Gianmaria Bruni at Silverstone in the Virgo Motorsport-entered F430 GT, headed for the final round with a commanding lead in the drivers' standings.

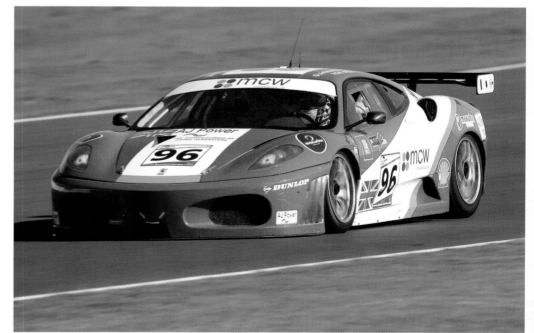

German technology dominates ALMS

Though Audi's R10 TDI still ruled the LMP1 field in 2007, the American Le Mans Series witnessed more manufacturer interest in LMP2 with competitive entries from Porsche and Acura, and a battle in GT2 between Porsche's new 997 GT3 RSR and Ferrari's F430 GT, reports **Andrew Cotton**.

The Sebring 12-Hours did little to quell expectations: Audi won overall, Acura's ARX-01a beat Penske's Porsche RS Spyder, and Ferrari and Porsche were separated in GT2 by two tenths of a second at the chequered flag. Yet there were undercurrents of trouble. Audi perceived that the LMP2 cars had an advantage and, despite winning again at St Petersburg, the R10 TDIs were defeated at the next eight races by Porsche. The R10 TDIs ran with an 81-litre fuel tank, down from 90 litres in 2006, had slower refuelling, and the IMSA refused to implement a five per cent reduction in air restrictor size for the LMP2 class. With a 150 kg weight advantage over the LMP1 Audis and a minimum weight of 775 kg, the LMP2s dominated on the often tight courses that characterised the series. Audi benefited from mid-season changes (a refuelling break and the air restrictor being eventually reduced for LMP2 from Lime Rock onwards), but the Penske team continued to win not only through speed, but also reliability. GT1 was a lonely place for the two Chevrolet Corvettes this year, joined only by the Team Modena Aston Martin at Sebring, and by a private Maserati MC12 from Road America onwards. The GT2 category saw Ferrari in dominant form.

At Mosport in Canada, Audi's McNish-Capello found themselves in the lead for much of the race before hitting gearbox problems ten minutes from the end. The double win went to the Porsche RS Spyders of Dumas-Bernhard and Maassen-Briscoe, seen here pulling away in the lead at the start. The smaller restrictor from Lime Rock onwards improved the Porsches' fuel consumption and did little to negate their competitiveness.

Audi's Allan McNish and Rinaldo Capello (pictured here at Mid-Ohio), put together a string of five LMP1 class wins from St Petersburg to Lime Rock in July, while teammates Emanuele Pirro and Marco Werner won at Sebring and twice more before the final round in Laguna Seca in October.

The GT classes of the American Le Mans Series could not have been more different. The GT2 category saw Ferrari in dominant form, winning eight of the first ten races with the Risi Competizione and Petersen White Lightning teams, while Porsche picked up the pieces of Ferrari in-fighting at Lime Rock and Mid-Ohio. Yet the GT1 class was the sole domain of the two Pratt and Miller Corvette C6.Rs for much of the year. The American team beat the Team Modena Aston Martin at Sebring, and were delighted to welcome back Maserati for the last five events, but it, too, was a privateer entry and could do nothing against the American muscle cars. Oliver Gavin and Olivier Beretta again had a magnificent season, winning seven of the first eight races, including this one at St. Petersburg.

Maserati retains its FIA GT crown

The FIA GT Championship is not afraid to try new things and that trend continued in 2007, reports **Andrew Cotton**. The Championship was the first to introduce success ballast, the first to develop a technically-based performance balancing system, the first to welcome the Maserati MC12, in 2006 introduced the GT3 regulations and in 2007 saw the arrival of GT4. It was the first year for two-hour races, with two compulsory driver changes, and the series led the drive to cut costs by introducing a limit on the number of tyres and brakes each weekend. In August, promoter and organiser Stéphane Ratel presented his plan to replace the existing GT cars with those built to GT3 regulations and continued his quest to become the first to have a World Championship for teams, and not for manufacturers. He is an ambitious man, but one who brings results; nine drivers, behind the wheels of Maseratis, Aston Martins and Corvettes, were separated by seven points with two races remaining.

The palace of former dictator Nicolae Ceaucescu was the centre piece of a stunning new circuit in Romania. The FIA GT Championship was the first international race series to visit the country in May, and nearly 70,000 spectators turned out in the rain to watch in awe as Maserati defeated Lamborghini, Aston Martin and Corvette. Although seventh in this particular race, Thomas Biagi headed the points table going into the season's finale at Zolder.

The epic Spa 24-Hours sits ill at ease with the two-hour format and cost-cutting regime that are new features of the series. This year's race was a classic, however, Marcel Fassler (teamed with Deletraz-Hezemans-Gollin) drove superbly behind the wheel of his Phoenix Racing Corvette to pressure the leading Maserati into a mistake in the wet less than two hours from the chequered flag.

Having won three races out of five for Peugeot, Stéphane Sarrazin and Pedro Lamy had a small lead in the drivers' championship going into the final LMS round at Interlagos.

Audi drivers Dindo Capello and Allan McNish celebrated their second ALMS title in a row by winning nine out of 12 races in the LMP1 class.

Maserati Vitaphone Racing Team driver Thomas Biagi took the FIA GT1 driver's title for the second time after his first win in 2003. Biagi's victory meant that Maserati collected all four titles on offer in the 2007 FIA GT championship (Drivers, Teams, Manufacturers and Citation Cup for gentlemen drivers).

LE MANS SERIES – DRIVER STANDINGS

Pos.	Driver	Car	Monza	Valencia	Nürburgring	Spa	Silverstone	Interlagos	Points
LMP1									
1	P. Lamy (P)	Peugeot 908 HDi	6	10	10	10	*		36
-	S. Sarrazin (F)	Peugeot 908 HDi	6	10	10	10	*		36
2	J-C. Boullion (F)	Pescarolo-Judd	8	4	6	8	8		34
3	E. Collard (F)	Pescarolo-Judd	8	/	6	8	8		30
4	M. Gene (E)	Peugeot 908 HDi	10	*	8	*	10		28
-	N. Minassian (F)	Peugeot 908 HDi	10	*	8	*	10		28
5	J. Barbosa (P)	Pescarolo-Judd	3	5	0	5	6		19
-	S. Hall (GB)	Pescarolo-Judd	3	5	0	5	6		19

* not classified
To be allocated points, a driver must drive at least 45 minutes during the race and a maximum of four hours

LMP2

	Driver	Car	
1	T. Erdos (BR)	MG Lola EX 264	36 points
-	M. Newton (GB)	MG Lola EX 264	36 points
2	M. Amaral (P)	Lola B05/40	30 points

LMGT1

	Driver	Car	
1	S. Ayari (F)	Saleen S7-R	40 points
-	S. Ortelli (MC)	Saleen S7-R	40 points
2	P. Goueslard (F)	Corvette C6.R	33 points

LMGT2

	Driver	Car	
1	R. Bell (GB)	Ferrari F430 GT	42 points
2	A. Simonsen (AUS)	Ferrari F430 GT	32 points
3	M. Lieb (D)	Porsche 997 GT3	29 points

LE MANS SERIES – TEAM STANDINGS

Pos.	Team	N.	Monza	Valencia	Nürburgring	Spa	Silverstone	Interlagos	Points
LMP1									
1	Team Peugeot Total	8	6	10	10	10	*		36
2	Pescarolo Sport	16	8	4	6	8	8		34
3	Team Peugeot Total	7	10	*	8	*	10		28
4	Rollcentre Racing	18	3	5	0	5	6		19
5	Charouz Racing System	15	0	8	5	2	*		15

LMP2

	Team	
1	RML	36 points
2	Quifel-ASM Team	30 points
3	Saulnier Racing	23 points

LMGT1

	Team	
1	Team Oreca	40 points
2	Luc Alphand Aventures	33 points
3	AMR Larbre Competition	30 points

LMGT2

	Team	
1	Virgo Motorsport	42 points
2	Team Felbermayr-Proton	29 points
3	GPC Sport	27 points

AMERICAN LE MANS SERIES – FINAL STANDINGS

Pos.	Driver	Car	SEB	STP	LB	HOU	SLC	LRP	M-O	ELK	MOS	DET	PLM	LS	Points
P1															
1	Dindo Capello	Audi R10 TDI	22	20	20	20	20	20	16	23	20	16	26	23	246
	Allan McNish	Audi R10 TDI	22	20	20	20	20	20	16	23	20	16	26	23	246
2	Marco Werner	Audi R10 TDI	26	16	16	16	16	10	20	19	16	20	16	19	210
3	Emanuele Pirro	Audi R10 TDI	26	16	16	16	16	10	20	19	16	20	0	0	175
4	Clint Field	Creation-Judd	19	13	13	13	13	16	8	0	0	0	0	0	95
5	Chris McMurry	Creation-Judd	16	0	10	0	0	13	10	13	13	0	14	0	89

P2

1	Romain Dumas (Porsche RS)	239 points
1	Timo Bernhard (Porsche RS)	239 points
2	Sascha Maassen (Porsche RS)	186 points
	Ryan Briscoe (Porsche RS)	186 points
3	Andy Wallace (Porsche RS)	128 points
	Butch Leitzinger (Porsche RS)	128 points

GT1

1	Oliver Gavin (Corvette C6.R)	246 points
1	Olivier Beretta (Corvette C6.R)	246 points
2	Jan Magnussen (Corvette C6.R)	184 points
	Johnny O'Connell (Corvette C6.R)	184 points
3	Max Papis (Corvette C6.R)	52 points

GT2

1	Mika Salo (Ferrari F430 GT)	202 points
1	Jaime Melo (Ferrari F430 GT)	202 points
2	Jörg Bergmeister (Porsche 911 GT3)	170 points
	J. Van Overbeek (Porsche 911 GT3)	170 points
3	Wolf Henzler (Porsche 911 GT3)	126 points

Key: SEB = Sebring 12-Hours; STP = St Petersburg; LB = Long Beach; HOU = Houston; SLC = Salt Lake City; LRP = Lime Rock Park;
M-O = Mid-Ohio; ELK = Elkhart lake; MOS = Mosport; DET = Detroit; PLM = Petit Le Mans; LS = Laguna Seca

FIA GT – FINAL STANDINGS

Pos.	Driver		ZHU	SIL	BUC	MZA	OSC	SPA	ADR	BRNO	NOG	ZOL	Points
GT1													
1	Thomas Biagi	Maserati MC12	3	10	3	5	10	14		2	8	6	61
2	Ryan Sharp	Aston Martin DBR9		5	5	10		5	10	8	4	10	57
	Karl Wendlinger	Aston Martin DBR9		5	5	10		5	10	8	4	10	57
3	Mike Hezemans	Corvette C6.R	4	8		6		18	4		10	5	55
	Jean-Denis Deletraz	Corvette C6.R	4	8		6		18	4		10	5	55
GT2													
1	Toni Vilander	Ferrari F430 GT	10	10	10	8	5		10	10		10	73
	Dirk Müller	Ferrari F430 GT	10	10	10	8	5		10	10		10	73
2	Stephane Ortelli	Ferrari F430 GT	8			10	10	8	8	8	10	4	66
	Gianmaria Bruni	Ferrari F430 GT	8			10	10	8	8	8	10	4	66
3	Matteo Malucelli	Porche 997 GT3 RSR		5	8		8	20	6	4	8	5	64
	Emmanuel Collard	Porche 997 GT3 RSR		5	8		8	20	6	4	8	5	64

GT1 Teams

	Teams	
1	Vitaphone Racing Team	115 points
2	Scuderia Playteam Sarafree	63 points
3	Jetalliance Racing	60 points

GT2 Teams

	Teams	
1	AF Corse Motorola	139 points
2	BMS Scuderia Italia	64 points
3	Scuderia Ecosse	60.5 points

GT1 Manufacturers

	Manufacturers	
1	Maserati	182.5 points
2	Corvette	115.5 points
3	Aston Martin	98 points
4	Lamborghini	32 points

GT2 Manufacturers

	Manufacturers	
1	Ferrari	251.5 points
2	Porsche	156.5 points

Key: ZHU = Zhuhai; SIL = Silverstone; BUC = Bucharest;
MZA = Monza; OSC = Oschersleben; SPA = Spa 24-Hours;
ADR = Adria; BRNO = Brno; NOG = Nogaro; ZOL = Zolder

BMW under assault

To win a world championship, you've got to be good. To win two, that puts
you in "all-time great" territory. So what should we call Andy Priaulx,
who was on course for his third successive World Touring Car Championship, asks **Charles Bradley**?
With two rounds remaining, Priaulx led the standings by 12 points from fellow BMW racer,
Augusto Farfus. With the series' success ballast system being as it is, it's unlikely that anyone
was going to close that gap, especially as the final round at Macau is one of Priaulx's favourites.
Once again, the Guernseyman concocted a perfect blend of speed and
racecraft to lead the all-action series from the front.
The competition was stronger than ever, with SEAT again fielding former British champions Yvan
Muller and Gabriele Tarquini, while Chevrolet had a two-time BTCC title-holder in Alain Menu and
former DTM champ Nicola Larini. Alfa Romeo had less factory support than ever, but that didn't stop
Brit James Thompson from winning races and also running in the top five in the standings.

Augusto Farfus proves the structural integrity of his BMW 320si after this last-ditch effort for pole position at the classic French street track of Pau ended in disastrous fashion. Apart from this imprudence at the famous Foch corner, the young Brazilian's switch from Alfa Romeo was impressive.

The 2005 and 2006 champion Andy Priaulx put in a very consistent performance over the season before the debacle at Monza. Used to millimetric cornering, as emblematically shown here at Pau, he went into the last race at another street circuit in Macau as the favourite.

Chevrolet was stronger than ever in 2007, and Alain Menu racked up multiple victories in the Lacetti. Here he negotiates one of the tricky chicanes at the Porto street track, the Portuguese venue making a popular debut on the WTCC schedule.

Seat and Alfa Romeo also took the fight to BMW, with the Spanish manufacturer resorting to diesel power in the middle of the season in an attempt to offset its straight-line speed deficit. Its TDI engines were immediately on the pace, with Yvan Muller scoring a landmark victory here at Oschersleben.

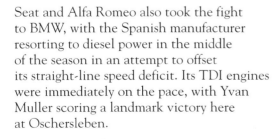

No love lost

From the very first lap of the season, this year's DTM was one of the most turbulent
since its rebirth eight years ago, reports **Charles Bradley**.
At the second corner of the inaugural race at Hockenheim, Tom Kristensen's innocent-looking spin
led to one of the series' biggest-ever pile-ups and landed him in hospital with serious concussion.
But even that sickening impact was rivalled by what happened at Barcelona,
for entirely different reasons. With the championship slipping away, Mercedes
appeared to allow its drivers to attack their Audi rivals with no holds barred.
Audi's series leaders Mattias Ekström and Martin Tomcyzk were harpooned off the track,
but Audi then made the situation even worse by retiring all its remaining cars to the pits,
with boos ringing out from the 40,000-strong crowd.
Audi said the decision was made because the tactics were "too rough". Quite whether
the series can survive such direct action, when only two manufacturers are taking part,
remains to be seen. The title still fell in Audi's lap after the final race, held again in Hockenheim.

Nürburgring. Bruno Spengler has carved himself out a place as Mercedes-Benz's DTM team leader in recent years, and led its line once again this season with some virtuoso race-winning performances. The Canadian was Mercedes' best title shot right up until the season's final laps at Hockenheim.

Audi and team leader Mattias Ekström, here pictured leading at Zandvoort, repeated their 2004 success. In Barcelona, the Swede was taken out by Mercedes' Daniel la Rosa, threatening his title bid before the season's finale, but in Hockenheim he managed to fend off rival Bruno Spengler in the closing stages to claim the crown.

The cockpit of the Audi A4 DTM car.

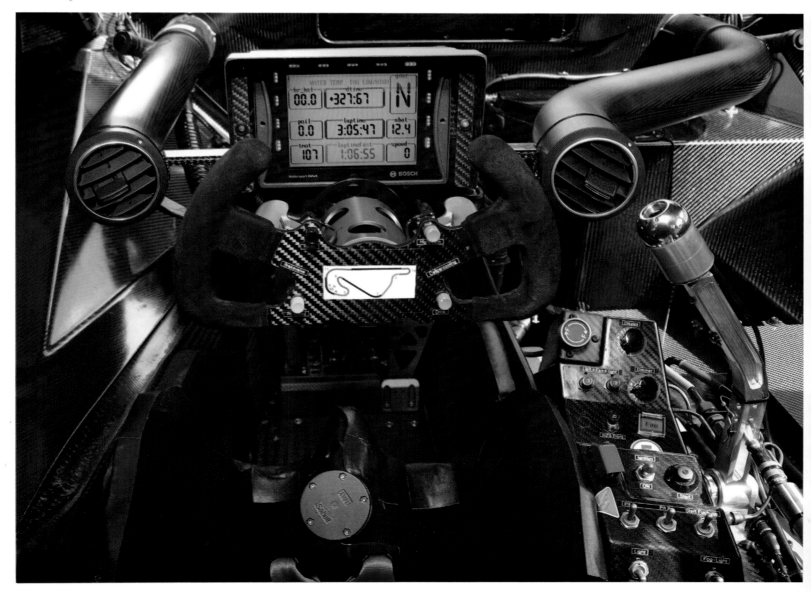

From strength to strength

The "Chase for the Cup" play-off system whereby the top 12 drivers after 26 races remain alone
with a points realignment to compete for the title made the destiny of the 2007 Nextel Cup somewhat
of a lottery, but there were plenty of other aspects making waves this year, notes **Charles Bradley**.
With the introduction of the all-new "Car of Tomorrow", NASCAR showed it could successfully change
the face of its age-old rulebook in the interests of safety without ruining the show.
The phased implementation of the new-look car (noticeably safer, less aerodynamic and cheaper to run)
meant that teams had to contend with parallel development programmes, but the superteams still ruled.
The biggest story of the year was fan favourite Dale Earnhardt Jr, who failed to make the Chase, bolting
from the family-run DEI team to join Chevy powerhouse Hendrick Motorsports next year. The arrival
of Juan Pablo Montoya gave NASCAR some worldwide credibility, and although he scored a race win on
a road course, he struggled to star on the ovals. He looks set to be joined by Indycar champion and Indy
500 winner Dario Franchitti and ex-World Champion Jacques Villeneuve next year.
The times, they are a changin'.

NASCAR hard man Tony Stewart pulled off a trademark move to steal victory away from Kevin Harvick in the Allstate 400 at the Brickyard. Indiana native Stewart's victory was followed by his traditional fence climb ritual, while Harvick was left complaining about the nature of Stewart's robust pass.

"And they're racing!" The Daytona 500 NASCAR Nextel Cup showpiece was led away at the start (left) by an all-Robert Yates Racing front row of David Gilliland and Ricky Rudd, but it was Kevin Harvick who came through with an unbelievable last corner manoeuvre that stole the victory from perennial bridesmaid Mark Martin.

Reigning champion Jimmie Johnson scored one of his six pre-Chase victories here at Martinsville. His title defence wasn't as impressive as his march to the crown last year, however, as he crashed out of the majors at Daytona and Indianapolis, both of which he won in 2006.

Ex-F1 star Juan Pablo Montoya races wheel-to-wheel with NASCAR hero Dale Earnhardt Jr at Sears Point. Montoya went on to score his maiden Nextel Cup victory here, aiding his domination of the Rookie of the Year standings. Earnhardt had such a miserable year that he quit his family-run team.

Andy Priaulx looked set to win his third WTCC title in a row with two races to go, but the penultimate round in Monza changed that: Yvan Muller made up a 14-point deficit during the Italian weekend and four other drivers still held a mathematical chance of taking the title going into the season's finale, in Macau.

Swedish driver Mattias Ekström had a superb season in DTM with Audi, becoming Champion for the second time despite only winning the opening round. Seven podium finishes in 10 races ultimately gave him a three-point advantage over Canadian rival Bruno Spengler.

With five races to go, all 12 drivers left competing in the "Chase for the Cup" still stood a chance of being crowned NASCAR Champion. Yet the two title favourites were 2006 winner Jimmie Johnson (right) and points leader Jeff Gordon (left).

WTCC – STANDINGS

Pos.	Driver	Car	Curitiba		Zandvoort		Valencia		Pau		Brno		Porto		Anderst.		Osch.		B. Hatch		Monza		Macau		Points
1	A. Priaulx (GB)	BMW	8	8	1	4	4	6	3	8	0	2	2	10	0	0	4	8	3	10	0	0			81
2	Y. Muller (F)	Seat	1	5	0	0	6	5	8	3	3	0	4	4	3	0	10	4	6	5	10	4			81
3	A. Farfus (BR)	BMW	6	10	4	8	0	0	2	10	5	8	0	3	0	1	2	10	0	0	2	0			71
4	J. Thompson (GB)	Alfa Romeo	0	0	0	0	10	10	0	2	0	4	0	0	6	4	6	5	8	2	6	6			69
5	J. Müller (D)	BMW	10	6	0	6	1	8	0	0	8	10	1	8	0	0	5	0	0	3	0	0			66
6	N. Larini (I)	Chevrolet	0	0	8	5	8	4	0	0	4	3	6	0	2	8	0	0	0	0	5	8			61
7	A. Menu (CH)	Chevrolet	0	0	10	0	0	0	10	1	1	0	10	6	1	6	0	0	10	0	4	0			59
8	G. Tarquini (I)	Seat	5	4	2	10	0	0	0	0	2	5	5	2	4	2	8	2	0	0	3	0			54
9	R. Huff (GB)	Chevrolet	4	0	0	0	0	0	5	5	0	0	8	0	10	0	0	3	4	6	1	5			51
10	J. Gené (E)	Seat	0	0	0	0	5	3	1	4	0	1	0	0	0	0	3	6	5	4	8	10			50

Pos.	Make		Curitiba		Zandvoort		Valencia		Pau		Brno		Porto		Anderst.		Osch.		B. Hatch		Monza		Macau		Points
1	BMW		18	18	10	14	7	14	7	18	18	18	7	18	5	5	9	18	5	18	5	5			237
2	Seat		10	11	8	14	11	8	14	10	9	9	11	9	13	10	18	10	11	9	18	14			227
3	Chevrolet		5	4	18	8	10	5	15	7	9	4	18	8	14	18	2	5	14	8	9	13			194
4	Alfa Romeo		0	5	3	3	11	12	3	4	3	7	3	3	7	6	9	5	9	4	7	7			111

DTM – FINAL STANDINGS

Pos.	Driver	Car	Hockenheim I	Oschersleben	Lausitzring*	Brands Hatch	Norisring	Mugello	Zandvoort	Nürburgring	Barcelona	Hockenheim II	Points
1	M. Ekström (S)	Audi	10	2	-	6	6	8	6	6	-	6	50
2	B. Spengler (CDN)	Mercedes-Benz	-	-	3	4	10	5	4	8	8	5	47
3	M. Tomczyk (D)	Audi	8	4	-	8	-	-	10	10	-	-	40
4	J. Green (GB)	Mercedes-Benz	3	-	1,5	3	3	-	-	4	10	10	34,5
5	P. di Resta (GB)	Mercedes-Benz	4	8	4	-	-	6	-	3	6	1	32
6	B. Schneider (D)	Mercedes-Benz	2	3	2,5	10	8	-	-	2	-	4	31,5
7	T. Scheider (D)	Audi	-	5	2	-	-	-	5	5	-	8	25
8	M. Häkkinen (SF)	Mercedes-Benz	-	-	5	5	5	10	2	-	-	-	22
9	G. Paffett (GB)	Audi	1	10	0,5	-	5	-	-	-	4	-	20,5
10	A. Margaritis (D)	Mercedes-Benz	5	1	-	-	2	-	1	-	5	2	16

Pos.	Team		Hockenheim I	Oschersleben	Lausitzring*	Brands Hatch	Norisring	Mugello	Zandvoort	Nürburgring	Barcelona	Hockenheim II	Points
1.	Audi Sport Team Abt Sportsline		18	6	-	14	6	8	16	16	-	6	90
2.	Originalteile/DC Bank AMG Mercedes		2	3	5,5	14	18	5	4	10	8	9	78,5
3.	Salzgitter/AMG Mercedes		3	-	6,5	8	3	10	2	4	10	10	56,5
4.	stern/Laureus AMG Mercedes		6	11	0,5	-	7	-	1	-	9	2	36,5
5.	Audi Sport Team Abt		-	5	2	-	4	1	5	6	-	11	34
6.	TV-Spielfilm/JAWA.de AMG Mercedes		4	8	4	-	-	6	-	3	6	1	32
7.	Audi Sport Team Phoenix		-	-	-	3	1	2	11	-	-	-	17
8.	TrekStor/Trilux AMG Mercedes		6	-	1	-	-	4	-	-	3	-	14
9.	Audi Sport Team Rosberg		-	6	-	-	-	3	-	-	3	-	12

* only half points were awarded due to steward errors

NASCAR – DRIVER STANDINGS

Pos.	Driver	Points	Starts	Poles	Wins	Top 5	Top 10	DNF	Winnings
1	Jeff Gordon	5880	31	9	6	19	25	1	$6,347,892
2	Jimmie Johnson	5812	31	3	6	16	19	4	$6,211,141
3	Clint Bowyer	5802	31	2	1	5	15	0	$3,745,944
4	Tony Stewart	5682	31	0	3	10	22	4	$5,718,671
5	Carl Edwards	5640	31	0	3	9	13	3	$3,981,112
6	Kyle Busch	5600	31	0	1	9	17	2	$4,057,943
7	Kurt Busch	5565	31	1	2	5	11	3	$4,499,906
8	Kevin Harvick	5552	31	0	1	4	12	0	$6,802,463
9	Denny Hamlin	5531	31	1	1	11	16	1	$4,335,789
10	Jeff Burton	5514	31	0	1	8	14	3	$5,321,013
11	Martin Truex Jr.	5502	31	0	1	6	11	3	$4,254,231
12	Matt Kenseth	5438	31	0	1	8	17	4	$5,261,499

Standings after 31 out of 36 races
Drivers beyond the 12th position are not contending for the Nextel Cup
Key: Pos.= Position; DNF= Did not finish

To the last tenth of a second

The 2007 World Rally Championship mirrored that of Formula 1 in that the outcome was never a foregone conclusion, reports **Keith Oswin**. Although it emerged that only two drivers were really capable of claiming the crown, Marcus Grönholm and Sébastien Loeb were rarely far enough apart for either to rest easy. Each played to their strengths as the season unfolded and with Ford and Citroën enjoying strong reliability throughout the year, this was a contest far more worthy of the name than in the past.

While Grönholm and Loeb fought it out for the crown, Ford's Mikko Hirvonen emerged as a future contender for the title with a string of podium finishes in support of Ford's retaining its manufacturers' crown. Victory on the inaugural Rally Norway was nothing less than he deserved.

Petter Solberg again struggled to reacquaint himself with the podium but the latest Subaru was clearly better than the one it replaced. However it was Australia's Chris Atkinson that proved the more adept at taming the wild beast, rewarded with a renewed contract for future campaigns.

Aside from the chase for the title, 2007 was the year in which Suzuki entered the top flight with its first ever World Rally Car, Grönholm announced his retirement from rallying while at the top of his game, and the sport was stunned by the death in September in a helicopter crash of former champion Colin McRae, and his young son Johnny.

2007 will be remembered for the battle between Ford's Marcus Grönholm and Citroën's Sébastien Loeb. Loeb won in Monte-Carlo with the new C4, dispelling suggestions that the car would suffer from teething problems. The duel came to a head in New Zealand where Loeb lost out on the final forest stage as Grönholm claimed victory by just 0.3 seconds – the smallest winning margin in WRC history.

Mikko Hirvonen proved a more than capable
second driver at Ford, winning in Norway and
maintaining Ford's bid for a second Manufacturer title
throughout the season with solid podium finishes.

The flamboyant Italian Gigi Galli flies his private
Citroën Xsara in Norway but his season faltered
through lack of finance, robbing the series of one
of its greatest and most likeable characters.

Subaru had a desperate season in 2006, and hoped
to put it all behind them but Petter Solberg's season
(here in Mexico) was only marginally better than last.
Nevertheless he signed a new contract to stay with the team

After the Rally Mexico (won by Loeb, illustrated on
the following double page) Portugal was one of three
new events for the 2007 series. Loeb passes through
a tiny Algarve village as he pushes the C4 WRC to
another victory. With Grönholm only fourth, this
was a useful points haul for the Frenchman.

Here Marcus Grönholm discovers the tricky
nature of the roads of Portugal on his way
to a disappointing fourth place.

Ford turned the screw on Citroën's title hopes with victory for Marcus Grönholm in Sardinia. Second place for Mikko Hirvonen put clear air between Ford and Citroën – a vital bit of breathing space.

Mistakes by Sébastien Loeb are always rare but when they happen they are costly. Rallye Sardinia ended with a wrecked car while his Ford rivals claimed a 1-2 result. The turning point?

Petter Solberg showed he was not down and out when he claimed third place at the Acropolis Rally in Greece. The Subaru literally flew on the toughest event of the year but victory was seemingly still a long way away for the embattled Norwegian former champion.

Dani Sordo emerged during the season as a solid
team-mate to Citroën number one, Sébastien Loeb.
In October's asphalt events in Spain (Rally RACC
Catalunya, pictured) and France (Tour de Corse)
the Spaniard drove superbly to assist Loeb
and keep his challengers at bay, notably
with his second place on home soil.

Sébastien Loeb isn't used to being challenged
but Belgium's Francois Duval actually led after the opening
day of the ADAC Rally in Germany in this private Citroën
Xsara until Loeb restored order to claim his sixth win.

New Zealand. Australian driver Chris Atkinson continued
to impress with his growing confidence in the Subaru.
Indeed he managed to outpace his team leader
on several occasions and will be staying for the future.

Suzuki made its World Rally Car debut in Corsica although the SX4 suffered a string of teething troubles. In the end Nicolas Bernardi brought the newcomer home in 31st place with some top 10 times on the final day to give the Japan-based team an idea of the winter work needed.

Sébastien Loeb went into the Catalunya (pictured) and Corsica rallies knowing that anything other than back-to-back victories would be a disaster for his title plans. He need not have worried as he duly romped home on both rounds to close the gap to Marcus Grönholm to just four points.

Ford Focus WRC

Though the emphasis of the 2007 World Rally Championship has centred mostly on the title fight between Marcus Grönholm and Sébastien Loeb, the battle between manufacturers raged equally fiercely, reports **Keith Oswin**.

With regard to the team line-up for 2007, little had changed at the front of the pack since the previous season. Ford and Subaru were still in the field and the only major difference was that Citroën had returned in an official capacity with the new C4 The regulations remained more or less the same (300-hp engines and a 1230 kg minimum weight limit in race trim). The rule that stated that engines had to last two successive races was, however, dropped in favour of a system whereby each car was allocated six engines per season. Each contestant could race up to 10 different chassis. The second string teams looked somewhat different, however. Out went Skoda once more leaving the supporting cast to comprise the OMV-backed Kronos team to run last year's Xsara for (mainly) Manfred Stohl and two privateer Ford teams including a returning Stobart-VK squad and the South American Munchi's outfit. Although the "official" teams still had to enter two cars for each event this requirement was quietly dropped for the minor teams in 2007.

FORD

Ford started its 2007 campaign as reigning Manufacturer champions after securing the 2006 title in a tense shoot out with Citroën in the closing events of the year.

The Blue Oval opened the season with the same car with which it ended the previous one, but behind the scenes Christian Loriaux was hard at work designing the new version of the Focus that would replace the '06 variant in Finland at the start of the second half of the year. Indeed, Ford's 2007 mount was quite an old hand at the WRC having been introduced in Australia on the last event of the 2005 season.

In 2006 the main reason why Marcus Grönholm was unable to add the Drivers' crown to Ford's team title was a lack of consistency – partly of his own doing and partly

Marcus Grönholm

Mikko Hirvonen

Malcolm Wilson, *team manager*

because the car let him down occasionally. In 2007 Ford worked hard to ensure the car delivered every time and by the mid-season break Grönholm had secured three wins, three seconds, a third and a fourth to lead the series.

With Mikko Hirvonen never out of the top five either, this was a team performance far better than in 2006 and formed the cornerstone of Ford's attack in 2007.

The Focus WRC is now a well-established car having first debuted on the championship (amid considerable controversy surrounding the legality of some of its components) in 1999. Since then the Focus has evolved from a fairly "standard" looking WRC campaigner into one of the most aggressively-styled examples on the startline, doubtless as a result of Ford poaching Belgian designer Christian Loriaux from Subaru where a car's appearance is equally as important as its performance.

The '06 version of the car differs from previous models in that the transmission is supplied from Ricardo instead of the ubiquitous Xtrac. The overall dimensions are shorter and wider than the cars used before but the longer wheelbase gives the Focus great stability and that may have been a key to its performance in the first half of 2007.

Amongst privateer teams, Stobart-VK Ford returned but Matthew Wilson was unregistered in 2007 to take away the pressure while his team-mates Jari-Matti Latvala and Henning Solberg were left to score points on a fairly regular basis with the 2006-specification Focus. A second Ford team, the Munchi's squad from Argentina, was also run by M-Sport for Federico Villagra and Luis Perez-Companc. It took a while for them to get onto the score sheet but the Argentine drivers samba'd their way into the top places by mid-season, again using last year's Focus to reasonable effect.

Citroën C4 WRC

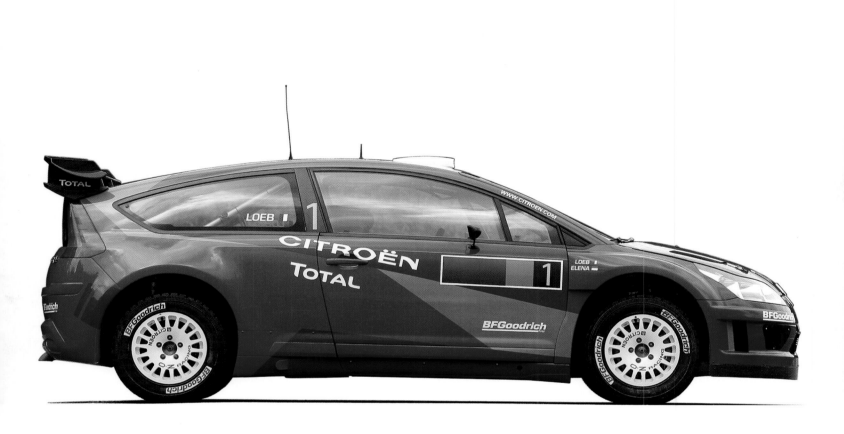

CITROËN

Having taken a sabbatical from the sport in 2006 and handed the reins of its motor sport programme to Kronos, Citroën Sport returned in an official capacity for the 2007 season with the brand new C4 model. Just getting the latest saloon/hatchback into international motor sport required some major re-engineering, not least because the sleek road car had been designed with a glass roof – something emphatically banned for rallying for obvious safety reasons.

The C4 is longer than the Xsara it replaces, and is therefore permitted also to be wider, further enhancing the essential stability of the car. Without some of the exotic electronic traction aids employed by the Xsara until they were outlawed at the start of 2006, this was a key element in making the C4 competitive. Remarkably, however, with the exception of the monstrous rear wing attached to the trailing edge

Sébastien Loeb

Dani Sordo

Guy Fréquelin, team manager

of the roof, the C4 retains closer visual links to the road car variant than most other WRCs in the pack at present. Triple champion Sébastien Loeb retains the role of "team captain" whilst team principal Guy Fréquelin settled on Dani Sordo as his team-mate, thereby injecting some much needed stability into the line-up, the absence of which may have been instrumental in Citroën losing the Manufacturers' title to Ford last year.

Loeb's crushing win in Monte-Carlo on the C4's debut shattered the pre-season speculation that the new car may suffer teething troubles. More victories followed but off-road excursions by the Frenchman in Norway and Sardinia flung the door open for his title rivals to step in and head the points by mid season.

When the FIA announced that the controversial one-make tyre contract for 2008-2010 was to be awarded to Pirelli,

Fréquelin immediately warned that Citroën's continued participation may be in doubt given that the company has a time-honoured link to French company Michelin (now competing under the BFGoodrich name). It is far from sure that his comments were anything more than mischievous speculation but nevertheless they served to underline the still-fragile state of the WRC…

In theory the 2006 Xsaras run by Kronos should have remained in close contact, but it wasn't such a clear cut thing once the season unfolded. Manfred Stohl put in some solid drives but by mid-year was clearly frustrated with the car's performance and considered it worse than the two-season old Peugeot he had campaigned last year. Yet tarmac specialist François Duval's fine second place in Germany showed that the Xsara still had some performance to boast.

Subaru Impreza WRC

SUBARU

Rule changes introduced for 2006 with regard to pairing of engines and other components meant that Subaru's usual ploy of introducing a new car a few events into the season had to be shelved. Whether this forced the team to introduce the 2006 Impreza earlier than planned is unclear but what was patently obvious was that the car was struggling to be even remotely competitive.

Beaten on several occasions by privateers, and easily so on occasion, the team's continued participation in the WRC came under question during the year.

Although Subaru entered the 2007 campaign with the old car (and scored points in each of the opening three events) it was able to launch the next version by Mexico. Pairing rules for 2006 were again changed for 2007, thereby allowing

Petter Solberg

Chris Atkinson

Richard Taylor, team manager

Subaru to do this. While fortune didn't smile on Petter Solberg and Chris Atkinson it was clear that the Impreza was heading towards competitiveness once more.

The main improvements were made in the areas of weight distribution, suspension geometry and differential set-ups, while the WRC2007 also featured new dampers plus a different radiator and intercooler arrangement compared to its predecessor.

Almost immediately it was clear that the car had shed some of its nightmare handling characteristics although there was still some way to go before we saw the iconic blue cars topping the time sheets in Greece for a few stages. Various personnel changes took place in order to stem the haemorrhaging of performance, most notably the return of technical director David Lapworth to identify and resolve the issues that had cost the team so much face.

The Impreza variant is now the oldest WRC campaigner in the pack. Introduced for the Monte-Carlo Rally of 1997, at the start of the World Rally Car era, it has been a tremendous success story and has survived largely through a process of evolution rather than revolution. Outwardly any changes appear to be cosmetic, as much a part of the processes employed to keep road cars fresh than for any competition reason, although beneath the skin there has been extensive development work over the years.

The next generation Impreza should be the most radical yet as the car will be more of a hatchback style than the current saloon model and it might just be the catalyst for Subaru to bounce back to the head of the pack once more.

MONTE-CARLO

Rallye Automobile Monte-Carlo · 18 – 21 January
Terrain: Asphalt
15 stages covering 328.54 km in a route of 1,185.02 km.

Pos.	Driver	Group	Time	Gap
1	S. Loeb	A	3:10:27.4	
2	D. Sordo	A	3:11:05.6	38.02
3	M. Grönholm	A	3:11:50.2	1.22.08
4	C. Atkinson	A	3:12:55.5	2.28.01
5	M. Hirvonen	A	3:12:55.7	2.28.03
6	P. Solberg	A	3:13:39.4	3.12.00
7	T. Gardemeister	A	3:14:05.5	3.38.01
8	J. Kopecky	A	3:15:06.8	4.39.04
...				
17	O. Burri	N	3:32:56.6	22.29.02

SWEDEN

Uddeholm Swedish Rally · 09 – 11 February
Terrain: Snow
20 stages covering 341.20 km in a route of 1,730.36 km.

Pos.	Driver	Group	Time	Gap
1	M. Grönholm	A	3:08:40.7	
2	S. Loeb	A	3:09:34.5	53.08
3	M. Hirvonen	A	3:10:22.2	1.41.05
4	H. Solberg	A	3:10:50.5	2.09.08
5	D. Carlsson	A	3:12:18.5	3.37.08
6	T. Gardemeister	A	3:12:34.9	3.54.02
7	M. Stohl	A	3:13:53.2	5.12.05
8	C. Atkinson	A	3:14:55.4	6.14.07
...				
16	O. Svedlund	N	3:25:29.2	16.48.05

NORWAY

Rally Norway · 15 – 18 February
Terrain: Snow
18 stages covering 358.72 km in a route of 1,127.62 km.

Pos.	Driver	Group	Time	Gap
1	M. Hirvonen	A	3:28:17.0	
2	M. Grönholm	A	3:28:26.5	9.05
3	H. Solberg	A	3:32:01.6	3.44.06
4	P. Solberg	A	3:32:18.1	4.01.01
5	J. Latvala	A	3:33:47.7	5.30.07
6	G. Galli	A	3:35:22.2	7.05.02
7	D. Carlsson	A	3:37:40.7	9.23.07
8	J. Kopecky	A	3:40:06.9	11.49.09
...				
11	P. Flodin	N	3:43:03.6	14.46.06

MEXICO

Corona Rally Mexico · 09 – 11 March
Terrain: Gravel
20 stages covering 366.06 km in a route of 849.55 km.

Pos.	Driver	Group	Time	Gap
1	S. Loeb	A	3:48:13.3	
2	M. Grönholm	A	3:49:09.1	55.08
3	M. Hirvonen	A	3:49:41.0	1.27.07
4	D. Sordo	A	3:49:57.0	1.43.07
5	C. Atkinson	A	3:50:37.4	2.24.01
6	M. Stohl	A	3:51:58.8	3.45.05
7	J. Latvala	A	3:52:24.1	4.10.08
8	M. Wilson	A	4:00:35.9	12.22.06
...				
10	M. Higgins	N	4:08:44.5	20.31.02

PORTUGAL

Rally de Portugal · 30 March – 01 April
Terrain: Gravel
18 stages covering 357.10 km in a route of 1,009.31 km.

Pos.	Driver	Group	Time	Gap
1	S. Loeb	A	3:53:33.1	
2	P. Solberg	A	3:56:47.0	3.13.09
3	D. Sordo	A	3:58:38.4	5.05.03
4	M. Grönholm	A	3:59:10.2	5.37.01
5	M. Hirvonen	A	4:00:41.2	7.08.01
6	D. Carlsson	A	4:01:46.3	8.13.02
7	G. Galli	A	4:03:12.7	9.39.06
8	J. Latvala	A	4:04:18.0	10.44.09
...				
16	P. Flodin	N	4:26:41.1	33.08.00

ARGENTINA

Rally Argentina · 04 – 06 May
Terrain: Gravel
21 stages covering 336.55 km in a route of 1,383.14 km.

Pos.	Driver	Group	Time	Gap
1	S. Loeb	A	2:52:03.8	
2	M. Grönholm	A	2:52:40.5	36.07
3	M. Hirvonen	A	2:54:19.0	2.15.02
4	J. Latvala	A	2:55:46.8	3.43.00
5	H. Solberg	A	2:56:13.9	4.10.01
6	D. Sordo	A	2:56:27.4	4.23.06
7	C. Atkinson	A	2:56:47.2	4.43.04
8	M. Stohl	A	2:57:24.0	5.20.02
...				
10	T. Arai	N	3:09:03.0	16.59.02

ITALY

Rally d'Italia Sardegna · 18 – 20 May
Terrain: Gravel
18 stages covering 342.86 km in a route of 1,061.84 km.

Pos.	Driver	Group	Time	Gap
1	M. Grönholm	A	3:48:42.0	
2	M. Hirvonen	A	3:49:11.2	29.2
3	D. Sordo	A	3:50:03.8	1:21.8
4	H. Solberg	A	3:50:18.6	1:36.6
5	P. Solberg	A	3:51:16.2	2:34.2
6	T. Gardemeister	A	3:53:44.1	5:02.1
7	M. Stohl	A	3:54:10.6	5:28.6
8	J. Hanninen	A	3:58:13.7	9:31.7
...				
15	G. Manfrinato	N	4:20:23.1	31:41.1

GREECE

Acropolis Rally of Greece · 01 – 03 June
Terrain: Gravel
23 stages covering 334.44 km in a route of 1,572.33 km.

Pos.	Driver	Group	Time	Gap
1	M. Grönholm	A	3:49:22.6	
2	S. Loeb	A	3:50:01.2	38.06
3	P. Solberg	A	3:50:56.7	1.34.01
4	M. Hirvonen	A	3:52:03.9	2.41.03
5	H. Solberg	A	3:54:15.3	4.52.07
6	C. Atkinson	A	3:55:54.3	6.31.07
7	J. Kopecky	A	3:57:38.4	8.15.08
8	M. Stohl	A	3:58:18.8	8.56.02
...				
15	T. Arai	N	4:10:08.9	20.46.03

FINLAND

Neste Oil Rally Finland · 03 – 05 August
Terrain: Gravel
23 stages covering 360.34 km in a route of 1,375.15 km.

Pos.	Driver	Group	Time	Gap
1	M. Grönholm	A	2:57:26.1	
2	M. Hirvonen	A	2:57:50.3	24.02
3	S. Loeb	A	2:58:36.0	1.09.09
4	C. Atkinson	A	3:00:28.9	3.02.08
5	H. Solberg	A	3:01:55.5	4.29.04
6	X. Pons	A	3:04:26.6	7.00.05
7	U. Aava	A	3:05:05.7	7.39.06
8	M. Östberg	A	3:06:58.0	9.31.09
...				
15	P. Flodin	N	3:18:01.8	20.35.07

GERMANY

ADAC Rallye Deutschland · 17 – 19 August
Terrain: Asphalt
19 stages covering 356.27 km in a route of 1,227.04 km.

Pos.	Driver	Group	Time	Gap
1	S. Loeb	A	3:27:27.5	
2	F. Duval	A	3:27:47.8	20.03
3	M. Hirvonen	A	3:28:46.6	1.19.01
4	M. Grönholm	A	3:29:04.0	1.36.05
5	J. Kopecký	A	3:30:34.6	3.07.01
6	P. Solberg	A	3:30:42.2	3.14.07
7	T. Gardemeister	A	3:31:05.0	3.37.05
8	J. Latvala	A	3:32:56.8	5.29.03
...				
19	J. Van Den Heuvel	N	3:56:50.7	29.23.02

NEW ZEALAND

Rally New Zealand · 31 August – 2 September
Terrain: Gravel
18 stages covering 353.56 km in a route of 1,255.98 km.

Pos.	Driver	Group	Time	Gap
1	M. Grönholm	A	3:52:53.9	
2	S. Loeb	A	3:52:54.2	0.03
3	M. Hirvonen	A	3:54:36.7	1.42.08
4	C. Atkinson	A	3:55:26.2	2.32.03
5	J. Latvala	A	3:55:30.8	2.36.09
6	D. Sordo	A	3:56:35.9	3.42.00
7	P. Solberg	A	3:56:48.6	3.54.07
8	U. Aava	A	4:02:10.2	9.16.03
...				
13	T. Arai	N	4:13:35.8	20.41.09

SPAIN

Rally RACC Catalunya · 05 – 07 October
Terrain: Asphalt
18 stages covering 352.87 km in a route of 1,359.96 km.

Pos.	Driver	Group	Time	Gap
1	S. Loeb	A	3:22:50.5	
2	D. Sordo	A	3:23:04.3	13.08
3	M. Grönholm	A	3:23:30.3	39.08
4	M. Hirvonen	A	3:24:16.3	1.25.08
5	F. Duval	A	3:25:19.2	2.28.07
6	P. Solberg	A	3:25:44.6	2.54.01
7	J. Latvala	A	3:26:28.7	3.38.02
8	C. Atkinson	A	3:27:12.9	4.22.04
...				
19	A. Aigner	N	3:45:30.1	22.39.06

FRANCE

Rallye De France - Tour De Corse · 12 – 13 October
Terrain: Asphalt
16 stages covering 359.32 km in a route of 1,117.20 km.

Pos.	Driver	Group	Time	Gap
1	S. Loeb	A	3:28:31.5	
2	M. Grönholm	A	3:28:55.2	23.07
3	D. Sordo	A	3:29:15.8	44.03
4	J. Latvala	A	3:31:02.0	2.30.05
5	P. Solberg	A	3:31:13.6	2.42.01
6	C. Atkinson	A	3:32:25.3	3.53.08
7	J. Kopecky	A	3:36:34.4	8.02.09
8	X. Pons	A	3:38:05.7	9.34.02
...				
10	D. Solá	N	3:46:29.1	17.57.06

Marcus Grönholm (left) or Sébastien Loeb? The fantastic competition between the two rally greats will sadly end with the Flying Finn's retirement at the end of the 2007 season. With three rounds yet to go, he held a narrow four-point margin over his French rival.

WRC STANDINGS AFTER 13 ROUNDS (OUT OF 16)

Pos.	Drivers' WRC	Monte-Carlo	Sweden	Norway	Mexico	Portugal	Argentina	Italy	Greece	Finland	Germany	New Zealand	Spain	France	Japan	Ireland	Great Britain	Points
1	Marcus Grönholm (SF)	6	10	8	8	5	8	10	10	10	5	10	6	8				104
2	Sébastien Loeb (F)	10	8	0	10	10	10	-	8	6	10	8	10	10				100
3	Mikko Hirvonen (SF)	4	6	10	6	4	6	8	5	8	6	6	5	0				74
4	Daniel Sordo (E)	8	0	0	5	6	3	6	0	-	-	3	8	6				45
5	Petter Solberg (N)	3	-	5	-	8	-	4	6	-	3	2	3	4				38
6	Chris Atkinson (AUS)	5	1	0	4	-	2	0	3	5	0	5	1	3				29
7	Henning Solberg (N)	0	5	6	0	0	4	5	4	4	0	0	0	0				28
8	Jari-Matti Latvala (SF)	-	-	4	2	1	5	0	0	-	1	4	2	5				24
9	François Duval (B)								-		8		4	-				12
10	Jan Kopecky (CZ)	1	0	1		0		-	2	-	4		-	2				10
11	Toni Gardemeister (SF)	2	3	-		-		3			2							10
12	Daniel Carlsson (S)		4	2		3		-										9
13	Manfred Stohl (A)	0	2	0	3	0	1	2	1	-	-	0	-	0				9
14	Gigi Galli (I)		0	3	2													5
15	Xavier Pons (E)		-	0		0				3	0	-	0	1				4
16	Urmo Aava (EE)		0	0		0		0	0	2	0		1	0	-			3
17	Mads Ostberg (N)		0	0						1								1
18	Matthew Wilson (GB)	0	0	0	1	0	0	0	0	0	0	0	0	-				1
19	Juho Hanninen (SF)						0	1		-			0	0				1
20	Guy Wilks (GB)								0	0	0							0

Pos.	Manufacturers' WRC	Monte-Carlo	Sweden	Norway	Mexico	Portugal	Argentina	Italy	Greece	Finland	Germany	New Zealand	Spain	France	Japan	Ireland	Great Britain	Points
1	BP-Ford World Rally Team	10	16	18	14	9	14	18	15	18	11	16	11	9				179
2	Citroën Total WRT	18	9	1	15	16	13	6	8	6	10	11	18	16				147
3	Subaru WRT	8	2	5	4	8	2	5	9	5	5	7	4	7				71
4	Stobart VK M-Sport Ford RT	1	5	10	3	2	9	7	4	4	5	5	2	7				64
5	OMV Kronos Citroën WRT	2	7	5	3	4	1	3	2	-	8	0	4	0				39
6	Munchi's Ford WRT		0		0		0	0	1	5			0	0				6

Pos.	Production WRC	Monte-Carlo	Sweden	Norway	Mexico	Portugal	Argentina	Italy	Greece	Finland	Germany	New Zealand	Spain	France	Japan	Ireland	Great Britain	Points
1	Toshi Arai (J)		3		8		8		10			10						39
2	Mark Higgins (GB)		-	10					5									15
3	Kristian Sohlberg (SF)		6	6		-		-										12

RALLYING :: **LISBON-DAKAR**

So near
and yet so far...

When the teams lined up in Lisbon for the start of the 2007
Lisbon-Dakar marathon there was little doubt that Mitsubishi
was the clear favourite for victory, **Keith Oswin** reports.
With 11 wins behind it and an unbroken run of success
since 2001, the "red team" was riding the crest of a wave.

However, over recent seasons relative newcomers
Volkswagen with its diesel-powered Race Touareg had
been making inroads into Mitsubishi's dominance.

Right from the start it seemed that the 2007 edition of the event
might just see a shock result. VW led from the opening superspecial,
initially with Carlos Sousa and soon afterwards with former
World Rally Champion Carlos Sainz, who took over the lead
for three stages. When Sainz slipped back the baton was passed
to a third VW driver, Giniel de Villiers, and as the event headed into
the ninth stage everything was looking good for the "blue team".

And then it all went wrong.

De Villiers suffered a terminal engine failure and Sainz slid out
of contention with major electrical problems. And as the VW dream
died in the sand, so Stéphane Peterhansel was on hand to take
over the lead and do little more than cruise through the final five
stages to record another win for Mitsubishi. Peterhansel ended the
event 7m 26s ahead of team-mate Luc Alphand and the buggy
of Dakar veteran Jean-Louis Schlesser. The highest placed VW
at the finish was that of American driver Mark Miller in fourth...

If nothing else the 2007 result may yet prove to be a final
chapter for the Japanese camp as there are signs that they
may adopt a similar environmental policy to VW
and design a diesel-powered Pajero for the 2008 edition.
Maybe the playing field will become a little more level but,
even so, Mitsubishi knew it had been in a fight this year.

Stéphane Peterhansel brought Mitsubishi its
seventh successive Dakar victory but, although
his winning margin seemed comfortable at the
finish, he only inherited the lead after the VWs
hit problems as the event moved into the closing
stages. Nevertheless, Peterhansel proved the
master of steering clear of trouble and eventually
cruised home to win by over seven minutes.

With 12 Dakar wins behind it there is no question that
Mitsubishi knows how to build a winning car. This
cutaway drawing shows that one of the key elements is the
suspension arrangement with twin shock absorbers at each
corner to soak up the demands imposed by over two weeks
racing across one of the most hostile terrains on the planet.
The car also has a fully adjustable damping and anti-roll
bar system. The roads vary from rock-strewn battlegrounds
to the deep soft sand that requires around 250 mm of
suspension travel to keep the four driven wheels working to
push the car onward, hence the use of independent, double-
wishbone coil spring set-ups. To help the car stop quickly
each 16-inch wheel encompasses a ventilated brake disc
with six-piston calipers and to ensure the Pajero covers the
vast distances driven each day it is fitted with a 500-litre
fuel tank (around 10 times that of a standard car) which
adds 400 kilos of weight to the car when full but gives a
range of around 800 km. The car also carries a rack of spare
wheels in the rear to effectively deal with the inevitable
punctures that would otherwise wreck a winning dream.

Joan "Nani" Roma presses on through the palm trees
towards a 13th place finish, the last of the official
Mitsubishis over the finish line. A low-speed roll in
the Mauritanian desert and a close encounter with
a tree stump which caused him a broken thumb on
the penultimate stage forced him out of contention.

Formation flying on the road from Zouerat to Atar! Carlos
Sainz's VW Touareg and Robbie Gordon's Hummer take
to the air over a trans-Sahara railway line. The American
finished eighth, one place ahead of the Spaniard.

Qatari driver Nasser Al Attiyah led home the BMW
challenge in sixth place. The reigning Production Car
World Rally Champion was running as high as fourth
at one point proving that experience doesn't always count
on the Dakar, but a sensitive driving style works just as well.

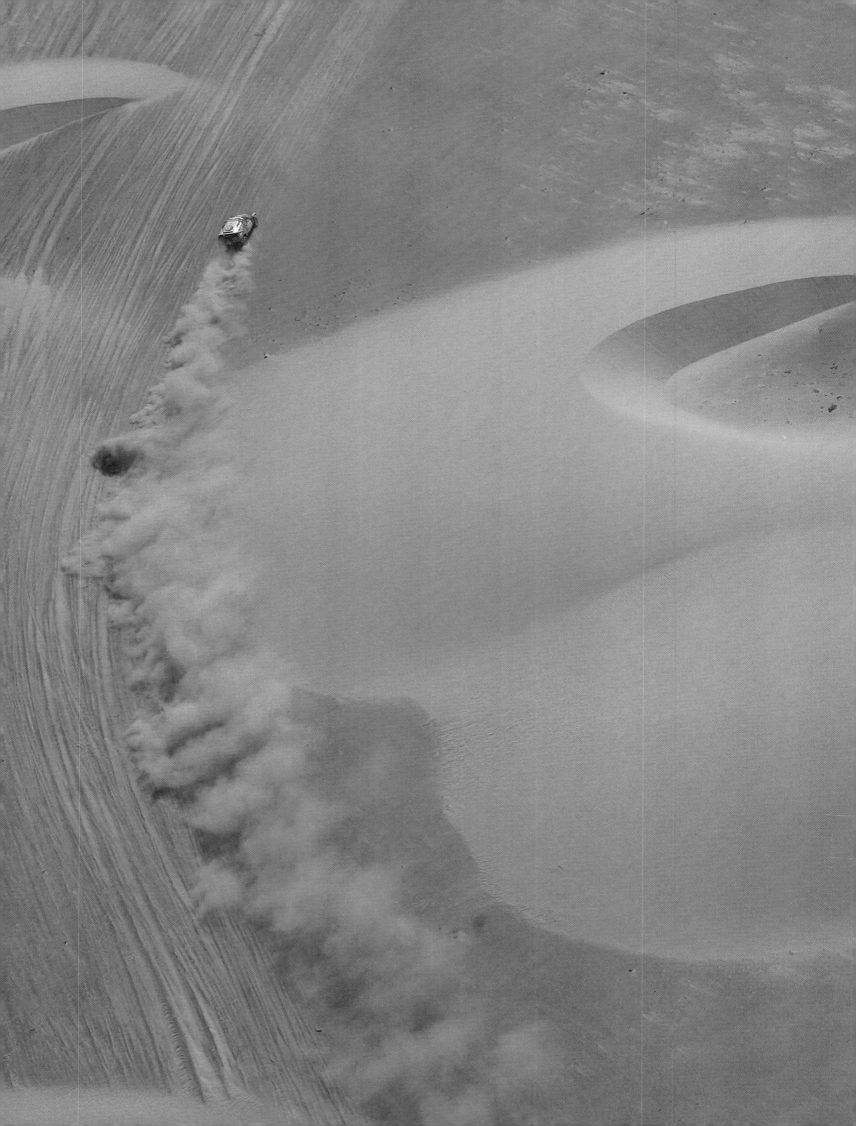

Jean-Louis Schlesser is a Dakar veteran and managed to add a couple of stage wins to his tally this year en-route to third overall behind the Mitsubishis. The Schlesser buggy is a familiar sight among the dunes.

Co-driver Jack Boyère gives driver Simon Jean-Joseph a push when their buggy gets stuck in soft sand atop a dune on the drive from Atar to Tichit. Sadly one-man-drive wasn't enough and the duo retired from the event on this stage.

Carlos Sainz gets a helping hand from team-mate Mark Miller but in the end it was to no avail. Sainz's lead had evaporated with an electrical fault on the same stage as Giniel de Villiers' engine failed – a double blow for VW.

The end of the road. Stéphane Peterhansel threads his way through the Senegalese fans on the final stage of the event as he turns his back on the Atlantic Ocean and heads to the finish at Lac Rose on the outskirts of Dakar. It was a win that had looked a distant dream a week earlier.

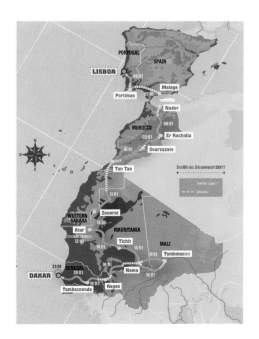

FINAL STANDINGS 2007 CARS CLASSEMENT GÉNÉRAL AUTOS

Pos.	N.	Team	Car	Time	Gap	Penalties
1	302	Peterhansel-Cottret (F/F)	Mitsubishi	45h 53' 37''		
2	300	Alphand-Picard (F/F)	Mitsubishi	46h 01' 03''	00h 07' 26''	
3	310	Schlesser-Debron (F/F)	Schlesser	47h 27' 34''	01h 33' 57''	
4	305	Miller-Pitchford (USA/ZA)	Volkswagen	48h 03' 53''	02h 10' 16''	
5	306	Masuoka-Maimon (J/F)	Mitsubishi	48h 38' 08''	02h 44' 31''	
6	309	Al Attiyah-Guehennec (QAT/F)	BMW	49h 25' 36''	03h 31' 59''	02h 12' 00''
7	313	Sousa-Schulz (P/D)	Volkswagen	51h 04' 31''	05h 10' 54''	
8	320	Gordon-Grider (USA/USA)	Hummer	52h 57' 44''	07h 04' 07''	13' 00''
9	303	Sainz-Perin(E/F)	Volkswagen	53h 19' 22''	07h 25' 45''	15' 00''
10	318	Henrard-Becue (B/B)	Volkswagen	54h 22' 06''	08h 28' 29''	
11	301	De Villiers-Von Zitzewitz (ZA/D)	Volkswagen	54h 38' 11''	08h 44' 34''	15' 00''
12	368	Errandonea-Garcin (F/F)	buggy	55h 16' 03''	09h 22' 26''	
13	304	Roma-Cruz Senra (E/E)	Mitsubishi	55h 30' 06''	09h 36' 29''	40' 00''
14	315	Shmakov-Meshcheryakov (RUS/RUS)	buggy	56h 04' 15''	10h 10' 38''	
15	307	Kleinschmidt-Thorner (D/S)	BMW	56h 22' 22''	10h 28' 45''	30' 00''
16	314	Monterde-Lurquin (E/B)	BMW	57h 28' 52''	11h 35' 15''	
17	336	Orioli-Rosolen (I/I)	Isuzu	57h 42' 33''	11h 48' 56''	
18	403	Gibon-Gibon (F/F)	Bowler	57h 53' 45''	12h 00' 08''	13' 00''
19	331	Housieaux-Polato (F/F)	Mitsubishi	57h 59' 47''	12h 06' 10''	
20	355	Novitskiy-Tyupenkin (RUS/RUS)	Mitsubishi	58h 17' 38''	12h 24' 01''	

(109 teams classified in the automobile category, 70 non-finishers)

Culture

Seriously nuts... and bolts

Any list of the world's entertainers contains many who love automobiles, but Jay Leno eclipses them all. Host of television's "Tonight Show" in the U.S., the comedian's Big Dog Garage is filled with great cars ranging from Stanley Steamers to Bugattis, from U.S. muscle cars to a McLaren F1.
A feature of Leno's collection is what you might call orphan automobiles. Along with the Porsche Carrera GT and Lamborghini Miura supercars and the classic Duesenbergs and Packards are the likes of a Saab 93, Citroën SM, a Monteverdi and a Mazda rotary-engine Cosmo sports car.
Then there are the huge steam- and petrol-driven stationary engines.
And the 'specials', on which **John Lamm** focuses, are truly manic!
All this is in a "green" garage with wind turbines and solar panels,
Leno determined to make the place energy independent.
Keeping it all working is a small but very talented crew, and when he's not at the studio or touring you're likely to find Leno at the garage, wrench in hand, working right next to them.

One of Leno's most famous machines is the tank car with a wheelbase of more than 15-feet. Why tank car? Under that long polished hood is a 30-litre V12 engine that once powered a U.S. Army tank. The transmission is an Allison 6-speed with double overdrive. Those who have ridden in the tank can testify to its ability to spin its wheels at most any speed and a wonderfully powerful sound.

When 800-plus horsepower proved too little in Leno's 10,000-pound tank car, he sent the engine to turbocharging guru Gale Banks. Off came the carbs and on went the type of Bosch fuel injection used on Formula 1 cars. Then came a pair of 91-mm Garrett turbos and what Banks figures is near 1,600 horsepower. At 145 mph, Leno says, the car, "…starts to walk around a little bit. So I'm happy to leave it at that."

This sleek and rather elegant single-seater is a Speed Six Bentley from 1931 with an engine that has been taken out to eight litres. The Bentley has been a race car most of its life and had several bodies. Leno added the fenders so he could drive it on the street. Note the huge reproductions of vintage posters that line many walls of Leno's Big Dog Garage.

Typical of the variety in Leno's garage. Far left is a 3-wheel car hand built by 17-year-old Bob Shotwell in the 1930s with a 4-cylinder Indian motorcycle engine. Next is Leno's tank and then the '32 Bowtie Deuce Roadster, a "modern classic" hot rod with a 580-horepower Chevrolet V8. At the right is the Boss Hoss motorcycle, weighing 1,200 pounds and powered by a GM V8 with 567 lb-ft of torque.

Possibly the most unique of Leno's motorcycles has a C18 Allison Rolls-Royce jet engine that once powered a Bell Jet Ranger helicopter. Designed by Frenchman Christian Travert and built by Marine Technologies in the U.S., the "Y2K" motorcycle sounds like a taxying jet. It's quick off the line but at 40 mph, Leno explains, it feels like the hand of God in your back pushing you forward.

Leno loves steam cars and has several Stanleys and a Doble with that powerplant. And this attempt at a steam-powered motorcycle. Built in the 1930s with an engine from 1902, Leno figures the machine "never really worked properly", and his crew is trying to remedy that. They've adapted the heat exchanger off a Titan missile as a boiler and the motorcycle now runs on propane.

Just inside Leno's garage is this huge flywheel he loves to get spinning with its 1870 Wright steam engine. Weighing 7 tons, the ancient engine is powered by a "green" natural gas-fired steam generator outside the garage. Leno loves to run the steam engine, oiling the mechanism as it huffs away. And when he shuts the steam off, that massive flywheel doesn't stop for 15 minutes.

Peter Kalikow's favourite cars

The Louis Vuitton Classic Concours Award rewards a car that won Best of Show in one of the major concours d'elegance in the world. The 2006/07 so-called "Best of the Best" award went to the 1961 250 GT California spyder which topped the classifications at the Ferrari Club of America Field and Driving Concours. **Aaron Jenkins** meets with its owner, Peter Kalikow, a major collector from New York.

AUTOMOBILE YEAR: How did you get into collecting?
PETER KALIKOW: I got the interest in cars from my family. My father thought Cadillacs were terrific; mom was into Rolls-Royces, before that Jaguars. The collection is currently 45 cars. I have 25 or 26 Ferraris, and have probably had around 45 Ferraris over the years.

AY: Why the interest in Ferraris in particular?
PK: When I was 15, I went to the New York Auto Show. I didn't know what a Ferrari was, but I go by this stand and see a '58 Pinin Farina cabriolet. I was actually mesmerized by this car, so I stood, looked at it, hung around. Then I start reading magazines, and in everything I read, there was a Ferrari story. I just became infatuated, became a big fan. I bought my first Ferrari, a 1967 330 GTC, nine years later. I say I've been a Ferrari fan for 50 years, a customer for 40.

AY: What do you look for in a car you're considering buying?
PK: I ask myself, would I like to drive to California in this car? Or, if I'm feeling more esoteric, how would it go from Milan to Paris? That's how I decide.

AY: Do you drive all the cars?
PK: I use them all. I use the 400 Superamerica a lot, the short wheelbase California spyder the most – it's like they designed the car around me – the long wheelbase California spyder second.

AY: Is there a favorite?
PK: The Pinin Farina cabriolet Series I is and was my favorite.

AY: How often do you show the cars?
PK: I like to go to four events: Villa d'Este, Pebble Beach, the Cavallino Classic and the Ferrari Club of America Nationals. I want people to see what the cars were like when new. Having and not sharing is not quite fair to the public – there are far more enthusiasts than cars, and they're entitled to see them.

AY: What did you think when your California Spyder won the Louis Vuitton Classic Concours Award?
PK: The surprise was total. I don't think there's anything more prestigious that you can win; it's the best of the best. Such a narrow field that contains all of these superb cars, it's a nice thing to win.

250 GT CALIFORNIA

400 SUPERAMERICA

AY: Like many of the cars, the California Spyder has been restored. what's your involvement during a restoration?
PK: I get involved in an extreme way. I choose the colours. I'm old enough to remember what the colours, paint and leather, were when new. If I don't use the original colour, I'll use a period-correct one. I have a bunch of paint chips and leather samples. I know the details. I deal with accessories, like the headlights, the correct brand and model number, like the air horns, correct shock absorber covers, air cleaner with correct tags... all the stuff you saw when you lifted the hood 40 years ago.

AY: You also collect new cars, and even had one made specially for you: the Kappa.
PK: The 612 Scaglietti is a great car to drive, I just thought it was a little short in the looks department. Pininfarina, the man, had a custom Lusso and a 275 GTB, and the changes to those cars were so subtle that many magazines used photos of them to represent the production car. That's exactly what I was looking for. So I went to Pininfarina, and got Ferrari's permission, and we did it.

AY: The Kappa is visually very understated, unlike the other one-off Ferraris that have appeared in the past couple of years...
PK: I was 62 years old, and it's a 62-year-old's car.

AY: In terms of understated styling, the Kappa is similar to a car you once planned to build: the Momo Mirage.
PK: When young I had the nutty idea I was going to build cars. As for the looks, it wasn't made for me; I was 24 then, and no-one my age could afford such a car. The styling was done for someone minimally 10 years older than I was at the time. I had Alfred Momo working with me. We went to Italy to build it, and rented part of the Stanguellini factory. Frua designed and built the bodies, we put in the running gear. We had a Chevy engine. Giulio Alfieri got special permission from Maserati to design the chassis. We had Alford & Adler front suspension, independent rear suspension that we designed and built in-house. We were supposed to build 12, but I don't know if we made it. I have five of the cars. I think a few got sold, but I've never seen another one elsewhere.

AY: What's the next car you'd like to add to the collection?
PK: I don't known. The market is a little overheated for me at the moment. Three of the cars have older restorations, maybe I'll fix them. I've never liked race cars, but I've been thinking maybe I should get one just to fill out the collection. Then again, I would really like to do another Pininfarina Special, like the Kappa.

250 GT CALIFORNIA

MOMO MIRAGE

612 KAPPA

Beauty Queens

Of all the events dedicated to classic cars today, the concours d'elegance are our favourites because, unlike historic racing, they mostly encourage the preservation of originality. Even American restorations, frequently overdone in the past, are now well documented and authentic. **Keith Bluemel** and **Jonathan Stein** attended the most select gatherings around the world, the ones that are considered by Louis Vuitton for their Classic Concours Award.

CAVALLINO CLASSIC
Palm Beach, Florida, 27 January 2007

The 2007 Cavallino Classic had the 166 MM barchetta as a feature car, and within the line-up was this 1949 example which won the Best of Show Competition Car class. It was the third built and is now owned by Brian Ross.

The quality of the concours Ferraris at the Cavallino Classic is exemplified by this aerial view (left) of the older examples which are arranged on the billiard table smooth croquet lawn at the host Breakers Hotel in Palm Beach. The concours is the highlight of the gathering each January which encompasses track time at Moroso Motorsports Park, a road rally, an airport party at Palm Beach International Airport and a brunch at the exclusive Mar-A-Lago Club owned by Donald Trump.

Among the 400 plus Ferraris registered for the gathering, there was a fine selection of Ferrari 250 GT models within the concours field, with this 1960 250 GT Berlinetta, owned by Tex and Tambi Otto, winning the Best of Show Road Car class against very strong competition.

This 166 MM was recently, almost literally, unearthed in the Arizona desert. The owner, Manny del Arroz, had it sympathetically refurbished, and won the Vintage Preservation Cup.

SHEL... | VIC ELFORD | BRIAN REDMAN | JOHN SURTEES MBE | SIR STIRLING MOSS | JOHN FITCH | ...ECON...

2007 AMELIA

General Motors GM
PRESENTS
The Great Road Races

AMELIA ISLAND CONCOURS D'ELEGANCE
Amelia Island, Florida, 11 March 2007

The 12th running of the Amelia Island Concours d'Elegance was held in March at the Ritz Carlton Hotel in northern Florida, where each year the organising committee gathers a phenomenal array of spectacular machinery to the resort's golf links, which is a delight for any classic vehicle enthusiast. Top left: this pair of Delahayes, a 1949 175 S model and a 1937 135 M model, respectively with Saoutchik and Figoni & Falaschi coachwork, make their way to the presentation arena.

One of Amelia's highlights is the seminar held in conjunction with the concours. This year's theme was The Great Road Races, and the panel included such heroes as Sir Stirling Moss, John Surtees, Vic Elford, and others, who entertained the public with the tales of their souvenirs. An unforgettable moment.

Great road races being honoured, a magnet for the racing enthusiast was the Targa Florio class, celebrating the centenary of the first running of the legendary Sicilian event inaugurated in 1906. Amongst a stunning array of cars that had competed in it, was this Porsche 907 driven by Elford/Maglioli to win the 1968 race, also winning its class in the concours.

The Best of Show Concours de Sport and Concours d'Elegance winners meet head to head for the presentation of the prestigious awards. In the foreground, a Ferrari 340/375 MM by Vignale bearing its 1954 Carrera Panamericana livery, owned by Bruce McCaw, faces a 1937 "teardrop" Talbot Lago T150 C-SS by Figoni & Falaschi, from the Nethercutt Collection.

CONCORSO D'ELEGANZA VILLA D'ESTE
Cernobbio, Italy, 21-22 April 2007

The jewel in the crown of European concours events is undoubtedly the Concorso d'Eleganza at Ville d'Este, on the shores of Lake Como in Italy. This two-day gathering, one by invitation only at the Villa d'Este, and one open to the public at nearby Villa Erba, may not be large in numbers, but the cars it features are among the best of their type in the world.

In the class for Designs by the Great "Carrozzieri" there was very strong competition between some outstanding automobiles, with virtually all the major Italian design studios represented. At the end of the day the award went to David and Ginny Sydorick's 1952 Ghia-bodied Fiat 8V Supersonic, making its debut after a lengthy restoration.

The overall Best of Show winner selected by the jury was this spectacular black ex-Count Trossi 1930 Mercedes-Benz SSK, currently part of the Ralph Lauren Collection.

This 1939 Bugatti Type 57 C convertible with coachwork by Voll & Ruhrbeck in Germany was the last Bugatti delivered to the country before the start of hostilities. It was the first time that owner James Patterson showed this car in Europe after a lengthy restoration when it was reunited with this original body, and it won the Coppa d'Oro Villa d'Este (public referendum at Villa d'Este).

The Trofeo BMW Italia (public referendum at Villa Erba) was awarded to the Alfa Romeo 6C 1750 GS Flying Star from 1931. It was with this very car, bodied by Carrozzeria Touring of Milan, that Mrs. Josette Pozzo won the Coppa d'Oro in the 1931 Concorso d'Eleganza Villa d'Este. Now owned by Arturo and Deborah Keller, the Flying Star returned to the historic site of its major triumph, claiming another prize some 76 years on.

The last six years have featured a design prize for the best contemporary concept cars. The 2007 Concorso d'Eleganza Villa d'Este Design Award went to the Ferrari P4/5 by Pininfarina. Commissioned by Ferrari *aficionado* James Glickenhaus in 2005, the P4/5 intentionally recalls the legendary Daytona-winning Ferrari 330 P4 of 1967 and adds exclusivity to exclusivity, being based on one of just 400 Enzo supercars built.

MEADOW BROOK CONCOURS D'ELEGANCE
Rochester, Michigan, 5 August 2007

Long one of North America's premier events, the Meadow
Brook Hall Concours d'Elegance was held for the 29th year
on the campus of Oakland University in Rochester Hills.
Unusually, there were three Best of Show Awards (all visible
in this picture): one for American vehicles, one for foreign
automobiles and a third for motorcycles. The Best Foreign
Car award went to Ray Scherr's short-wheelbase 1938
Alfa Romeo 8C 2900B bodied by Touring of Milan (in the
foreground), whilst the Best of Show award for American
Cars went to Ethel Lanaux's 1931 Chrysler CG Imperial
Victoria Cabriolet.
The motorcycle class celebrated four-cylinder machines of
all ages, with Edward Bortner's 1938 Indian Four garnering
Best of Show (top right).

THE QUAIL, A MOTORSPORTS GATHERING
Carmel Valley, California, 17 August 2007

Limited to 3,000 guests and 120 cars,
The Quail is exclusive by American standards.
For 2007, the "Motorsports Gathering" marked
Briggs Cunningham's 100th birthday.
Fittingly, Best of Show went to Dr. Frederick
 Simeone's 1952 Cunningham C4R (below),
with which Phil Walters and John Fitch won
the 12-Hours of Sebring in 1953.

Right: celebrating 50 years of the Ferrari
250 GT cabriolet series I by Pinin Farina,
The Quail assembled a class of 16 of the
sublime Italian masterpieces in various colors.
Although they appeared similar, virtually
all of them varied in details that ranged
from headlamp and bumper treatments
to interior trim.

PEBBLE BEACH CONCOURS D'ELEGANCE
Pebble Beach, California, 19 August 2007

It was fitting that the grandest North American Concours
would feature the grandest American automobile.
The Pebble Beach Concours d'Elegance celebrated
the Duesenberg Model J and SJ. Between 1929 and 1931,
just 481 examples of the Fred Duesenberg and E.L. Cord
masterpiece were produced. The strong competition
in the 18-car class included a 1930 SJ Murphy Convertible
Coupe and a 1931 J Murphy Coupe both seen here
in the foreground.

Aston Martin was another famous manufacturer honoured at Pebble Beach in 2007. In what was clearly one of the finest marque displays ever assembled, 38 Astons filled four classes, with a span of 81 years. This 1956 DB3S owned by Peter Livanos won the Aston Martin post-war race cars class.

Winner of the Most elegant sports car trophy, this resplendent DBR1/2 owned by Adrian Beechcroft boasted a second place in the 1959 Le Mans 24-Hours, driven by Paul Frère and Maurice Trintignant.

One of the most spectacular classes was for "Aston Martin Post-war Coachbuilt Cars," and included four of the exquisite 1961 DB4 GT Zagatos, of which 1 VEV had the most illustrious racing history.

In a world that generally celebrates exotic European coachwork, the 2007 Pebble Beach Concours d'Elegance broke with recent practice and presented its prestigious Best of Show award to Harry Yeaggy's Duesenberg Model SJ "Mormon Meteor" special. With a sleek one-off body penned by Herb Newport and an SJ engine modified by Augie Duesenberg, Ab Jenkins had driven the car continuously for 24 hours on the Bonneville Salt Flats to set a world record of 135.47 mph in 1935. Later it was modified with a Curtiss V12 aero engine before being further altered for road use. Carefully researched and restored to its original specifications, few could challenge the provenance or beauty of the big yellow Duesenberg.

THE LOUIS VUITTON CLASSIC CONCOURS AWARD
Frankfurt, Germany, 12 September 2007

Approximately one month after Pebble Beach,
a distinguished group of designers and collectors met during
the Frankfurt auto show to determine, for the third time,
a 'Best of the Best' award attributed by Louis Vuitton.
The contenders were the six Best of Show winners from the
events reviewed on these pages.

The judging panel included (from left to right in the image
below): Olivier Boulay (Mercedes-Benz),
Shiro Nakamura (Nissan), François Melcion (Rétromobile),
Leonardo Fioravanti (Fioravanti, panel co-chairman),
Fabrizio Giugiaro (Italdesign), Christian Philippsen
(*Automobile Year* publisher and panel chairman),
Laurens van den Acker (Mazda), Wahei Hirai (Toyota
Group), Jean-Pierre Ploué (Citroën), Chris Bangle (BMW
Group), Patrick le Quément (Renault), Lorenzo Ramaciotti
(Fiat Group), Anthony Lo (GM) and Luc Donckerwolke
(Seat, not pictured).

Guiding the group were the LVC Concours Award rules
that state "The judging criteria will primarily take into
consideration the elegance and the refinement of the
coachwork, exterior and interior, the mechanical beauty,
the relevance of the form and function, as well as the
authenticity, historical importance and rarity."

A detailed presentation was prepared for each candidate,
supported by a selection of pictures projected on a large
screen. And the winner was ... one of the all time greats,
the gorgeous 1938 Alfa Romeo 8C 2900 with coachwork
by Touring, Best of Show at Meadow Brook. When Bob
Lutz, chief judge of the concours, was presented with the
suggested result, he said with a happy smile "I can live with
that". Who couldn't?

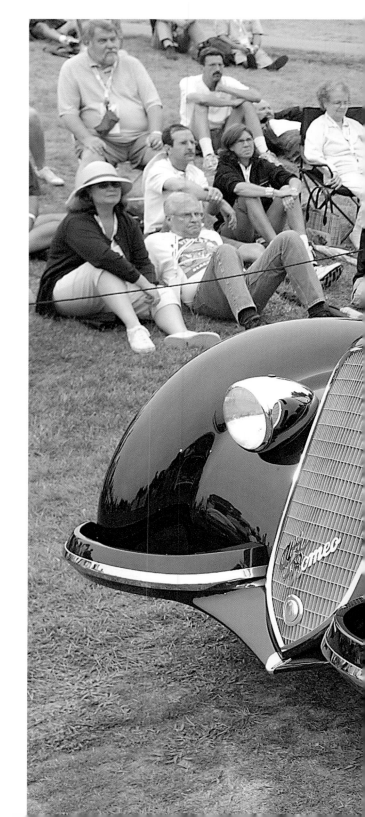

The auction world sees red

The top-selling trio of auction cars for 2007 had two things in common, explains **David Brownell**: they were all Ferraris and all were sold by RM, two at their successful Maranello sale and the third at their annual Monterey auction. But the top-grossing sale of the year was the Gooding & Company Pebble Beach auction with a total of $61,350,000 made during the two-day event.

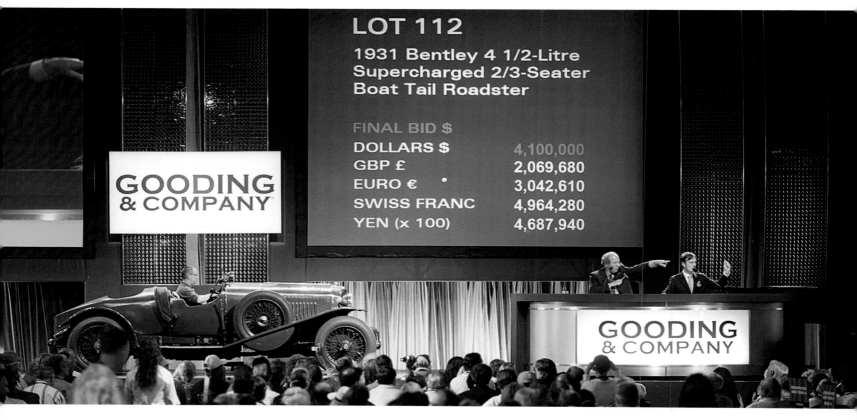

LOT 112

1931 Bentley 4 1/2-Litre Supercharged 2/3-Seater Boat Tail Roadster

FINAL BID $

DOLLARS $	4,100,000
GBP £	2,069,680
EURO €	3,042,610
SWISS FRANC	4,964,280
YEN (x 100)	4,687,940

GOODING & COMPANY

While an impressive number of stunning, rare and highly desirable cars crossed the block in 2007, one car which didn't appear made perhaps more news than many of the others. That was the Type D Auto Union GP car scheduled for Christie's Rétromobile auction. Following extensive pre-sale publicity the racecar was suddenly withdrawn after Christie's had received some allegations that the car's history was not as presented. They asked Audi Tradition to assist in further research and it was revealed that the chassis number attributed to the car was incorrect, and its race results different from the ones advertised. All credit to Christie's for doing the right thing, too late unfortunately.

Then quite unexpectedly after the August California auctions, Christie's announced the disbanding of its Motorcar Department. The staff joined Bonham's, extending the reach and depth of that firm.

It has been a somewhat jumpy market in the lower price range in 2007, with the muscle cars, particularly, leveling off from their previous activity. But the best models of top marques had no trouble sustaining or exceeding previous price levels. Not only Ferrari but Bugatti, Bentley, Packard, Alfa Romeo and Mercedes-Benz, among other great names, saw undiminished demand and some record high prices for the best examples. Cars carrying great originality continued to rise as well. The general category of veteran and vintage cars continued to do well, especially if they were London-Brighton Run candidates, a famous marque or offered exceptional performance for their age.

As in the 2007 fine arts auction market, there was no lack of qualified buyers for the crop of outstanding motorcars offered in Europe and the U.S. this year. Will 2008 bring more of the same?

1939 Auto Union Type D

1962 FERRARI 330 TRI/LM

€6,868,125, $9,281,250, £4,659,187
(RM, Maranello, 20/5/07)
1962 Le Mans winner driven by Phil Hill/
Olivier Gendebien. Ex-NART driven by
Pedro Rodriguez/Graham Hill. Crashed
at Le Mans 1963. Restored and driven daily
from '65 to '73. Copperstate 1,000 veteran.
Fantastic appearance. One of the most
significant Ferraris ever offered for sale.
Bought for Argentine museum.

1953 FERRARI 340/375 MM
COMPETIZIONE

€4,230,765, $5,717,250, £2,870,060
(RM, Maranello, 20/5/07)
One of three built. Ex-works car,
5th at '53 Le Mans, first at Spa 24-Hours
piloted by Farina/Hawthorn. Factory upgrade
to 375 specs. Condition good or better than
new throughout. Beautiful, brutal,
with a great racing history.
Also going to Argentine museum.

1959 FERRARI 250 GT
CALIFORNIA SPIDER

$4,950,000, €3,663,000, £2,484,900
(RM, Monterey, 19/8/07)
One of nine long wheelbase alloy-bodied
examples. Sent direct from factory to 1959
Le Mans for U.S. racer Bob Grossman.
Painstaking restoration back to street
appearance. Double Pebble Beach Concours
winner.

VETERAN, EDWARDIAN & VINTAGE CARS

**1884 De Dion-Bouton
et Trépardoux dos-à-dos**
$3,520,000, €2,604,800, £1,767,040
(Gooding, Pebble Beach, 20/8/07)
Oldest operating motorcar extant, originally
owned and driven by Comte De Dion
and successfully raced by him as well. Excellent
running order and appearance. Selling price well
beyond consignor's expectations.

1890 De Dion-Bouton et Trépardoux
€615,850, $832,231, £417,780
(Christie's, Paris, 17/2/07)
Complete and in remarkably original condition.
Not running when sold but with some proper
fettling could be ready for the London-Brighton
and other veteran runs. A fascinating and scarce
survivor of motoring's pioneer era. High bid was
over 450 per cent above top estimate!

**1902 Wolseley 10 HP rear entrance
tonneau**
£161,600, $321,905, €238,210
(Bonhams, London, 30/4/07)
Substantially original example and a veteran of
the London-Brighton Runs. 10-hp two-cylinder
power, charming patina, Irish Museum
provenance and in same ownership for decades.
Sold for $140,000 above low estimate.

1907 Packard Model 30 runabout
$403,000, €298,220, £202,306
(Bonhams & Butterfields, Quail Lodge, 17/8/07)
Low mileage award-winning example,
full provenance from new, restored
from completely correct original example.
One of the great American veterans sold
at an unsurprising price level.

**1909 Rolls-Royce Silver Ghost Roi
des Belges tourer**
$1,485,000, €1,098,900, £745,470
(Gooding, Pebble Beach, 20/8/07)
Rebodied in the style of the original Silver
Ghost. First carried a Hooper limousine body.
Current body crafted in 1972. Rescued from
English junkyard in 1946. Pebble Beach
and Amelia Concours award winner.

**1923 Rolls-Royce Silver Ghost Piccadilly
roadster**
$342,500, €253,450, £171,935
(Bonhams & Butterfields, Brookline, 21/4/07)
American-built Rolls with in-house custom
coachwork. Concours winner at 2005 Rolls-Royce
Owners Club National Meet. Attractive, sporty,
very well and correctly finished in all areas.
A record price for a Piccadilly.

1924 Lancia Lambda Fourth Series tourer
$104,500, €77,330, £52,460
(Christie's, Monterey, 16/8/07)
Somewhat shabby but essentially complete car
that would restore well. May have slightly later
engine. Top missing. Popular, highly innovative
model; the basis for a good vintage rally
and road car.

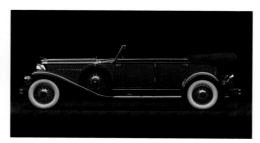

1930 Duesenberg J convertible berline
$902,000, €667,480, £452,804
(Christie's, Monterey, 16/8/07)
LeBaron coachwork on "matching numbers"
car. Won highest Classic Car Club award.
Professionally restored and maintained.
Said to drive superbly. Fabulous interior.

**1931 Rolls-Royce Phantom 1 Regent
convertible**
$403,000, €298,220, £202,306
(Bonhams & Butterfields, Quail Lodge, 17/8/07)
American-built Rolls with Brewster coachwork
superbly restored from a low mileage original car.
Numerous concours awards, full history
and documentation, highly attractive automobile
sold for $100,000 over high estimate.

1931 Bentley 4½ litre supercharged boat-tail roadster
$4,510,000, €3,337,400, £2,226,400
(Gooding, Pebble Beach, 20/8/07)
Had to be the newest, most original Blower
Bentley extant with only 3,500 miles showing
from new. Dramatic boat-tail style Gurney
Nutting coachwork, rode and drove like
the new/old car it was. Record-breaking price.

1932 Packard Twin Six Phaeton
$1,650,000, €1,221,000, £828,300
(RM, Amelia Island, 10/3/07)
Breathtaking restoration on one of the most
handsome Packard body designs of all time.
Claimed to be one of just two survivors of this
style in the 1932 Twin Six line-up. Pebble Beach
"Most Elegant" award winner. Totally stunning
Classic in all respects.

1932 Bentley 8-litre short chassis coupé
$962,500, €712,250, £483,175
(RM, Amelia Island, 10/3/07)
Mayfair Carriage Co. coachwork. Lovely low
profile appearance with some slight patina to add
to its charm. This "British Duesenberg" had great
presence, matching numbers and the distinction
of being the next-to-last Eight produced of the
original 100.

1933 Delage DS8 coupé roadster
$3,740,000, €2,767,600, £1,877,480
(RM, Monterey, 19/8/07)
1933 Paris Salon car. Stunningly low body,
all white finish as new complemented by green
leather with cream piping. A certain contender
for Best in Show at a host of concours.

1933 Lincoln KB convertible sedan
$495,000, €346,500, £249,490
(Gooding, Oxnard, 21/10/06)
Older professional restoration still shows to prize-
winning level. Dietrich body, one of six extant
of total 15 built. Open style front wings added
to attractive appearance. Robust price.

1935 Duesenberg SJ Town Cabriolet
$4,400,000, €3,256,000, £2,208,800
(RM, Monterey, 19/8/07)
Bohman & Schwartz coachwork. Original owner
Ethel Mars was CEO of famed candy company.
One of just 36 supercharged Duesies originally
built. Spectacular Art Deco styling inside and out.

1937 Duesenberg SJ town cabriolet
$2,805,000, €1,963,500, £1,409,110
(RM, Phoenix, 19/1/07)
Astonishingly original car right down to the
tyres. Last Duesenberg built; Rollston custom
body, factory supercharged, spectacular style,
full provenance from new. Unique among
Duesenbergs.

**1937 Mercedes-Benz 540K Special
Roadster**
$2,530,000, €1,872,200, £1,270,060
(RM, Monterey, 18/8/07)
Rakish Mayfair Carriage one-off coachwork. Full
professional restoration with admirable attention
to detail. Sparkling performance thanks to light
body and supercharger. Sold for low estimate.

1938 Bugatti Type 57C Atalante coupé
$852,500, €630,850, £426,250
(Christie's, Greenwich, 3/6/07)
Originally a Gangloff Stelvio cabriolet, rebodied
to current Atalante configuration years ago.
Needed total restoration. Several Bugatti
specialists thought price was market-correct.

PRE-WAR RACING CARS

1907 Renault AI 30/35 HP Vanderbilt Racer
$1,100,000, €814,000, £552,200
(Gooding, Oxnard, 21/10/06)
One of a small group of 60-hp "street legal" replicas of the 1906 GP de l'ACF winner ordered by Vanderbilt Cup Race founder William K. Vanderbilt for himself and some of his wealthy sportsmen friends. Pebble Beach award winner, one of five survivors.

1911 Mercer 35R Raceabout
$1,595,000, €1,180,300, £800,690
(Gooding, Oxnard, 21/10/06)
Restored from a very correct car and winner of numerous awards at major concours and national club meets. Veteran of Monterey Historics and good for nearly 100 mph. New World's record for the most desirable of Edwardian era American sports/racing cars.

1926 Bugatti Type 39A Grand Prix
$1,175,000, €869,500, £589,850
(Bonhams & Butterfields, Brookline, 21/4/07)
One of ten originally built. Ex-works racer piloted by Costantini to two seconds and a third place finish in 1926 GP season. Factory replaced frame. Actively vintage raced, ready for road or rally. Very well restored and presented. Full and fairly priced.

1929 Alfa Romeo 6C 1750 Super Sport roadster
£487,040, $970,200, €717,950
(H&H, Cheltenham, 1/3/07)
Four-seater coachwork by Carlton Carriage Co. 1929 Irish GP winner. Fresh engine rebuild. Shows some honest wear inside and out, a look much favoured by English collectors in particular. Impressive winning bid well over high estimate.

1937 Kurtis "Tommy Lee Speedster"
$440,000, €325,600, £220,880
(RM, Monterey, 19/8/07)
One-off styling inspired by Cord. Brutally fast 250-bhp Offenhauser power. Indycar genius Frank Kurtis fabricated body and chassis for legendary playboy Tommy Lee. Outstanding restoration.

1938 Delahaye Type 135 Special
$1,320,000, €924,000, £662,640
(RM, Phoenix, 19/1/07)
Originally part of Ecurie Bleue, successful pre-war racing team. Spent 20 years in Argentina, then back to Europe for another restoration that it wears today. Great vintage race and rally potential.

GT CARS

1951 Bugatti Type 101 coupé
$990,000, €732,600, £495,000
(RM, Marshall, 21/4/07)
Nearly new restoration in concours condition inside and out. One of eight built. Ex-Harrah Collection. 1951 Paris Salon factory show car. Price reflects soaring Bugatti market.

1953 Aston Martin DB2/4 Bertone drophead
$847,000, €626,780, £425,195
(RM, Marshall, 21/4/07)
One of two built. Literally flawless in all areas from the front bumper to the original fitted luggage. A outstanding car even among other post-war Astons with its Italianate style and gorgeous proportions. Sold strongly for 40 per cent over high estimate.

1954 Moretti Tipo 750 Gran Sport GT coupé
£95,000, $190,000, €144,400
(Bonhams, Goodwood, 22/6/07)
Splendid restoration with meticulous attention to detail. Concours winning potential. Beautifully proportioned so its minuscule size isn't readily apparent. Perhaps the finest example extant.

1954 Dodge Firearrow
$1,100,000, €770,000, £506,000
(Barrett-Jackson, Scottsdale, 22/1/07)
Ghia-bodied "dream" car, fully functional
with Dodge Hemi V8. In top concours condition
throughout including unique black and white
"diamond" theme interior and custom luggage.

1956 Maserati A6G/2000 Berlinetta
€143,747, $184,000, £96,365
(Bonhams, Gstaad, 17/12/06)
Allemano coachwork. Formerly part of famous
Rosso Bianco Collection. Engine and gearbox
removed from car when sold. Generally sound
cosmetics but needs a good tidying.

**1957 Mercedes-Benz 300SL "Gullwing"
coupé**
$715,000, €529,100, £357,500
(Gooding, Pebble Beach, 19/8/07)
Special order "strawberry" factory colour,
under 10,000 miles from new, perfectly preserved
with fabulous patina. In irreplaceable condition
throughout. A true time capsule.

1959 Aston Martin DB4 GT
$1,650,000, €1,221,000, £828,300
(RM, Monterey, 19/8/07)
One of six factory lightweights built from
DB4 GTs. Total specialist restoration
in 2001-2002 with a few tweaks and upgrades,
resulting in a true dual purpose vintage
racer/tourer. Full provenance from new.

1959 Ferrari 250 GT California Spider
$4,455,000, €3,296,700, £2,236,410
(Gooding, Pebble Beach, 20/8/07)
Long wheelbase in better than new condition
with flawless paint. First place winner at Pebble
and Ferrari National Meet. Incomparable
"no excuses" motorcar in every respect. Simply
the best there is and worth every penny.

1962 Maserati 5000 GT Series II
$1,100,000, €814,000, £552,200
(Gooding, Pebble Beach, 19/8/07)
Frua custom coachwork had special front-end
treatment, one-off colour, and a record player
installed! Pebble Beach award winner. One
of three built. Superb appearance throughout.

1963 Ferrari 250 GT Lusso
$2,310,000, €1,709,400, £1,159,620
(Christie's, Monterey, 16/8/07)
The Steve McQueen Lusso. Superb restoration
by consignor plus the cachet of celebrity
ownership by "car guy" McQueen. As a lovely
but non-famous Lusso it would likely have made
$800,000 instead.

1970 Lamborghini Miura S
$473,000, €350,000, £237,450
(RM, Monterey, 18/8/07)
Recent professional paint and interior restoration.
Carries SV split-sump engine block and SV road
wheels. Full history known from new. Appeared
to be road-ready. Excellent example.

1973 Ferrari 365 GTS4 "Daytona Spider"
$2,035,000, €1,505,900, £1,021,570
(Gooding, Pebble Beach, 19/8/07)
A virtually new car with under 90 miles from new
and the last of 124 Spiders built. Meticulously
preserved time capsule sold for well above high
estimate.

POST-WAR RACING CARS

1938/51 Marchese Championship race car
$99,000, €73,260, £49,700
(RM, Monterey, 19/8/07)
Extensive Indy 500 history, originally powered
by Miller straight eight, replaced by Offy 270
in 1947. Finished as high as 4th at Indy. Restored
to 1951 appearance. A bargain at the price.

1951 Talbot-Lago T26GS
€1,163, 812, $1,572,720, £789,500
(Christie's, Paris, 17/2/07)
Originally with cycle-wings, it was changed
to closed-wheel body for Le Mans regulations.
Raced by Pierre Levegh with mixed success
including epic 23-hour solo drive at the Sarthe
in 1952. Well restored, shown at Pebble Beach
in 2006. A true French racing icon.

1952 Jaguar XK 120 competition roadster
$231,000, €170,940, £120,120
(Gooding, Pebble Beach, 20/8/07)
Fresh $150,000 restoration in 2004 to present
specifications including 320-bhp 3.8 engine.
Concours winner, vintage rally participant
and vintage racing candidate with breathtaking
performance.

1955 Ferrari 750 Monza Spider
$1,540,000, €1,139,600, £773,080
(RM, Monterey, 19/8/07)
Very well known and successful California racer.
Only 750 built without a headrest.
20-year restoration culminated in multitude
of concours wins including Cavallino Classic,
Greenwich, Amelia.

1961 Porsche RS 61 Spyder
$880,000, €616,000, £440,760
(RM, Phoenix, 19/1/07)
One of 14 built. '63 European Hillclimb
Champion. 5th in '61 Nürburgring 1000 km.
Very well restored, strong runner. Equally ready
for concours field or vintage racing grid.

1961 Maserati Tipo 63
€446,000, $583,450, £298,880
(Bonhams, Gstaad, 17/12/06)
Ex-Briggs Cunningham team car. Victorious
in U.S. racing. Ran 1961 Le Mans.
Most successful of all rear-engined "Birdcage"
Masers. Second long-wheelbase Tipo 63 built.

1962 Maserati Tipo 151 Berlinetta
€1,432,270, $2,046,097, £1,023,050
(Bonhams, Gstaad, 17/12/06)
Cunningham Le Mans team car. From the famous
Rosso Bianco collection. Painted in original U.S.
racing colours. Only complete surviving Tipo 151
of the three originally constructed.

1963 Cooper Monaco Type 61
$935,000, €691,900, £469,370
(RM, Amelia Island, 10/3/07)
Very well finished and presented. Cobra-powered
for formidable performance. Appeared to be
race-ready and is vintage race eligible both
in the U.S. and Europe. Finished in American
racing colours of blue and white but it's really
an Anglo-American hybrid.

1965/81 Shelby 427 Daytona Super Coupe
$1,320,000, €924,000, £660,000
(Russo & Steele, Scottsdale, 19/1/07)
Although titled a 1965 it was not built until 1981
and did historic racing after that. Never raced in
the '60s as it didn't exist then. Second generation
coupé bodywork. Excellent order throughout.

1966 Shelby Cobra 427
$702,000, €491,400, £351,000
(RM, Ft. Lauderdale 9-11/2/07)
A "real" 427 with correct numbers, excellent
cosmetics and nicely patinated interior. Sold
for a strong price, even for an authentic 427.
It was already resold in Monterey for $770,000.
Even so, it may still look like a relative bargain
in the future.

**1981 Lancia Beta Montecarlo Turbo
Group 5 prototype**
€225,000, $303,750, £153,900
(Bonhams, Monaco, 21/5/07)
1981 Le Mans Group 5 class winner.
Also finished well at Nürburgring and Monza.
Retired to museum display from 1983 to '93,
then to the vendor's private collection.
Very important post-war Lancia.

1991 Peugeot 905
€907,790, $1,226,742, £615,825
(Artcurial, Paris, 19/2/07)
Fresh restoration to 1992 World Sport
Championship EV1 specifications by Peugeot
Talbot Sport. Fastest qualifier at the Sarthe
in 1992. Immaculately presented and ready for
historic racing. A world record for the marque.

SINGLE SEATERS

1959 Moretti-Branca Formula Junior
£40,250, $79,000, €55,300
(Bonhams, Monaco, 21/5/07)
Pioneering mid-engine design ran at Monaco
in '59. This car campaigned at Garda, Rouen,
Monza, etc. Fiat 1100 power with inverted 600
gearbox. One of two known to exist.

1970 Lotus 72
£286,000, $572,000, €400,400
(H&H, Kempton Park, 25/7/07)
New world record for Lotus 72. Ex-Works car
driven by John Miles, Graham Hill, Jo Siffert and
Emerson Fittipaldi. Ready for a full restoration.
New owner intends to go vintage racing.

1983 Ferrari 126 C2B F1
€417,360, $564,000, £282,565
(RM, Maranello, 20/5/07)
Patrick Tambay's team car with several podium
finishes including first at San Marino in '83.
Authentically redone to factory standards
and presented very well. A proven winner ready
for historics.

CURIOSITIES

1957 Chevrolet Bel Air convertible
$129,600, €95,900, £65,060
(RM, Toronto, 13-15/4/07)
Boasted fuel-injected V8, host of factory goodies
including fender skirts, spinner hubcaps,
dual antennas, continental kit, Wonderbar
radio, power steering, brakes and top. Superb
restoration on rust-free example of America's
Sweetheart with all the right stuff.

1966 Amphicar convertible
$77,000, €56,980, £38,500
(RM, Lapeer, 9/6/07)
Older restoration that presented quite well inside
and out. They were once described after testing
by an American car magazine as "a lousy car and
a worse boat" but collectors keep buying them for
big money.

1966 Fiat transporter
$297,000, €219,780, £149,094
(Gooding, Pebble Beach, 19/8/07)
Original, somewhat scruffy and rusty condition
but it has the right name painted on the doors
of the cab. Just the thing for bringing a brace
of vintage Ferraris to historic racing events.

Automobile Year 1907

Historian **David Burgess-Wise** takes a look back at some exceptional automotive events that occurred 100 years ago.

1907 was a year in which endurance was the watchword, with events as disparate as Rolls-Royce's 15,000-mile observed run with the Silver Ghost and the Peking-Paris race won by Itala demonstrating that the motor car had come of age as a means of transport. Perhaps the most remarkable feat of 1907 was Felice Nazzaro's three victories in the three major races of the year, all run under different formulas. But the end of the era of racing on public roads was foreshadowed by the opening of the world's first purpose-built circuit at Brooklands. And it was on the brand-new Brooklands track that S. F. Edge averaged over 60 mph for 24 hours in a 65 HP Napier to set another endurance record.

Two months after the start of the Peking-Paris race, Scipione Borghese's Itala reached Paris, three weeks ahead of its rivals. The victorious "mad motorists" were met by waving crowds and a "small army" of cars. "We were not heroes," claimed the modest Borghese, "we were simply patient... We concentrated on nothing but getting the day's stage done well."

100 years ago, one of the most epic contests in the history of motor racing started from Peking on the 10th of June 1907, bound for Paris, some 8,000 miles distant. Much of the route across Asia was trackless desert. The Peking-Paris Race was the brainchild of the French newspaper "Le Matin", which wanted to prove that "as long as a man has a car, he can do anything and go anywhere". Entries came from de Dion-Bouton, Contal, Spyker and Prince Scipione Borghese, whose 7.4-litre Itala is seen here on its way out of Peking.

The first French Grand Prix in 1906 had been a two-day affair, but proved so great a strain on the drivers that for 1907 the race was confined to a single day. Run to a fuel consumption formula, the Grand Prix was held on 2 July over 10 laps of a triangular 77 km circuit east of Dieppe. Nazzaro's victorious 15.25-litre Fiat averaged 70.5 mph/104.7 km/h. For the first time, Italian Grand Prix cars were painted red.

A remarkable triple was achieved by the Italian Fiat driver Felice Nazzaro, who won all three of the season's major races, each run to a different formula. In April he won the Targa Florio in Sicily driving a 7.4-litre car at an average speed of 33.5 mph – here he passes through the hilltop village of Caltavuturo – and in June, in an 8-litre car, he was victorious in the Kaiserpreis held in the Taunus mountains. His ride for the French Grand Prix in July had an engine as big as the two previous cars combined!

The year 1907 saw the opening of the world's first purpose-built race circuit at Brooklands in Surrey. The track, which was the centre of British motor racing until its closure in 1939, took less than nine months to build. A private venture which almost ruined landowner Hugh Locke King, the 2.78-mile circuit was Britain's first concrete roadway, with 200,000 tons of concrete laid on earth bankings by manual labour.

Automobile Year 1957

1957 was a year of mixed fortunes, with petrol still rationed in many European countries
due to the closure of the Suez Canal after the 1956 war, and the introduction of radar speed
traps in England. Petrol shortages inspired the appearance of a variety of utility "bubble cars",
mostly powered by single-cylinder engines displacing no more than 200cc. But demand for new
cars soared as rationing was lifted and the year saw the launch of some significant models such
as the Jaguar XK 150, the Aston Martin DB Mk III and the Bentley Continental Flying Spur.
At the other end of the scale, Fiat introduced the diminutive rear-engined two-cylinder Nuova 500.
On the sporting front, the Vanwall challenge became reality, with victory in three Grands Prix,
but even so Fangio won his fifth and final World Championship. Historian **David Burgess-Wise**
reviews the cars, the races and the events that made the headlines 50 years ago.

Mechanical misfortunes eliminated 10 of the 18 starters in the 90-lap British Grand Prix at Aintree. When a persistent misfire in his Vanwall slowed race leader Stirling Moss, he took over the car of team-mate Tony Brooks on lap 26. He rejoined the race in ninth position, regained the lead on the 69th lap and maintained it to the end to record Vanwall's first *Grande Epreuve* victory and set a new lap record at 90.6 mph.

Juan Manuel Fangio recorded his fifth World Championship title in 1957, which he recalled as "the best year of my career". Signed for Maserati, he began the season with a decisive victory in the Argentine Grand Prix and went on to win a further three F1 championship Grands Prix, win six other races, finish second in two and come fourth in Morocco after slowing for a false flag signal; he retired in only three races.

The 500-mile race at Monza in June saw nine American Indianapolis racers pitted against three Ecurie Ecosse Jaguars; all had to lap at over 140 mph to qualify. The race was run in three 170-mile heats, two of which were won by Jimmy Bryan's Dean Van Lines Special, which was declared overall winner on aggregate and set a new lap record of 175.73 mph.

The 1957 Le Mans 24-hour race was a clean sweep for Jaguar, with privately-entered D-Types finishing 1-2-3-4-6. Here, the winning Ecurie Ecosse D-Type of Ron Flockhart and Ivor Bueb leads the Ferrari of Lewis Evans/Severi round the "kink" at the entrance to the Tertre Rouge. It covered 2,732 miles at an average of 113.85 mph to give Ecurie Ecosse its second consecutive victory.

The 1957 Mille Miglia proved to be the last running
of the Italian classic road race after Alfonso "Fon"
de Portago's Ferrari crashed with fatal results for its
crew and a number of spectators. Photographer Louis
Klemantaski was passenger in Peter Collins' Ferrari,
and the "Kidderminster Kid" maintained a commanding
lead until a broken differential forced his retirement
at Parma, less than an hour from the finish. Indeed,
Collins beat Stirling Moss's 1955 Mercedes record
as far as Siena (100.66 mph against 99.81 mph).

Based on the Chrysler Imperial, Ghia's Type 400 was the world's biggest production car. It adopted the Torinese carrozzeria's "Dart" line with enormous tail fins that were alleged to be essential for stability at speed. Ghia planned to build just 25 of these Imperial limousines for sale in hard currency areas at a cost of $15,000 each, however apparently only two were ever built. A long-playing record unit was a standard feature.

The year 1957 marked a major turning point in the history of Pinin Farina, for company founder Battista "Pinin" Farina decided to retire, leaving the company in the hands of his son Sergio and son-in-law Renzo Carli. Among the year's show cars from Pinin Farina was the Alfa Romeo Sestriere pillarless coupé with a sliding door on the driver's side and exceptionally thin screen pillars.

Unveiled at the Turin Show at the end of October was Bertone's aerodynamic 125 mph/200 km/h "Sprint Spinta" prototype on the Alfa Romeo Giulietta chassis with a tuned 1,290 cc engine and five-speed transmission. With slight modifications, it went into production as the "Sprint Speciale"; a total of 1366 examples was built before production ended in 1962.

Based on the Fiat 500, the Ghia Jolly shown at Turin featured wicker seats and the option of a fringed top to shield its occupants from the Mediterranean sun. The Jolly was adored by wealthy playboys like Fiat chief Gianni Agnelli, who carried a Jolly on the deck of his luxury yacht like a kind of shore-going dinghy that served as a stylish runabout in port.

Publisher
Christian Philippsen

Production manager
Johann Lemercier

Design & layout
Gattocubico, Modena (Italy)
Elisa Domenichini
Gianluca Pace

Translations
Simon Arron
Geoff Day
Wordshop

Le Mans hour chart
Alan Eldridge

The publisher expresses his heartfelt
thanks to the following persons
for their invaluable and friendly
support to *Automobile Year*:

Anne Asensio; Massimo Delbò;
Pierre Dupasquier; Peter Kalikow;
Patrick le Quément & Jean-Marie
Souquet (Renault); Robert Lutz (GM);
Joanne Marshall; Professor Gordon
Murray; Adolfo Orsi; Francesco Pelizzari
(Automobilismo d'Epoca);
Jean-Pierre Ploué (Citroën); Peter Sachs
(The Klemantaski Collection); Karl
Baumer & Nuevit Kavacikli
(BMW Mobile Tradition); Sam
Livingstone (Car Design News);
Ginger Ostle (Car Men); Luigi
Macaluso (Girard–Perregaux);
David Gooding & Dawn Ahrens
(Gooding & Company); Alberto
Fumagalli & Lorenza Cappello
(Italdesign-Giugiaro); Yves Carcelle,
Christine Bélanger & Juliette de Gonet
(Louis Vuitton Malletier); Patrick
Oliva & Jean-Pierre Lamour (Michelin);
Claude Hugot (Nissan); Yves Junne &
Stéphane Ract (Motul); Pete da Silva
& Kenton Elliot (A1GP); Manrico
Iachia & Alexandra Carvalho
(Europ Assistance); Franz Danner
& Jochen Münziger (Mazda); Douglas
Freedman (Motor Club Events)

Photoengraving by Vaccari Zincografica, Modena (Italy)

Printed by NIIAG, Bergamo (Italy)